Overcrowded

Design Thinking, Design Theory
Ken Friedman and Erik Stolterman, editors

Overcrowded

Designing Meaningful Products in a World Awash with Ideas

Roberto Verganti

The MIT Press
Cambridge, Massachusetts
London, England

This book was set in Stone Serif and Stone Sans by Toppan Best-set Premedia Limited. Printed and bound in the United States of America.

Library of Congress Cataloging-in-Publication Data

Names: Verganti, Roberto, author.
Title: Overcrowded : designing meaningful products in a world awash with ideas / Roberto Verganti.
Description: Cambridge, MA : The MIT Press, [2016] | Series: Design thinking, design theory | Includes bibliographical references and index.
Identifiers: LCCN 2016018208 | ISBN 9780262035361 (hardcover : alk. paper)
Subjects: LCSH: New products. | Product design.
Classification: LCC TS170 .V47 2016 | DDC 658.5/752--dc23 LC record available at https://lccn.loc.gov/2016018208

10 9 8 7 6 5 4 3 2

To

Alessandro

Matilde

Agnese

the gifts of life

Contents

A Gift Note

Everyone is a creator of meaning.
We create meaning through the humans we love.
But we also create meaning in the humbleness and responsibility of our everyday work.
Each one of us through our profession—
managers, designers, scholars, students, artists, scientists—
generates products, services, events that carry meaning to the life of people.
We may bring happiness, relieve pain, open new opportunities.
Beyond our own awareness, each one of us has an impact on the life of others,
through the vision we nurture and the new things we advance.

Early morning. My eyes closed, I feel the warmth of my bed, the kind light of the sunrise seeping through the curtains. The sheets are crisp. My mind is fresh.

The alarm clock sounds. I know there is a train passing by the station in about one hour. My daily commute is waiting for me. But I feel the coziness of the blankets.

Why should I wake up?

Why should I ever wake up with a smile, catch that train and go to my office?

I turn, and I see a book lying on a shelf next to the window. A book on innovation. It has been lounging there for a while, forgotten after I read through it to prepare a class. I ponder what this book would suggest as an answer. It would probably invite me to wake up to "solve problems," like many other innovation books that have lain on our desks in the last fifteen years. They offer us an implicit perspective on why we work, why we offer things to others, and why we innovate. Their tacit assumption is that there are *problems* in the world; people, customers, have *needs* and problems. We wake up in the morning to help solve those problems better.

Which is good. But maybe there is a more powerful perspective, something more to pull us out from these warm blankets. We wake up to "find meaning." That is: there are *opportunities* in the world; people have a *purpose* in life. We wake up in the morning to help create things that make more sense, that are more meaningful.

This book is for those of us who see life not as a problem but as an opportunity. Who believe that people are not driven by need but by purpose. That existence is not a solution but a gift.

In short, this is a book about the search for meaning. The search for meaning through innovation.

MEANING FOR PEOPLE

Meaning for whom?

First, for the receivers of our creations; for the people who treasure the products and services we offer. When they wake up in the morning, they search for meaning.

People have always searched for meaning. This search is deeply embedded in the history of humanity. Indeed, meaning has been the cynosure of philosophy, of major branches of psychology (logotherapy, in particular), of contemporary sociology. But the search for meaning has never been as relevant as today, when people live in a world awash with ideas, bursting with options. A world where everything is possible and the big question in life is not "how?" but "why?"

Yet many innovation theories seem to miss this fundamental perspective of life. They silently propound a picture of life rooted in the last century, a life driven by need. They implicitly suggest that we look at customers as "walking sacks of problems to be solved." We have to admit that even if these theories are labeled as user-centered, or human-centered, even if they are technically human, they are deeply inhuman. They treat people as "beings," but they dissect what makes these "beings" humans: the search for meaning.

I do not believe in this.

I have the lucky chance to have three children. When they came into life, I did not mean to create a sack of problems and needs. I did not tell them: "Sorry you came into this world, now you have problems to be solved." I celebrated their life. I wished to offer them a gift. The gift of life.

An opportunity. Yes, of course people have problems and needs, and our responsibility is to help solve them. But I believe there is much more in life.

If you want to create things that people love, that are meaningful, you will hardly get there just by solving problems. Think about love. Love is one of the feelings in life that carries more meaning, but also more pain. If you want to solve problems, simply avoid falling in love. Problem solving and love really do not get along well together.

MEANING FOR YOU

Second, this book is about your own search for meaning. It is about the reason you wake up in the morning and catch that train.

Solving problems requires an aseptic, impersonal attitude; a naive mind, free of judgments, free of preconceptions, free of your personal values. Which is reasonable when you solve someone else's problems. But creating meaning demands much more: it demands that you start from your values, from what you believe in, from your vision of the world. It's like a gift. A person will never fall in love for a gift she simply asks for. The gift needs to come from you, from your own search for meaning. If you do not love it, how could she love it? The search for meaning gives you the chance not only to solve problems, not only to innovate, but to innovate in a direction that *you* believe is more meaningful to people and to this world. "Meaning" is what connects you and the recipients of your creations.

I turn again in my bed. Time is short. I have a meeting at my business school. As I enjoy the last moments of warmth, thinking about the creation of meaning for others and for myself, I realize I have overlooked an important dimension connected to my work: what about the creation of business value?

I smile. Well, if something is meaningful both for the people who receive it and for the people who create it, how can't business value easily ensue? My mind goes back to all the projects we did in these years, to the entrepreneurs and managers I met who are driven by meaning. Entrepreneurs and managers who have generated much more business value than others who start from business value itself. They are makers of precious gifts.

Time to get up. There is a scent of tea in the air ...

THE GIFT MAKERS

A book may also be seen as a gift. Like every gift, it has a wrapping and a content. The wrapping is the pages, the text, the figures. The content is the thinking, the reflection, the research.

The wrapping of this book comes from me. But the content comes from the invaluable work and the inspirations of many whom I wish to acknowledge and thank.

First, the sparring thinker: Åsa Öberg. Without her insights, reflections, feedback, this book would just be an empty package. I owe her especially the core of the framework: the two principles of inside-out innovation and criticism. And many other principles I have clumsily tried to apply in life. Namaste Åsa.

Second, the radical circle: close friends who have enriched my understanding. Starting from the team at Politecnico di Milano: Claudio Dell'Era, Emilio Bellini, Naiara Altuna, Tommaso Buganza, Paolo Landoni, Emilio Bartezzaghi, and all the others who have been helping with concrete practical support in our research projects and collaborations with corporations. A special acknowledgment is for Gianluca Spina, my sparring thinker in earlier adventures: thanks Luca for all your silent support. I miss you.

This radical circle has been alive thanks to institutions that have provided funding for the theoretical research underpinning this book: the European Union (through the projects Light.Touch.Matters, Cre8Tv.eu, Deep, EU Innovate, Prindit Wellbeing, DESMA), Copenhagen Business School, Mälardalen University, California Polytechnic University (three schools that hosted me as visiting professor), and of course Politecnico di Milano.

Thanks also to scholars with whom I have shared part of the journey: Ezio Manzini, Francesco Zurlo, Anna Meroni, Cabirio Cautela, François Jegou, Sara Ferrari, Don Norman, Gary Pisano, Steve Prokesch, Rob Austin, Daved Barry, Finn Thorbjørn Hansen, Keith Goffin, Erik Tempelman, Paul Hekkert, Celine Abecassis-Moedas, Marcus Jahnke, Per Apelmo, Carina Söderlund, Anders Wickström, Rami Shani. Finally, all the managers and innovators who have believed in us and have engaged with us in projects for the creation of new meaningful directions. As it is impossible to mention all of them, I just recall those who have contributed also to the methodological development: Rob Chatfield and Nicki Morley, Victor

Aguilar, Troy Nimrick and Matthew Hodgson, Joseph Press, Gianluca Loparco and Gerhard Vorster, Anna Wróblewska and Piotr Voelkel, Anne Asensio, Monica Menghini and Bernard Charlès, Valter Pieracciani, Benedetto Vigna, Alexander Genov, Marco Fregonese, Marcello Vignocchi, Carlo Magistretti, Massimo Mercati. And, last but not least, Douglas Sery at the MIT Press.

Third, the interpreters: scholars in other fields whose work has been a theoretical foundation for my reflections. I have met some of them only through their creations. Here I wish to point out two studies to which I owe many insights: the analysis of collaborative circles in art by sociologist Michael Farrell, which helped me to better capture the dynamics of criticism in pairs and circles; and the study on perception, interpretation, and seeing new things by cognitive scientist Alexandra Horowitz. I hope they will condone my repeated sourcing of their reflections.

I also frequently reference the work of IDEO. In a peculiar way: as the foil in my argumentation. Their framework of Design Thinking is indeed the quintessential embodiment of the principles of creative problem solving: starting from users, understanding their needs, ideating, nourishing a naive mind, deferring judgment, and avoiding criticism. Principles that this book will challenge. Not because they are inherently wrong. These principles are right, but only for a particular type of innovation: solving existing problems in a better way. This book will explain that those principles falter when we want to find breakthrough directions, to create meaningful gifts that people fall in love with. The thinking of IDEO is as indispensable for this book as is the thinking of Farrell and Horowitz. It enables us to understand what innovation of meaning is by highlighting also what it is not, by creating contrasts, by stimulating a critical reflection. And, as we will see in these pages, criticism is fundamental if we are to move into new spaces, to innovate. I will sometime stretch some of their concepts and create polarizations between problem solving and innovation of meaning, although of course reality is never black and white. I hope they will forgive me for taking this liberty. I admire their work. Simply, it serves a different kind of innovation.

During this journey, as I was doing research and projects on innovation of meaning, I learned that you cannot renew things if you do not renew yourself. One has to lose oneself to eventually find "oneself as another" as Paul Ricoeur put it, a major source for this book. People see my photo in my previous book and then they see me now and ask me where that man is with eyeglasses, a pinstripe suit, and cufflinks. He went lost. Maybe he had to. Definitely he could have done it in a less painful way for others around him. Francesca, Alessandro, Matilde, Agnese, no word can express my gratitude for you having been there, notwithstanding all my mistakes, without ever complaining.

The initials of my children, Alessandro, Matilde, and Agnese, create the word "AMA," which in Italian means love. It was not done on purpose. We only realized it years after we picked those names. Maybe there is a meaning in that.

Milano
June 2016

1 Innovation of Meaning

Thriving in an Overcrowded World

"Tony," says Matt, "I want to start a company. And I want to start a company with you."

"What do you want to do?" asks Tony, as he enjoys his lunch.

"I want to build a smart home company."

"You're an *idiot*," bursts out Tony with his loud powerful voice. "No one wants to buy a smart home. Smart homes are for geeks."

Pause.

Let's imagine we are sitting at the next table and happen to listen to this conversation. In our hands we hold a classic handbook on innovation management, one of the many that have been produced in the last two decades. Tony's voice explodes in our ears right as we are reading a key passage in the book: "How to innovate—*Principle 1: do not criticize the ideas of others.*" Indeed, theories of innovation in recent years have insisted that we *defer judgment*. Criticism impairs the creative process.

So we expect the conversation between Matt and Tony will stop there, in frustration.

No. Hold on, hold on! They keep talking! Let's listen.

"You know," says Tony, "I'm into a house-building project right now. A house on Lake Tahoe. It will be the dream home for my family. I want it to be full of things I love. And I want it to be energy-efficient. Filled with state-of-the-art technology. But there are many things that are really frustrating. Take thermostats, for example. They are absolutely, utterly hideous. I think we can do better. I want to create a thermostat *to love*. I can use *my home project* as a research facility to understand how the current products work and how a future thermostat could look. How it could be very different and reinvented. Why don't you just build me a thermostat? Why don't you join me and start a company for this?"

Pause.

We are really bewildered. Are these two guys really going to start a business? This way? By taking inspiration from their own home project? Don't they know that you don't create products based on what you love? *You shouldn't start from yourself.* You should start from what users want. You should get ideas from outsiders, from creative communities. It's also written here in the book: "How to innovate—*Principle 2: innovation comes from the outside in; you need to start from users and outsiders.*" Indeed, user-driven innovation, crowdsourcing, and open innovation have been the innovation mantras of recent years. These two guys are really crazy!

Flash forward five years. These two guys, whose full names are Tony Fadell and Matt Rogers, did indeed start a new company: Nest Labs. Which they sold in 2014 to Google for the hefty ticket of US $3.2 billion. Their first product is a thermostat that people love. Nest Labs has sold about one million thermostats in three years, at a notable price of US $249 each. Between 2011 and 2014 these thermostats combined saved nearly two billion kilowatt-hours of energy. Nest Labs, coming from nowhere, is now leading the revolution of the connected home.[1]

THE QUESTION

Puzzled and disconcerted, we look at our handbook on innovation management, lying on the table of the restaurant. And wonder: Why was the prediction of the book wrong? How is it possible that Fadell and Rogers succeeded? They did exactly the opposite of what innovation studies have suggested in the last decade: they did not conduct creative brainstorming sessions; rather they *criticized* each other. They did not crowdsource ideas from outsiders; rather, they built their vision *starting from themselves.*

Yet it turned out that people loved the thermostat of Nest Labs, much more than the new thermostats that its competitors developed by following "good practice" in innovation.

Nest is not the only case of organizations that succeeded by following a different path to innovation. Companies such as Apple, Yankee Candles, Kuka Robotics, Philips Healthcare, and Nestlé have created breakthrough businesses by using a similar approach: an ability to be *critical* and to *start from your own vision.*

Meanwhile many corporations have practiced the good principles for innovation suggested by the handbook: they have engaged in brainstorming exercises, have scrutinized users, have accessed massive amounts of ideas from outsiders. In doing so, they have enhanced their capability to improve existing products. Yet they struggle to capture the big opportunities of the competitive landscape. Notwithstanding all their investments in innovation, they witness other companies enjoying the biggest chunks of the pie. The point is not that they miss ideas. They are *overwhelmed by ideas*. But they *keep going in the same direction*.

Why? What is *missing* in the innovation approaches that have been promoted in the last decade?

How to be innovative in a *world full of ideas*? Where the biggest challenge is not to create another idea, but to make sense of a wealth of opportunities?

How to develop *one robust vision* that is meaningful to customers, to us, and to our business?

THE LEARNING

In the last years I've been fascinated by these questions. And I've not been alone. Other likeminded scholars have also developed reservations about the two mantras of recent innovation discourse: (1) to be innovative you need to create more ideas; and (2) you need to start from outsiders. There was emerging evidence, from my studies and those of other researchers, that this was not always the case. Some unexpected findings, for example, were reported in my earlier book *Design-Driven Innovation*:[2] it seemed that breakthrough innovation did not come from users. *Design-Driven Innovation* was an inspirational book. The positive feedback it received encouraged my team to dig deeper. We wanted to move from inspiration to action. To craft and experiment a process that could better fit a changing world: a world awash in ideas, but in desperate search of breakthrough visions.

Along the way we had the lucky chance to meet executives who also shared our wonder. Caught in the frustration of their innovation efforts, seeing the limited return of brainstorming, crowdsourcing, and user-driven processes, overwhelmed by ideas whose value proved positive but limited, these managers have approached us with the wish to explore a new path. In a context where innovation processes increasingly tend to look all alike, they wanted *to innovate the way they innovated.*

This book shares what we have learned along the journey. Which, in a nutshell, can be summarized in three statements:

- In the current scenario, overcrowded by ideas, having additional ideas adds marginal value, both for businesses and customers. Indeed it destroys value by making things even fuzzier and more difficult to discern.
- Amid this wealth of opportunities, value comes from envisioning which direction makes more sense. It does not require more ideas, but one *meaningful* vision. Not to improve how things are, but to change *why* we need them. The winners are those who make existing problems old and redefine the scenario: those who make customers fall in love by offering not something better, but something more meaningful.
- To create meaningful things we need a process whose principles are the opposite of the ideation and outside-in innovation that has populated the innovation discourse in recent years: we need criticism and to start from ourselves.

In this book we will first examine the rationale for these findings, and then we will share our learning in terms of methodologies: a process and tools that organizations can use to create meaningful offerings. First let's summarize the content of the following chapters, starting from the core: there is not only one kind of innovation.

TWO KINDS OF INNOVATION

Whether we are talking of products, services, processes, or business models, there are always two levels of innovation (figure 1.1).

Innovation of solutions. This concerns better ideas to solve established problems. It's a new *how*, a novel way to address the challenges that are considered to be relevant in a marketplace. A novel solution may introduce incremental or even radical improvements, but always in the same direction: they are "more of the same" innovations.

Consider for example the thermostat industry. Before Nest Labs was founded, companies in the industry assumed that value came from providing users with better *control* of their home temperature. They therefore launched novel solutions with this purpose in mind: *how* can we enable

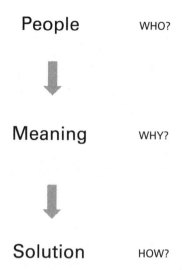

Figure 1.1
Two types of innovation: innovation of solutions and innovation of meaning.

families to better control the temperature in their home? Innovation focused on creating digital programmable thermostats, with several new features that enable a more precise and customized programming (such as touchscreen displays, day-of-week settings, user temperature calibration). These were definitely better solutions. Better *how*. And people did buy these new thermostats. But were they meaningful? Did people really loved to program them?

Innovation of meaning. This concerns a novel *vision* that redefines the problems worth addressing. It takes innovation one level higher—not only a new *how* but especially a new *why*: it proposes a new reason why people use something. A new value proposition, i.e., a novel *interpretation* of what is relevant and *meaningful* in a market. A new direction.

For example, Nest Labs has succeeded by proposing a novel meaning for thermostats: people do not use them *because* they want to *control* the temperature, but *because* they want to be comfortable in their home *without having to control the temperature*. A Nest thermostat is informed by smart simplicity: it does not require programming because it learns by itself what temperature the user likes and how to save energy. One just needs to start up the thermostat with simple manual regulation (through a straight-forward rotary interface that acts as an on/off switch), and after three days its software learns about temperature habits in the family. The thermostat is also equipped with sensors that understand when there's no one home, so that the heating is automatically turned down. And the software platform is open, so third parties can participate in this new meaning: how to save people from fussing with temperature control. For example, Jawbone enables users to wirelessly connect its UP24 wearable bracelet to the thermostat, so that if a person is waking up earlier than usual in the morning, the heat turns on automatically. "Tech people say [to me], why have a thermostat at all—why don't you have phones control everything?" says Fadell. "But I say homes are for families, and you have to make sure you design for the family, not just one person: kids, your wife, your grandparents need to be able to use it."[3]

Nest Labs' vision went exactly in the opposite direction from the incumbents in the industry: Nest designed products that "feel like home" rather than making them overly techy or pretentious.[4] This vision redefined what is meaningful in the market: comfort rather than programming; trusting the device rather than controlling it; simplicity rather than sophistication. Most of these features would never be recognized by firms that want to put users in control of the temperature, and some would even be banned as outlandish (especially the use of the simple rotary interface instead of a touchscreen). But when customers saw Nest's new interpretation, they found it more meaningful, and fell in love.

Creating innovations of meaning brings your interaction with customers to a higher level: the level of love. It focuses on what worth really is: *value* for a person. People do not fall in love with a better performance. That's a date. Love for a person, as well as for anything in life, comes from meaning. The best metaphor for describing innovation of meaning is to think at it as a "gift." The Nest thermostat is a gift to customers, from Tony Fadell, Matt Rogers, and their team. It's not an answer to an explicit need, or to a problem (people did not explicitly ask for it). Nor is it something that customers can design themselves. Nest offered people a discovery of something unexpected, a new possibility that people could find more meaningful.

CREATING VALUE THROUGH INNOVATION OF MEANING

Nowadays most organizations operate in a context where innovation of meaning is the *key source of value creation.*

On the one hand, because *customers search for it.* The fact that people search for meaning is well known. Several studies of customer behavior have shown that people fall in love with things that are more meaningful to them. They fall in love with the why, not the how.[5]

In our current world, however, the main driver of value is not just meaning, but *new* meaning. Customers nowadays face an unprecedented scenario: their context changes at an extreme speed, and therefore their problems and search for meaning keep changing. Companies that focus on innovating solutions often find themselves launching a great new product that unfortunately solves a problem that meanwhile has become old. There is no value in a better performance if this performance is no longer meaningful. Of course, if no other competitor proposes a new meaning, then the pure focus on solutions can still work. But as soon as someone comes up with a product that plays on a new, more meaningful dimension, solutions that seemed advanced suddenly look obsolete. Think of the traditional manufacturers of thermostats: they kept launching new products that enabled better control of temperature. Meanwhile, however, temperature control had become a meaningless problem, because of Nest's new proposal. Suddenly, the sophisticated programmable thermostats, the "better solutions" that required a lot of R&D investment, looked awkward.

What is relevant therefore today is not simply meaning, but the *innovation* of meaning. In a changing world, people change; therefore what is meaningful changes. The only way to build a connection of endless love is to keep *innovating the meaning* of what we offer.

On the other hand, innovation of meaning is relevant not only from the perspective of customers but also of business strategy. In fact, innovation of solutions has *lost its differentiating power.* We live in a context where ideas are abundant and technologies are easily accessible. Thanks to the widespread impact of the innovation paradigms of the last decade (such as open innovation, crowdsourcing, or design thinking), firms nowadays can easily invite ideas from outsiders, and they widely adopt processes to empower the creativity of their own teams. The consequence is that *solutions nowadays are not in short supply.* They are widely available and cheap. What is in short supply, instead, is the ability to make sense of this abundance of ideas; to propose a new interpretation, a new vision, in an unfathomable world. Moving innovation one level higher, to meanings, is nowadays necessary to *make a difference.* And it is the way to *capture the value* of previous investments in creativity: the more we adopt open innovation, crowdsourcing, and design thinking, the more we need to empower our capability to make sense of a wealth of opportunities.

Other organizations, in different industries, have followed a strategy similar to Nest: they have captured a large share of value by innovating meaning, rather than by simply improving solutions. Deloitte Australia for example has changed the meaning of risk management services: instead of looking at risk as something negative that destroys value, it proposes risk as a positive factor that clients may leverage to create competitive advantage. AirBnB has changed the meaning of lodging from a safe rest in a standard room to an opportunity to meet new people and immerse oneself in the authentic life of a place. We will discuss in depth several cases (for example, Yankee candles, Philips Healthcare, Apple, Uber, Waze, Kuka Robotics, STMicroelectronics, Vibram, IKEA, Spotify) and provide, in the appendix, a broader variety of examples in different environments: in business-to-consumer and business-to-business markets; in products and in services (see figure 1.2).

How did they do it? How did they create meaningful innovations that people love?

THE PRINCIPLES

The perspective of innovation of solutions has dominated the discourse on innovation in the last fifteen years. This perspective assumes that users have a need or a *problem* and are searching for the best *solution*. Innovation therefore is seen as an activity of *creative problem solving*. Which implies that organizations innovate by understanding the users' needs (what problems customers currently have), and then by *creating ideas* to better solve those problems.

Studies have therefore proposed methods to improve the creativity of organizations, both internally (e.g., brainstorming, design thinking) and externally (e.g., open innovation, crowdsourcing), the underlying assumption being that the most difficult thing to find is a great solution: the higher the number of ideas, the higher the chance of finding a better solution to users' problems. These methods of "creative problem solving" vary in their specific steps and processes, but they are all based on two fundamental principles.

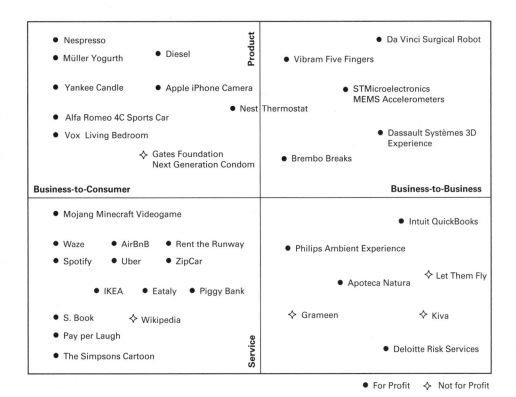

Figure 1.2

Examples of innovation of meaning in different industries (see the appendix for descriptions).

The first concerns the *direction* of the innovation process: creative problem solving moves from the *outside in*. We start by going *out* and observing how users use existing products; then we involve *outsiders* to propose novel ideas; and even when it comes to our own contribution, we are advised to "think *outside* of the box."

The second concerns the *mindset*: innovation of solutions is built on the art of *ideation*. The assumption is that the more ideas we generate, the better the chance of finding a good one.

This book shows that innovation of meaning comes from a process that is exactly opposite. It requires starting from the *inside out* rather than from the outside in; and it is grounded on *criticism* rather than ideation (figure 1.3).

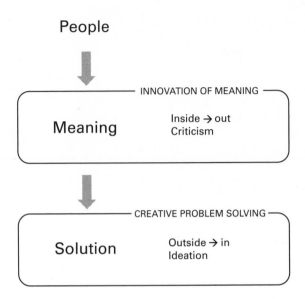

Figure 1.3
The principles of innovation of meaning (vs. innovation of solutions).

Innovation from the inside out

Tony Fadell started from himself. He wanted to create a thermostat that people could love. And "people" for him initially meant him and his family. If I do not love it, how could customers love it? Of course, later in his journey he eventually did classic user analysis. But he did not start from there. He started from the inside.

To be more precise, he started from an inner malaise: he hated all of the thermostats he had to choose from for his house. And still now, when he is thinking about new products, this malaise is a major driver. "After the thermostat we plan to do the same thing for every unloved product in the home and make them all magical,"[6] says Fadell. During an interview he pointed to an ugly beige gadget glued to the outside wall that controls the pool's temperature at his home in Tahoe. "That stupid thing was there before we got here, and it doesn't even try to blend in. It's staring at me, and somehow, I'm going to fix it. And just look at those horrible [security] cameras up there!"[7]

He did not start from users. And he did not even start from outsiders to get ideas, which is what creative problem solving has preached for the last decade. And what Nest's competitors did. Why did he succeed and they did not?

Outside-in innovation (such us open innovation or user-driven innovation), which has been so popular recently, is based on a strong assumption: the most difficult thing to find is a new idea, but once we have a great one in front of us, it can be easily recognized, even if outlandish and introduced by outsiders. This is true for innovation of solutions, since solutions can be put, more or less easily, on a scale of judgment according to how well they enable us to solve a given problem. But it does not apply to innovation of meaning. The reason is that meanings have a different nature than solutions. They are new interpretations of what is good and what is bad (in the case of Nest: comfort and simplicity instead of temperature control and perfect programming). There is no scale of judgment, because what we innovate *is* the scale of judgment itself. Proposing new meanings, new interpretations, is relatively simple, especially in a world full of opportunities. What is difficult instead is understanding which of them really makes sense. The more options there are, the more they all look similarly interesting and at the same time arbitrary. Even if outsiders bring us novel visions, in the confusion of stimuli we end up seeing only what we can (and want to) see.

Think about the thermostat industry. Most ideas that are today incorporated into the Nest thermostat were already known, but no one recognized them. In 2009, two years before Nest Labs was founded, the U.S. Green Building Council, the American Society of Interior Designers, and NEWH launched a public design competition for ideas on sustainable suites. The winners showcased a smart thermostat that sensed the presence of people in the room (as eventually Nest did).[8] The idea was known, public, and free, but the industry did not get it. In 2012 Honeywell filed a lawsuit against Nest for infringing seven of its patents, which means that the ideas were already there in front of Honeywell's eyes. But it could not recognize their value and use these patents to create value. Nor could customers help in understanding what was meaningful. A top executive of the Environmental and Combustion Control division of Honeywell said in an interview that the company had already tested similar solutions to Nest's but "we found that consumers prefer to control the thermostat, rather than being controlled by the thermostat."[9]

The point is that everyone in an organization has, explicitly or more likely implicitly, a sense of direction for where to go in the future. This sense of direction inevitably acts as a filter on the insights we collect along the way. We tend to pick customers that support this direction and listen only to what we want hear (the name of the division of this Honeywell executive says a lot about what she was prone to listen to). This is not a problem if we are looking for better solutions along an existing scale of judgment. But an innovation of meaning is a change of direction, a change of scale. We will never recognize it by starting with outsiders' ideas, even if the proposal is there in front of our eyes. And even if we timidly try to explore an outlandish path, this path will be dismissed at the first challenge.

We can outsource the development of solutions, but not of visions. They are the lenses through which we look at things, the heart through which we give meaning to our place in the world. We cannot merely borrow someone else's eyeglasses. And definitely not their heart. This is why Nest Labs *is not an idea* coming from a crowd or from users. Instead, it's a *vision*, coming from Fadell and Rogers.

Starting from ourselves, from what *we* would love people to love, has two benefits.

First, as said, everyone in her heart always nurtures a sense of direction, a silent hypothesis of what people would love. It's inevitable. By exposing this inkling of hypothesis we make our cognitive frame *explicit*; we make it visible to others who can then target it and *challenge* it.

The second reason to start from the inside is even deeper. Our initial hypothesis is not a negative preconception that we want to fight. Rather, it is something precious. We need it. It's the foundation on top of which we forge meaning. No one can go in a direction that is not meaningful for herself. Solutions can be borrowed from the outside, because they enable us to achieve a target, but the target, the direction, has to come from ourselves. In a recent interview I asked Steve Wozniak, cofounder of Apple, what his attitude was when he developed the Apple I and II. He answered: "People will never love a product you do not love. If you do not love it yourself they feel it ... they smell it ..."[10]

Indeed, people cannot love a gift we do not love. A gift is a meeting between two loves: what *the receiver* would love (the gift is not for us of course); but also what *we* would love this person to receive (i.e., our *authentic* belief for how *we* can make her life better). Creating meaningful products, like making gifts, is an act of responsibility and pleasure. Responsibility because, through the gift, *we* have a chance to create a more meaningful world. It's the way we contribute to people's life. Pleasure because when we love the gift, we pleasure ourselves in *making* it.

So *the gift is for the receiver, but the act of making the gift is for us.* When this happens, we create meaning. People will smell it even before seeing it. And they fall in love.

Criticism

The second fundamental difference between innovation of solutions and innovation of meaning concerns the *mindset.* Creative problem solving is built on the art of *ideation.* Innovation of meanings instead requires the art of *criticism.* For two reasons.

First, because the process starts from the inside. Since we start from ourselves and our own hypotheses, we need to be sure that what comes from us is meaningful to other people, that we are not getting stuck in old interpretations. Criticism is the way to *challenge* our own cognitive frame; it's the way to question how we make sense of the environment. It helps us to shake us off and get rid of a past that might not be meaningful anymore.

There is a second, more important reason why we need criticism: it enables us not only to move beyond the past but also to *create the new.* When we propose a new vision, we simply start from the inkling of a hypothesis. Our initial proposal is blurred, vague. Just a *sense of direction,* whose value and implications are unclear. Not only to others; even more to ourselves. Criticism enables us to dig deeper, confront our hypothesis with the hypotheses of others, and find a new, more powerful interpretation that lies underneath.

The word "criticism" comes from the Greek *krino* (*κρίνω*), which means "I *judge,* I *value.*" Although the English word often carries a sense of negativity, in reality it has no particular negative or positive disposition. It rather indicates *the practice of going deeper* when interpreting things. A movie critic does not necessarily produce a negative critique. She simply helps us understand better the content of an artwork. Some critiques can be positive, some negative, some both. But a good critique is always deep. It strives to unveil what is *beneath the surface of things.*

Criticism is the dynamics that spurred the conversation between Fadell and Rogers at the restaurant and that led to the creation of Nest Labs. Their conversation was between two trusted peers (they had previously worked together at Apple, where Fadell was the main engine behind the iPod). It aimed not at killing but at developing a better interpretation. A "creative criticism" that formerly also marked Fadell's interaction with Steve Jobs at Apple. "He thought I asked too many questions," says Fadell. "I would just keep asking, 'Well, what about that? What about that?' And he'd say, 'Enough already.' It would frustrate him. But then he'd ask me a ton of questions, and he could frustrate me, and I'd be like, 'Steve, leave me alone.'"[11] Fadell suffuses Nest Labs with creative tension. His colleagues compare his style to that of the Mountain in Game of Thrones, the towering brawler known for beating his opponents to a pulp.[12] "When you make someone really upset, that might mean you are on the right track," explains Fadell.[13] Yet his purpose is not to smash and kill but to go deeper, build a powerful vision, beyond easy ideas. "There have been times when Tony's banging his fist on the table and yelling at people and demanding excellence," says Rogers. "But at the same time, he is incredibly caring and passionate about their development."[14]

It's criticism nurtured by a common will to move beyond old interpretations, a commitment to a new shared vision. A criticism that, if properly conducted, may be a source of much more encouragement and energy than any compliant and amenable ideation session.

The process of getting to a novel meaningful interpretation therefore is totally different from the classic ideation process. A new meaning is not created through quantity, i.e., by generating as many ideas as possible and then selecting the best one. Instead, it is created through quality: by taking a few initial visions and making them clash: focusing on their differences in the search for a novel deeper interpretation that can explain what lies beyond each of them. It's a process of *clashing* and *fusing* the different perspectives that we inevitably have inside ourselves. While brainstorming suggests *deferring* judgment, innovation of meaning creates *through* judgment. It's the art of criticism that enables us to discover the new, to turn the blurred internal hypotheses we start with into a final robust vision that people love.

Criticism is an art that we rarely nurture, unfortunately. To be handled with care, because it is rooted in *tensions*. The wrong kind of criticism would simply kill the process and destroy the potential of a great vision. So how should we do it? How should we embark on this quest for a deeper interpretation? How to combine creativity and criticism (apparently an oxymoron)? The challenge is not trivial, considering that Tony Fadell himself, a serial innovator, has not always succeeded in this practice.[15] And indeed the journeys of several people who have created meaningful products have been punctuated by failures as well as successes (Steve Jobs is probably the most acknowledged example). How can we learn from these successes and failures?

THE PROCESS

Our wondering about the limits of creative problem solving did not stop at those two principles. We wanted to understand how companies can actually make meaningful innovations happen: how those principles translate into a robust, viable process.

We therefore set out on a long journey: almost a decade of direct experience in how to make products that people love. First we learned from companies that successfully did it in the past. Then we assembled the best of what we learned into a prototypical process that could be replicated in different contexts, industries, cultures. Finally we tested this process in several projects with a variety of organizations. We were lucky, because along the way we met managers who were willing to try a new path, to enjoy the benefit of being pioneers. Over the years the process has changed from the initial blueprint and has become robust, although of course we keep studying, experimenting, improving. In this book we will share this process, with the hope that you will become part of it. What you will see here is open to adaptation to your specific purpose and context. Our invitation, however, is not only to practice what you will find in these pages, but also to try different avenues, expand the range of available methods, and share your findings. The more we improve and share, the more we empower others to create meaning.

Figure 1.4 summarizes the process for innovation of meaning (the details and the actionable tools are illustrated in the course of the book). It is the natural consequence of the two principles we discussed above: moving from the inside out and criticism.

Being an inside-out process, it starts from *us*, as individuals. We begin by envisioning our own hypothesis about *what we would love people to love*. This is the process that happened in the minds and hearts of Rogers and Fadell before they met that day at the restaurant. We will provide guidelines on pulling together a team of "us," of individuals within our organization who have a great potential to envision meaningful hypotheses. And we will

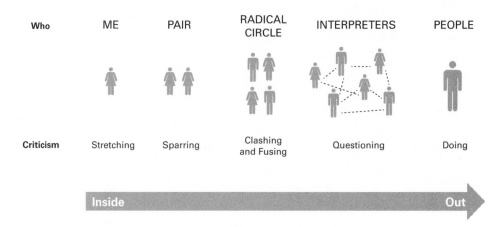

Figure 1.4
The process of innovation of meaning.

provide methods on how to nurture and leverage our own insights. This first phase is opposite to what happens in creative problem solving. Not only because we do not start from users, but also because the way we envision possible hypotheses is not based on ideation, but on reflection and self-criticism. Rather than generating several ideas, we need to envision just a few hypotheses (even just one), but to envision it well. Rather than focusing on *how* problems can be solved, we focus on the *meaning* of our proposal, on *why* customers would love it. Rather then working in teams, we need to envision our own hypothesis individually and autonomously; this way we increase the ability to dig deeper in our vision without watering it down. Autonomy also means that we can personally pick the envisioning method we feel most appropriate to ourselves (intuitive, qualitative, quantitative, etc.; this book will propose a wide array of options); this increases the heterogeneity of the proposals, and therefore expands the space of possible directions. Rather then conducting a quick brainstorming session, we take more time to reflect on our hypotheses (typically one month). We start by envisioning a few hypotheses, perhaps intuitively, than take some distance from them, and after a while we *deliberately* reflect on what we have been proposing, try a new method, challenge our assumptions, improve our insights, then leave them again for a while, until our confused intuition takes a better form.

After this first step that starts from the inside, the process moves outside ourselves, in order to be sure that we are not stuck in our own assumptions. The purpose is to create something that *customers* will love. We therefore need criticism. But in a careful way, because our initial hypotheses are still weak and unclear, even to ourselves, especially the most outlandish ones. So we need to open up to criticism *gradually*.

The most delicate way to practice the art of criticism is by working in *pairs*. Pairs are two individuals who have envisioned similar directions. By challenging each other they will naturally tend to go deeper in their reflections, without killing their visions. This is the dynamic we observed between Fadell and Rogers at the restaurant: harsh criticism between two pals who have a great trust and respect for each other. And this is the dynamic that Fadell experienced earlier with Steve Jobs. A dynamic that resembles what happens in boxing between sparring partners who are training for big matches: they explicitly search for each other's weaknesses and hit hard, not to knock down the partner but to make him stronger. Similarly, in innovation of meaning, sparring partners attack the weaknesses in each other's hypotheses, without fear, because they know that fundamentally they believe in a similar scenario. Working in pairs is one of the most powerful (and neglected) ways to develop breakthrough visions. When we believe in something totally novel, whose form we struggle to understand even ourselves, we are too weak (and even scared) to expose our half-baked thinking to a larger team, as it would be killed in a second. But with a trusted sparring partner we can dare to share and be criticized, with the purpose of making our shared vision stronger for later harsher criticism.

If criticism from a sparring partner aims at going *deeper,* the next step aims at moving to a *newer* direction. We want to compare and combine *different* hypotheses in order to search for unprecedented interpretations. To this purpose, the pairs assemble into a larger group that we call a *radical circle*. Radical because its purpose is to develop novel visions; circle because its participants have been carefully selected and they work closely together, typically in the format of an intense workshop. Given that pairs come with hypotheses that are significantly different from each other, criticism during the workshop will be more abrasive. And this is what we search for at this stage. The individual hypotheses are now stronger and clearer, they will not succumb. Rather, the circle will naturally work in the search for what lies behind the apparent contrast between two visions. A novel meaning that the individuals and pairs, from their specific perspective, could not see. This is the core of the process of clashing and fusing: contrasts and tensions are favored for the sake of innovation. We will see methods that support these dynamics of innovating through criticism: for example the identification of a common enemy, the development of scenarios, the focus on delighters, the use of metaphors.

The following step of the critical process entails opening up further, this time to real outsiders, i.e., people *outside our organization*. First, to *interpreters*, i.e., experts from far-flung fields who address our strategic context but from different perspectives. Interpreters help us reflect even deeper on the implications of our emerging vision. Finally, to *customers*, i.e., those who will hopefully love our proposal. Fadell and Rogers, in a more advanced stage of their process, did open up to outsiders. They eventually went into people's houses to check whether their direction was indeed meaningful. But when they did this they already had a strong vision, which they wished to test and challenge. Innovation of meaning therefore still of course leverages the value of outsiders. But it does it later in the process, *once we have a new framework* through which to interpret their feedback and insights. Their involvement is therefore profoundly different from what happens in popular open-innovation, crowdsourcing, and user-driven approaches. The main role of outsiders in innovation of meaning is *not to provide ideas*; rather, it's to *challenge* the innovative direction that we propose and make it stronger and deeper. What outsiders here have to bring are good *questions*, rather than good ideas. In other words, they contribute to *criticism*, not to ideation.

POSITIONING INNOVATION OF MEANING

The process illustrated in this book is therefore significantly different from what has been promoted by the mainstream innovation discourse in the last decade. Indeed it practices principles that innovation thinkers have often banned as useless, even demonized as detrimental: starting from ourselves, and being critical. This difference is not just in the principles. It continues in every detail of the process: working autonomously, taking time, reflecting, using different tools instead of one common method, finding a peer, selecting a few outsiders, meeting customers later in the process.

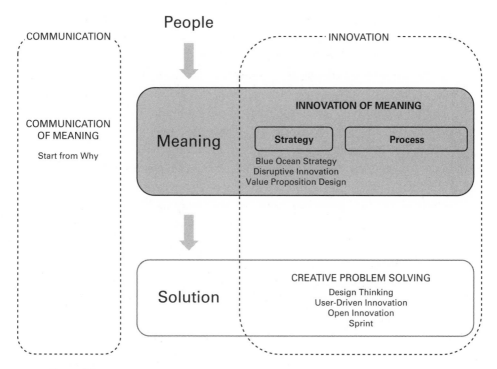

Figure 1.5
The portfolio of innovation processes: how innovation of meaning complements and completes other approaches to innovation. (The shaded area is the focus of this book.)

I'm not claiming that creative problem solving is wrong. At all. Simply, we are talking here of *different kinds of innovation,* which of course require *different processes.* Figure 1.5 illustrates how innovation of meaning compares to other approaches to innovation.

As said, innovation of meaning concerns the why of things. It proposes a new, more meaningful, reason why people use a product. It's a vision toward a new direction.

Outside-in processes based on ideation (which we gathered under the umbrella of "creative problem solving") instead support the innovation of solutions. The creation of a better how along an existing direction. Many innovation approaches proposed in recent years are extremely effective for this kind of innovation: for example open innovation, crowdsourcing, design thinking. Conversely, they definitely are not suitable to develop new meanings (well … of course the opposite is also true: inside-out processes based on criticism are not suitable to improve existing solutions).

So these two levels of innovation have their own specific processes. And every organization needs both: new meanings to create the foundation for value creation, to make customers fall in love with our products, to navigate and lead the changes in the scenario. New solutions to ensure that we provide the best performance within a given meaning, and that we keep improving. The secret of every organization and every leader is to master both. They complement each other. We need an innovation project portfolio where changes of meanings are followed by waves of improvements of solutions, and then again by creation of new meaning.[16]

With one deep awareness. Whereas twenty years ago the capability of organizations to creatively solve problems was limited, and approaches such as open innovation and design thinking helped to fill a dramatic gap, nowadays innovation of solutions has lost much of its differentiating power. In a way, creative problem solving is a victim of its own success: the more companies adopt it, the more organizations and society easily create novel ideas, the more ideas become a cheap accessible currency which, alone, hardly makes a difference. Using an analogy, design thinking and open innovation are becoming the "total quality management" of our time. A must. We need to do it. But not a differentiator. We do not create competitive advantage through them. We do not delight people and make them fall in love.

Innovation of meaning is the next step in the innovation path of organizations. In a scenario awash with ideas, where technologies and solutions are increasingly accessible but problems and meanings keep changing, it helps to *make sense* of this wealth of opportunities in order to capture their potential.

Figure 1.5 also illustrates the positioning of this book vis-à-vis other frameworks recently discussed.

A first connection is with the reflections of Simon Sinek on the importance of "why."[17] We definitely position at the same level: at the level of meaning (the why) instead of the level of solutions (the how). And we definitely share the same observation: in the current scenario, firms that capture the biggest chunk of value, that make customers (and employees) fall in love, are the ones that start from the why, from the meaning, not from the solution.

The main difference is that Simon takes the perspective of *communication*. Here instead we talk of *innovation*. He focuses on the power of meaning to communicate (to customers and people in our organization). We focus on how to *create* new meaning. In the awareness that in our ever-changing world, value creation comes from *new* meaning. Here you will find how to innovate it. Simon inspires you on how to communicate it and leverage it.

A second connection is with theories in the realm of strategy and the creation of new *value propositions*. For example the frameworks of the *blue ocean strategy* of Chan Kim and Renée Mauborgne,[18] and of Clayton Christensen's *disruptive innovation*.[19] Again, we definitely position at the same level here. Innovation of meaning is indeed a change of direction, a journey into a blue ocean. It instantiates what Kim and Mauborgne call *value innovation*, that is, a change in the parameters customers use to give value to products. Similarly innovation of meaning relates to Christensen's and Ulwick's "jobs to be done,"[20] and to the value proposition design of Osterwalder.[21] The difference with these frameworks is not only terminological. (We refer to "innovation of meaning" for a reason: people and customers do not think and feel in terms of jobs or value propositions, but in terms of meaning. The perspective of meaning therefore helps to build more empathy with customers.) The main difference is that, whereas the frameworks above propose canvases in the realm of *strategy*, here we dig deeper and move into implementation: we illustrate the *process* used to create new meaning (i.e., to create a blue ocean, or new jobs to be done, or a new value proposition). We have collaborated with managers who were accustomed to these strategic frameworks, and they welcomed the process described in this book, since it enabled them to put these strategies into practice.[22]

We will see how to incorporate the strategic canvases proposed by these frameworks (and by many others in the same line, such as Kano's model of value, the framework of discovery-driven innovation, experience design, lead users, etc.) into a viable, coherent organizational process: especially how to identify the right people to involve in the process and how to build the proper mindset: starting from the inside out and practicing the art of criticism.

The last connection is with the practices of *lean and fast development* (e.g., the sprints, the identification of a minimal viable product, followed by iterative development).[23] These practices deal with the development of products and services and effectively complement our process. Indeed, we will leverage these practices in our final pages.

THE SCRIPT OF THE BOOK

This book is structured in three parts. Part I digs into *value creation*. It introduces the concept of innovation of meaning, why it is important nowadays, and how it is a key element of an *innovation strategy*. First, we will take the perspective of *people*: we will illustrate why customers fall in love with new meanings (chapter 2). Then we will take the perspective of *businesses* and show why innovation of meaning is a major *differentiator* (chapter 3). Beyond the fundamental observation that organizations nowadays compete on meanings, we will focus on a specific question: does *my* business, in *this moment*, need an innovation of meaning?

Then we move into implementation. In particular part II focuses on the *principles* that underpin the process of innovation of meaning: innovation from the inside out (chapter 4) and criticism (chapter 5). The reason for a focus on principles (before moving into the description of the process and tools) comes from a basic observation: what we lack in our world are not solutions but directions. Not the how, but the why. We do not lack methods and tools for innovation (which have been significantly overproduced in the last decade). We lack a clear idea of which one to use, when, and *why*. The purpose of this section is to provide the core capabilities, so that you will be able to pick the methods that are most meaningful *for your specific organization and context*.

Part III of the book then illustrates the process and tools for innovation of meaning, i.e., the methods that we have applied when we worked with firms to create products that people love. Chapter 6 focuses on the first step: how to *envision* new meanings, starting from us as *individuals*. Chapter 7 focuses on the next two steps: how to clash and fuse different visions by working in *pairs* and in a *radical circle*. In particular we will describe the methods and tools of the meaning factory, a two-day intense workshop based on the art of criticism. Chapter 8 finally focuses on the last two steps, which involve outsiders: the *interpreters* and the *customers*. We will show how to find and select the interpreters, how to interact with them in a one-day intense meeting (the interpreter's lab), and how to involve customers in the creation of breakthrough meaningful products.

Given that each part has a different purpose, the style and language will evolve during the book: in part I, which deals with values, I will inevitably let my heart surface through the narration. I hope you will concede this. The point is that we will talk about why people fall in love with meaningful things: how can one talk about love by switching off his heart? In part II, which deals with principles, I will turn to a more academic tone. Just a little, no worries ... you will not get lost in a scientific dissertation. Just what is needed to support the foundations of our reflection, which is grounded on the robust shoulders of other notable thinkers. We will connect you with the theories that sustain the strategy and process, so that you may develop the mindset, skills, and capabilities before moving into implementation. In part III, which deals with the process and tools, I will use a pragmatic, sometimes even meager tone. The language of handbooks, tapestried with more schematics and fewer words.

In a way, these are my three natures: the person, the scholar, the engineer. I did not plan for them to surface like this. But things sometimes happen in an inevitable way. I hope you will put up with these changes of tones and differences in focus. And that you can resonate with at least one of them. That at least one of these three voices can inspire you to build your own story, with your own multiple personalities, in the fascinating journey to creating meaning in our world.

Part I   The Value

Why Innovation of Meaning Matters

Why is innovation of meaning important?

The meaning of things has always changed over time. And meaning has always been central in the life of people. Yet it has hardly been central in innovation frameworks. Why? Why in the past could organizations survive without bothering too much about innovation of meaning? And why does their survival now depend on their ability to propose new meanings? Does *your* business, in *this moment*, need an innovation of meaning?

Part I addresses these questions from two perspectives. Chapter 2 takes the perspective of *people*: why innovation of meaning is important for customers; why they fall in love with new meanings. The answer will lie in two changes of the scenario. First, an overabundance of options, in a complicated world. People, today, are not lacking possible solutions. When one has to choose a product or a service, the possibilities are many; in this sea of opportunities, the challenge is to understand which option is meaningful for them as individuals. The focus of people's attention has therefore moved from the how to the why, from "how can I solve this?" to "is this meaningful to me?," from "I need this" to "do I need this?" Second, the speed of change: in the past meanings in society evolved slowly; an organization could simply wait and adapt. Nowadays the meaning of things changes at a dramatic pace. Think about the meaning of television: as smart phones have diffused among teenagers, TV screens have moved from being the enemy of a family ("Do not watch TV for so long!") to being one of its best fellows ("Guys, can we please watch TV tonight? It would be so cool: everyone watching the same screen instead of staring at your own phone?"). This radical change of meaning occurred in just a few months. A big bang that did not allow time for reaction. One can only proactively ride these changes.

Chapter 3 takes the perspective of organizations: why innovation of meaning creates value for businesses. Why it is a major *differentiator*. This is due to two converging phenomena. On the one hand customers search for it (see above). On the other hand, only a few organizations know how to do it effectively. Firms have become extremely productive in generating ideas of solutions, especially thanks to the web and to creative methods such as design thinking. But the more ideas they create, the more they see a confused landscape in which they struggle to find a meaningful direction. In a way, the success and diffusion of problem solving is one of the major causes of its own loss of relevance, and of the prominence of innovation of meaning. Ideas are abundant. Meanings are rare. And value, in business, is in what's rare.

2 The Search for New Meaning

The Value for People

"There was a time when the default assumption that almost everyone had is that you get married as soon as you could and then you start having kids as soon as you could. The only real choice was 'who' ... not when. Not what you do thereafter."

Barry Schwartz had just started his TED talk. A psychologist and a professor, he was wearing unusual attire for such an event: saggy gray shorts, sneakers, and a loose plain T-shirt. "Nowadays, everything is very much up for grabs. ... I teach wonderfully intelligent students and I assign twenty percent less work than I used to, and it is not because they are less smart; it is not because they are less diligent; it is because they are preoccupied, asking themselves, 'Should I get married or not? Should I get married now? Should I get married later? Should I have kids first or a career first?'"

This passage deeply captivated me. In a few words, Schwartz captured one of the most distinctive changes in our society: the shift *from the search for solutions to the search for meaning.*

Indeed, until recently many of the problems in people's lives were substantially predefined: graduating, meeting a life mate, finding a job, setting up a house, having children, making a career. These things were determinate in culture, and rooted in the structure of society. They gave meaning to life. They gave a direction. People did not question the problems to address. They focused on finding the most appropriate solution: which degree to pursue, whom to partner with, how many children to have.

In a few years, the world has dramatically changed. The availability and accessibility of solutions has increased, but the questions have simultaneously become undefined, slippery, erratic. To the point that even some of the fundaments of humanity, such as partnering and giving life, are queried.

Let alone more mundane questions such us: "Should I buy a car"? In the past, one of the main recreations of newly hired graduates used to be speculating about which car to pick with their new salary. Nowadays millennials in urban areas wonder whether they need a car at all, notwithstanding that the range of car models keeps increasing to please any taste. A study commissioned in 2014 by the car-sharing company Zipcar shows that more than 35 percent of young people are actively looking for alternatives to owning an automobile, and 24 percent are changing their habits thanks to mobile applications such as Uber and public transportation apps.[1]

One of the cyclonic changes in our society is that people do not have a crystallized, conformed and stable idea of what is meaningful. Their life is not just focused on finding solutions to predefined problems, but on finding what questions to address in a world where problems are undetermined and constantly changing. They are in constant search of meaning; they seek purpose more than solutions. Their delight, and their challenge, is to understand where to go rather than how.

Doing innovation in a world where people search for meaning is totally different from doing innovation in a world where people search for solutions. In this chapter I propose that in our context, organizations that thrive are those that propose new meanings. I will show why people fall in love with new meaningful visions; in other words, I will show why innovation of meaning has an unprecedented *value* from the perspective of *people and society*.

I start by articulating the fundamental trait of our world: people, as never before, are in search of *meaning*. They savor making sense of a life that is increasingly rich of opportunities, intricate and unfathomable. And since life keeps *changing*, they are in constant search of *new meaning*.[2]

We will then see that this search for new meaning deeply affects how people interact with products, services, and organizations. In the past, when people were searching for solutions, they picked the *product* that performed *better*. Their need was determinate, the performance was given, and companies competed on offering the best solution. What happens now, when people search for new meaning? Their need is not determinate. The performance is not given. Instead, they pick the *vision* that makes *more sense*. In this context companies compete by helping people understand what is good for them, as individuals in a world that is complex and unsteady.

To support our reflections, I will leverage only one case, based on a familiar consumer product, in order to keep things simple and focus our attention on what we want to know: why do people nowadays fall in love with new meaningful visions? The next chapter will then elaborate, showing how similar dynamics happen in every industry, in products and services, in consumer and industrial markets, in profit and not-for-profit organizations. So please bear with me for a moment, even if I do not pick other examples that are closer to your reality. They will come next.

This chapter's case concerns one of the humblest products ever. Something that normal logic would consider as remotely connected to innovation as ever. Something that should have disappeared by now, forgotten in the cemetery of extinct product species. And yet, instead, a product that has radically changed in recent decades, and that people value and love more than ever.

WARMTH

"Mum, do we have a candle?"

"Yes, we have one," answered my mother, her voice coming from somewhere in the living room. "It's with the matches in the cabinet next to the entrance door, on the first shelf."

I moved in the total darkness, slowly and carefully, toward the entrance hall. In the early eighties, in Italy, it was still not rare to have a sudden interruption of electricity; especially in the mountains during a thunderstorm. I sparked a match and watched the room getting faintly illuminated as the wick started to burn. Then I moved toward the electricity panel, to check if the problem was in our circuitry or from the utility provider.

It was the only candle we had in our small flat in the mountains. In our apartment in Milan we had two. One served the same purpose: to illuminate in case of power failure. It mostly rested forgotten in some remote drawer. The second one was a votive candle with a decoration of the Madonna that I got for confirmation, and was not supposed to be lighted up.

Fast-forward to today, three decades later. There should be no candles in people's homes anymore. Indeed, both those purposes of candles have lost their value. If the power ever goes off, people always have their mobile phones close to hand, whose flashlight applications are way more convenient and efficient than any flame. And votive candles are becoming rare fixtures in secular homes, even in a country with a strong Catholic tradition like Italy.[3] We are in the third millennium. The candle industry should have disappeared by now. Yet, when I visited my mother last weekend, a nice candle was welcoming me on the dinner table next to a steaming stew and polenta. I looked around: her home was well equipped with dozens of candles, well displayed.

People buy candles more then ever. The industry is up and running. Candle sales took off in the 1990s and peaked in 2000, growing at a rate of at least ten percent each year.[4] In the 2000s people kept buying candles, notwithstanding the economic recessions. In Europe the consumption of candles between 2008 and 2013 remained relatively stable in volume (around 600,000 tons per year), but increased in revenue by 18% (from 1.332 million euros to 1.567 million euros).[5] These figures would be the envy of many industries. Why do people buy candles? Spending even more than they do for electric bulbs? Even if candles are less convenient, less durable, more expensive, more dangerous, and perhaps unhealthy. Even in years when families' finances are limited and many cannot afford the luxury of useless objects reminiscent of an older time?

But candle are not useless and old. They are contemporary. They are meaningful. People love them. Simply put, their purpose has radically changed. People do not buy them as a backup for power failures, nor for religious reasons. Not because they illuminate better or last longer. There is no market for those uses anymore. People buy them because they create emotional warmth in the home when welcoming friends or when alone.

According to the National Candle Association of the United States, nine out of ten candle users say they use candles to make a room feel comfortable or cozy. More specifically, 71% of people use them to create a romantic environment; 67.7% say candles put them in a good mood; and 54.4% say candles help them relieve stress. And they do not leave their candles forgotten in some remote drawer: the majority of US consumers use their candles within a week of purchase.

Of course, the kinds of candles that thrive in the current market are significantly different from the candle I was lighting at my mom's place in the mountains. A new purpose (emotional warmth) requires a new solution. If we look more carefully at the figures, we see that sales of the traditional simple candles, like votive candles, which may cost as little as 50 cents, are struggling. On the other hand, the segment of high-end sophisticated candles has soared. People nowadays may buy large pillar or jar candles that cost from US $30 up to US $200. In particular, the main driver for purchase is not luminescence or durability, not safety or convenience, but scent. Fragrance is by far the most important characteristic in candle purchases, with three-fourths of buyers saying it is "extremely important" or "very important."

This new scenario has had a dramatic impact on businesses operating in the industry, for bad or for good. On the one hand, many incumbent historical firms have failed to fully capture the shift in the market. Take for example Price's Candles. Founded in 1830 near London, at the beginning of the twentieth century it was the largest manufacturer of candles in the world. In 2001, just as the market for candles was soaring thanks to the new scented products, Price's Candles filed for administration. On the other hand, other firms, especially newcomers, have flourished. Possibly the most outstanding example is Yankee Candle.

The Yankee Candle Company may be considered a start-up in the centuries-old industry of candle manufacturing. Founded in the 1970s in South Hadley, Massachusetts, by a teenager who made candles for his mother, the company rapidly grew to become a dominant market leader. In 2012 Yankee Candle held 44% of market share for premium scented candles, with a turnover of US $844 million and more than five hundred company-owned stores in the United States. In 2013 consumer product maker Jarden bought Yankee Candle for $1.75 billion, the largest acquisition made by the corporation to date.[6]

From the perspective of traditional chandlers, the candles made by Yankee Candle are nonsense. The wax is typically contained inside a thick jar, covered by an outsized label. The flame is therefore often screened and nonvisible; definitely not the best solution for an illumination device. What makes their candles unique, however, is their fragrance, which is visibly depicted on the large label. Yankee Candle has more than 150 fragrances, ranging from traditional flower and fruit bouquets such as Jasmine or Apple, to mood- and context-inspired scents such as Summer Wish or Beach Walk, to more venturesome twists such as Bacon and Riding Mower, targeted at men.

I have been fascinated by the dynamics of innovation in the candle industry. Perhaps because of the time I spent in Scandinavia in the past three years: I have come to appreciate the emotional value that candles have in Nordic culture, where there is an invisible etiquette on how to arrange candles to bring warmth in the long, cold nights. Perhaps because I am amused by how candles are diffusing in more southerly countries, such as southern Europe and the southern United States, with a translation more focused on scent (more relevant in hot weather) than on light. Most of all because I am impressed by how the industry has addressed the market evolution with variable success. Some businesses have struggled to interpret what was happening in people's lives, even if they had long experience. Others instead have gifted us with products that people love. Surely this industry is a perfect synecdoche: it provides a clear, simple example of what is happening in many other industries, and in society at large. So let's use this simple case to introduce a framework that may enable us to understand why people love meaningful products, and then we will apply this framework to other, more complicated settings.

MEANING

Figure 2.1 is our starting framework. It gives form to a basic concept: people search for meaning. Whenever they act, whenever they do something in life, there is a meaning behind it.

By "meaning" here we refer to the *purpose* people try to achieve: *why* they do things. To achieve this purpose, they may use solutions (products or services), which is *how* they do things. For example, I lit a candle (the solution) in my mother's home in the mountain *because* I wanted to illuminate the room when the power went off. Illuminating the room was my purpose. Three decades later my mother placed a candle on the dinner's table *because* she wanted to welcome me with warmth; welcoming was the new purpose, the new meaning.

Although this starting framework looks simple, in reality it stands on layers of concepts, definitions, theories, reflections, debates, and unsolved questions, especially connected to what "meaning" is. We will not dig into this rich discussion here. Not because it is irrelevant, but for reasons that I will explain a few lines below, and that are connected to the deep essence and insight of this book. First, however, let's clarify what "meaning" is in the framework of figure 2.1.

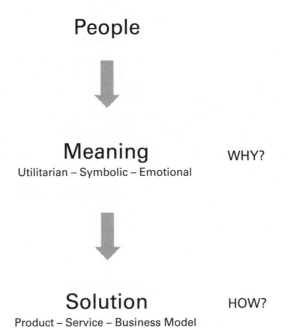

People

Meaning   WHY?
Utilitarian – Symbolic – Emotional

Solution   HOW?
Product – Service – Business Model

Figure 2.1
People search for meaning.

"Meaning" can have at least three main acceptations, according to English dictionaries.[7]

1. The thing, idea, or feeling that a sound, word, sign represents (e.g., "the meaning of the word 'friendship'");

2. The things or ideas that somebody wishes to communicate (e.g., "by offering you this gift I mean we are friends"), and the ideas that writers, artists, musicians try to express in their work (e.g., "the meaning of this song is about friendship");

3. The special importance or *purpose* of something; the sense of purpose that makes you feel that your life is valuable (e.g., "friendship means a lot to me; friendship gives meaning to my life").

All these concepts are strongly related to each other, and they all apply to our framework. But the third one, i.e., meaning as purpose, is the main focus of this book.

Coming to the example of candles, the first concept is connected to the meaning that an object called "candle" has. There are signs that make us interpret a candle as a candle: for example a wick surrounded by wax that creates a visible flame. In a way, objects and products "speak" to us through a language. Designers indeed often denote this as a "product language," determined for example by a product's shape, colors, or materials. And a product language can of course be a subject of innovation. A Yankee Candle surprises us because of its odd language that does not comply with what we would expect: the wick is not visible, but rather is hidden behind a hefty label that shades the flame. This new language, and in particular the outsized label indicating the fragrance, is however perfectly coherent with the new purpose of a Yankee candle: to create a scented environment. Although in this book we will consider this semiotic perspective on meaning (i.e., the language of things), this is not the core of our framework. In fact, the language of products refers more to the dimension of how than to the dimension of why.[8]

The second acceptation of "meaning" is connected to what one wants to express through an action or an artifact. What was my mother meaning by welcoming me with a candle? Here the focus is on communication and interpretation. This concept will play an important part in our reflection (indeed, every product brings a message and every meaning eventually is based on a narration, whose power depends on how it is communicated and interpreted).[9]

Our framework, however, expressly points to the third concept of meaning: "the special importance and *purpose* of something that make you feel that your life is *valuable*." In other words, the framework focuses our attention on *why* people do things, and their value. People buy Yankee Candles *because* they want to welcome friends in a cozy warm environment and put themselves in a good mood. This is *worth* more to them than a bright lightbulb shining in a room.

When we say that "people search for meaning," we explicitly refer to the fact that nowadays people are captivated by the "why" before they get into the "how." Before they decide which car to buy, they ask themselves why they should buy a car, and whether they ever need it. The purpose of things is not determined and instead is open up for discussion, reflection, interpretation … and innovation.

Meaning can have three types of purpose that typically occur simultaneously: a *utilitarian* meaning that expresses the practical utility of things (I light a candle because I want to cover, with its fragrance, the bad smell of smoke from the kitchen), a *symbolic* meaning that expresses how an action enables us to send messages to others (I light a candle because I want to show that I care for visitors), and an *emotional* meaning that expresses the value of an action for ourselves (I light the candle because it reminds me of Christmas or because my senses are pleased by its scent).

ORDINARY MEANING

So now we have specified what we mean here by meaning: it is the purpose, *why* people do things. Yet the richness and indeterminacy of this concept (meaning as purpose) is still considerable. The search for meaning in life has been reflected upon for centuries, especially in philosophy, and the subject is still totally open for discussion (luckily enough). This book, in any case, is rooted in the insight that nowadays people *do* search for meaning, in *everyday* life. In other words, in our society the question of the meaning of life has left the books, essays, and classrooms and entered the quotidian life of every person. In the past there were basically two categories of people who asked this question every day: teenagers and philosophers. I spent nights in front of fireplaces with my high school friends, talking about religion, where we come from, where we go, what life is all about. And this was nothing different from what our parents and their parents had done at the same age. The difference is that people nowadays keep wondering about the meaning of life even when they are adults (perhaps interacting with friends not in front of a fireplace but by posting aphorisms on Facebook). They may find temporary answers but hardly definitive, in a multifaceted, ever-changing society. Previous generations, instead, found answers as they moved into adulthood; they found a direction that had less frequent changes and was more easily suggested (determined) by a clear and stable institutional culture. As Barry Schwartz indicates, they slowly focused on the solutions without challenging the questions any more.

Then, only philosophers had the important role of questioning and challenging the institutional culture, nurturing a precious debate with proper theoretical instruments. But the search for meaning in life is now a subject for *everyone*, for the layperson.[10] It permeates our ordinary actions. Not only the major choices of our life but also the most humble ones, such as buying a car or lighting a candle. It affects the way we buy and use products and services. Behind any small action there is always a meaning, and there has always been. The difference is that people now are ready (and willing) to reconsider that meaning.[11]

Thus we are not setting out in this book to examine the different theories about the meaning of life. The point of our framework is that nowadays people are in search of meaning in their prosaic everyday actions. It's *ordinary* meaning. They find it by themselves.

WHY NEW MEANING IS RELEVANT NOWADAYS

We have seen that the search for meaning is not unprecedented. People have always searched for meaning. But in the past we could create products and manage businesses without caring too much about this dimension. Especially, innovation frameworks could neglect it. So why is meaning so relevant *today*, to the point of becoming the lens we need to wear when thinking about innovation? Why is meaning a protagonist in the ordinary life of people? Why are people delighted, now more then ever, by the discovery of *new* meaning? There are three possible lines of argument: opulence, opportunities, and change.

Opulence?

When I ask these questions, the answer I often get is: because we live in an opulent society. That is, the basic needs of people are today mainly satisfied (especially in western societies). As people become wealthier, they can afford to wonder about why to buy and use things. This explanation leverages the well-known model of the hierarchy of needs proposed by Maslow:[12] more advanced needs (such as the need for love, esteem, and self-actualization) become relevant only when the more fundamental needs are met (such as physiological needs or the need for safety).

At first sight, this hypothesis seems reasonable. But in reality it is not the strongest driver of an increased interest in meaning. A few months ago a friend visiting Burma sent me a photo of a stilt house. The family living there was not wealthy, at least according to western standards. Yet the structure of the building was rich in decoration, which had no functional utility. Why? Why did they invest time and resources in these creative decorations? In a need that belongs to the highest level of Maslow's scale, though their basic needs were not fully satisfied? The answer is that humans dance, sing, love, and search for meaning regardless of wealth or basic needs, as suggested by our ancestors who decorated caverns millennia ago. Rather, I would turn this argument upside down. A focus on meaning, rather than on solutions, is the best way to address people around the world regardless to wealth, especially at the so-called "bottom of the pyramid."[13] Because people, wherever they are, search for meaning.

Opportunities and the creation of identity

A more convincing hypothesis is advanced by Barry Schwartz in his book *The Paradox of Choice*.[14] Schwartz's point is that we live in a society that is overcrowded by opportunities. He does not spotlight opulence, but variety and indeterminacy. For example, the simple choice of cookies in a normal supermarket confronts us with hundreds of possibilities. The larger the number of opportunities, the less determined is the direction. "Our identity has now become a matter of choice," says Schwartz "We don't inherit an identity, we get to invent it. We have to reinvent our self as often as we like." His conclusions significantly depart from a Maslowian perspective that people search for meaning because lower levels of needs are already fulfilled. In his view, instead, more opportunities (personal, professional, and material) undermine happiness. "I believe that many modern Americans are feeling less and less satisfied even as their freedom of choice expands," writes Schwartz, and explains why, the larger the options, the more one gets lost: infinite choice gives a sense of regret for the opportunities we miss, it puts the blame for our failures completely on ourselves, it raises expectations. Infinite choice leads to paralysis rather than liberation. "Increased choice may actually contribute to the recent epidemic of clinical depression affecting much of the Western world."[15]

Unfortunately, businesses often miss Schwartz's insight and invest in more variety even when this does not make things more meaningful. We conducted a study to analyze product choice in the Italian furniture industry, and found that the least successful companies offer greater variety than the leaders. The most-appreciated firms instead focus on a clear identity and propose one distinct vision to people.[16] You may think also about the choice of phones or computers. I visited today the website of Nokia mobile devices (in reality it was a Microsoft website, since the Seattle giant recently acquired the struggling mobile business of Nokia). There are 70 models for sale (and I did not count the different colors and memory expansions, which rapidly lead to hundreds of choices). The Apple website has only 4 models. Yet guess which product people love (you can also imagine my dismay when, right after the departure of Steve Jobs, Apple launched iPhone 5C in colors). The increase in variety is not necessarily wrong. But it is not necessarily right either. Unfortunately, many businesses believe that more choice is better, assuming that people know what they want; you just have to give it to them. In reality, as shown above, people do not know exactly what they want. And if they know, they are always open to reconsidering and renegotiating: they are in a search process. Simply putting more meaningless things up there on the shelf does not necessarily make this search more effective.

Still, we do not wish for a world with fewer options. And in any case, the increase of opportunities is a long tide that ineluctably marks the evolution of our society. We cannot (and possibly shouldn't) stop it. We can, however, understand its dynamics more deeply and embrace it in a better way. A dynamic that is probably more visible with millennials, or the "me me me generation," as Joel Stein named them in a cover article in *Time*.[17] The main occupation of millennials is, apparently, building an identity, to the point of being accused of excessive narcissism. Adults in reality are not much different (use of Facebook, a significant identity-building device, is much higher in adults than in teenagers). The more the options we can pick from in terms of personal connections, lifestyles, beliefs, norms, the more the need to create an identity. In a context where institutional and traditional culture (such as religion and political ideals) becomes weak and no longer helps to clear up the confusion, this identity is not given. It cannot be borrowed from the outside. Everyone has to *create* and *build* it herself or himself. "What to do? How to act? Who to be? These are focal questions for everyone living in circumstances of late modernity," writes sociologist Anthony Giddens, "and ones which, on some level or another, all of us answer, either discursively or through day-to-day social behaviour. They are existential questions."[18]

Summarizing our reflections on this second contextual change: whether having more options is good or bad in people's lives, in any case having more options changes the source of value. In a context with low variety, the challenge is to build more solutions, more how. In a context with more choice, the challenge is to find the right direction, the right why. Hence the relevance of meaning.

Change

Until now we have been talking of meaning. However, our point, to be more precise, is that people are delighted by the discovery of *new* meaning. The key observation, which leads to our investigation of innovation, is that meanings change. To be honest, meanings have always changed in the history of humanity. The value of things, what society was looking for, evolved over time. In the past, however, the change of meaning occurred more slowly and more rarely. Slowness implied that business had time to reactively observe the changes in how customers gave meaning to things: the meaning slowly crystallized into needs, and needs into behaviors, which could be observed through user analysis techniques. In addition, rarity implied that after a shift in meaning occurred and a new product was offered to meet the new needs, competition could focus for years on performance improvements.

Nowadays innovation of meaning happens rapidly, frequently, and continuously. People's search for meaning never reaches an end. Perhaps it may slow down periodically, but then it goes into sudden accelerations. The reason for this continuous change can be exogenous (something happens in our life that is beyond our control, for example our partner gets a job offer in another city) or self-generated (we *want* to find a new meaning). Indeed, people have a latent aspiration for change and discovery, as sociologist Zygmunt Bauman discusses. Bauman uses the metaphor of "liquid modernity" to describe this constantly unstable status, in which people flow from one situation to another, like fluids.[19] Using our framework, this implies that people are not simply searching for meaning, but are *constantly* searching for *new* meaning. They continuously renegotiate meaning and are *always* open to new interpretations. "The question mark," says Bauman, "has moved from the side of the means to that of the ends."[20]

MEANINGS AND SOLUTIONS

The context described above, and which some enlightened sociologists, philosophers, and psychologists have powerfully captured in advance, has strong implications for how people interact with products and services.

The search for *new meaning* is silently and constantly at the center of people's behavior, and they are delighted by whoever supports them in this search. This includes organizations and businesses that, whether they are aware of it or not, contribute to people's everyday search for new meaning. Organizations address this search by proposing new visions (depending on the framework, other authors may call them value propositions or value innovations). For example Yankee Candle offers a vision that candles can make you feel better because of their fragrance. This is a delightful proposal to people who find meaning in a welcoming home. A vision, in other words, is a proposal of a direction, of a why. It's an organization's own interpretation of what could be meaningful to people; of what people could love. It's a vision because it expresses an organization's ability to see a path, to find significance in a complex environment that is full of opportunities, to picture a scenario that makes sense.[21]

A solution is instead the incarnation of this vision. It's the how offered by an organization that makes it possible for people to go in a meaningful direction. A large jar with a Beach Walk fragrance is Yankee Candle's solution for those who want to welcome friends who visit after a trip to Hawaii. It shows the fragrance on a large label instead of making the flame visible, because perfuming is the purpose of this candle/solution. In general, solutions may be products, services, processes, or entire business models and ecosystems (such as the Apple iPhone and its related iOS App Store).

INNOVATION OF MEANING

Meaningful visions are designed as much as solutions are. Indeed, creating a new vision, a new direction, implies making sense of things, which is exactly what design is all about.[22]

Innovation of meaning is what businesses do to address people's search for new meaning, to make people fall in love. People who need new solutions buy new products; people who search for new meaning buy new interpretations, new visions.

Finding meaning through innovation

In particular, innovation may contribute in two ways to people's search for new meaning:

- On the one hand it may enable new meaningful *directions* (i.e., it *expands* the space of opportunities). Think for example about the market of mobile phones around 2005, in which many innovations aimed at proposing new purposes for phones: as camera phones to take photos (e.g., Nokia's series N8 phones), as music players (e.g., Motorola's Rockr, the first phone integrated with Apple's iTunes), as business devices to write emails (e.g., BlackBerry's phones).

- On the other hand, it may offer a *clearer interpretation* that helps to make sense of a situation that has become too complex (i.e., it *cleans up* an excess of opportunities). For example, the iPhone proposed *one* new powerful vision of smartphones as personal devices, which eventually became the dominant interpretation in the market.[23]

The nature of innovation of meaning

Innovation of meaning is profoundly different in nature from innovation of solutions (see table 2.1):

- Innovation of solutions creates a new how, leaving the why unchanged. (It even reinforces the existing why. For example: creating a wick that generates a brighter flame implies reinforcing the concept of candles as tools to illuminate.) Innovation of meaning still consists of a new solution (a product, a service, a brand, a business model, or most likely a combination of these), but this solution also has a new why. There is a new purpose for people to use it. It embodies a new meaning.

- Innovation of solutions is an *answer*: it assumes that people have a *need* (e.g., it assumes that people need candles that last longer). Firms have to understand this need and devise an answer. Innovation of meaning instead assumes that people has no clear need but an area of inquiry, of exploration, of clarification. It is a *proposal* from us to people that addresses their search for meaning. When customers see an innovation of meaning, they *discover* a new possibility (e.g., I discover a new way to make friends feel better when they visit me: by lighting up a fragranced Yankee Candle).

Table 2.1
Differences between innovation of solutions and innovation of meaning

Innovation of Solutions	Innovation of Meaning
How (act)	Why (meaning)
Answer (need)	Discovery (proposal)
Negativities (problem)	Positivities (gift)
User (using)	Person (living)
Compete on performance (better)	Compete on value (meaningful)

- Innovation of solutions addresses *negativities*: it assumes that people have *problems* to be solved. Innovation of meaning addresses *positivities*: it assumes that people do not always think in terms of problems; and if they do, they are open to questioning them. What people have, instead, is a search for value, for worth, for opportunities. Candles do not solve the problem of illuminating our rooms, but they offer us a new positive opportunity: they enable us to connect with our friends and ourselves. Innovation of meaning often emerges as a *gift*: something people do not expect, but love once they see it.[24]

- Innovation of solutions addresses the how and therefore focuses on *users*, on those who use a solution. Innovation of meaning instead moves one level higher (see figure 2.1): it addresses the why, which does not pertain to the user but to the *person*. It does not restrict its focus to the act of *using* (e.g., how people light up a candle's wick), but it embraces the why of *living* (why we feel good when friends visit our home in a cozy atmosphere). This is why innovation of meaning has a higher potential to be disruptive by moving beyond existing users and product categories.

- The worth of innovation of solutions can be measured on a standard scale of performance. It aims at making things better (e.g., improving the luminosity of a candle's flame). Innovation of meaning instead redefines the scale of performance, it redefines what is valuable for people. It cannot be put on a scale (is it better to have a brighter flame or a more fragranced room?), because it *changes* the scale. It brings competition to what worth really is: *value* for a person.

Both innovations are relevant. People need better solutions to existing problems, and also new opportunities and possibilities. They have needs and dreams, negativities and positivities. And firms do both: new solutions that improve existing ones, and new meanings that radically change what is already on the market. Indeed, after a new meaning is created, a stream of solution improvements has to follow, to make the new direction increasingly powerful. So after Yankee Candles proposed its meaning of welcoming friends through candles, it followed up with an intense stream of solutions to implement this vision: from new kinds of fragrances to new formats, from custom-based packaging to accessories, from new materials to applications in new environments (like fragrances for cars and small spaces).

Of course, innovation of solutions is far more frequent than innovation of meaning. However, the remarkable change in our world is that the latter is not a rare event anymore. It happens continuously, as we have seen before. Right at this moment, as you are reading these lines, there are probably several organizations that are working on new solutions. But there is certainly at least one organization that is working on a new meaning. And, unlike for solutions, to completely overturn a competitive scenario there is no need for several meaningful visions: one is more than enough.

Why people fall in love with new meaningful visions

So now we can come back to love. And perhaps it is clearer now why what makes people fall in love is not a new solution but a new meaningful vision.[25]

Because we fall in love with the one who proposes something more, with the unexpected, with what we cannot build ourselves alone, with what we discover we like only after we see it. We do not fall in love with what we already know, with the expected (this we just build ourselves, or we buy it, until we buy something else).

Because we fall in love with the positivities, not the negativities. Love is a gift, not an answer to a problem (that's a psychologist). You may even be the best at solving one problem, but once the problem is solved, what's next? Love does not come this way. It's a striving for the beauty of the world.

Because we fall in love with what is meaningful for us, not for a better standard performance. You can't measure love on someone else's scale. You cannot even measure love on a scale. The one who promises a better performance is just doomed to loneliness among a multitude of the lonesome fighting for a better performance. When we love something that is meaningful, valuable, we do not even think in terms of performance (rather, we are even happy to forgive lack of perfection on some dimensions).

Because we fall in love when we are considered people, not users.

And ... endless love? This is why we talk of *new* meaning: endless love, in a changing world, only comes with *change*. Love is a shared journey: meanings change, endless love remains.

3 Competing through Meaning

The Value for Businesses

"Yes ... but ..."

This is probably your reaction after chapter 2. I can picture our conversation as if we were sitting next to each other on a sofa, sipping a cup of hot chocolate (well, perhaps you would drink something fancier) after listening to my reflections on meaning.

"Yes ... this story of the candles was nice. I might agree on the scenario and the framework."

"Thanks," I would reply, grateful for the appreciation.

"And these reflections about love," you might add. "You come from a country, Italy, that loves the love of love. Italians seek beauty for the sake of beauty ..."

I would smile: "That's a kind of stereotype that has been irreparably harmed by the latest political events in my country. Touché. I take in your remark. Love is important and delicate. We can't play with this word."

"And then, this story of your mom. Mothers are not the only ones in this world who buy products."

"Please, leave my mom out of the debate. I warn you. I'm Italian, you know?" I would start to get a little nervous here.

"You are the one who mentioned her in the previous chapter," you would properly reply.

"Touché, for the second time. Listen, before you knock me down with a third blow, would you please tell me what makes you concerned?"

Then you would let it out: "Yes, I like these stories, and they might be true for candles and love, but ... but how is this connected to *business*? I mean to those mundane things like profit, growth, job creation, competition, and wealth? And is this happening in *any* industry, aside from candles? How is this connected to *my* business?"

Touché, for the third time … because these are important questions that I have postponed. The previous chapter, indeed, discussed the value of meaning from the perspective of people: those who search for meaning. In this chapter we will mirror that reflection with the perspective of businesses and organizations: those who propose new visions.

We will start by addressing your first question: How does innovation of meaning create *business* value? Why is it *relevant* in current competition? And especially *when* is it relevant? What are the contextual drivers that lead to new meaning? When it is likely to occur? (I.e., when is it likely that in an industry a new vision succeeds, hopefully proposed by you rather than by a competitor?)

During this discussion we will introduce new examples of innovations of meaning, which will also help to address your second question: Does it happen in any industry? In the second part of the chapter we will complement these examples with a more extensive map of cases from a broad *variety of industries* and businesses: in products and services, in consumer and industrial markets, in profit and not-for-profit organizations. These cases are arranged in the appendix in an essential schematic format, with the purpose of giving you fast access to a large range of contexts and situations. Hopefully, this map will cover areas that are close to your business. So that, after journeying through this chapter, we will have addressed your doubts about whether there is any industry, business, or context that is immune to innovation of meaning.

Eventually, this chapter aims to create a better understanding of why in *your* industry there is an urge for a new meaning *now*, why there are definitely some competitors who are working on claiming this space, and why you may not want to be the second one in.

WHERE VALUE IS IN A WORLD AWASH WITH IDEAS

The rules of markets are sometimes very simple. Value is where two conditions hold simultaneously: demand is high, and supply is scarce. There is nothing more precious than something that is much desired but hard to find.

There is no doubt that in recent years the demand for innovation has been at its highest peak, and still is. This holds not only for innovation of solutions, but also, as seen in the previous chapter, for innovation of meaning. They are both in high demand. These two types of innovation, however, are significantly different in terms of supply. New solutions are not in short supply, while new meanings are.

It may seem bold, almost offensive, to posit that new solutions are not rare, after a decade of studies that have invited firms to create more ideas. But my point is indeed aligned with these claims. It leverages their positive consequences: ten years of studies and celebrations of ideas eventually had an impact. Nowadays new solutions are in large supply.

Consider for example the number of ideas generated in relation of the Deepwater Horizon oil spill. On 20 April 2010 an explosion destroyed a drilling rig in the Gulf of Mexico, taking the lives of eleven people and starting a chain of events that resulted in the largest marine oil spill in the history of drilling. Faced by the disappointing early attempts to stop the spill, the US Federal Government and BP launched the Deepwater Horizon Response website in a desperate search for ideas from whoever could contribute. In a few weeks, more than 20,000 ideas were submitted by a scattered global community of scientists, engineers, and entrepreneurs (even from Hollywood celebrities such as Scarlett Johansson).[1]

Ideas for solving problems are not today's rarest asset. Indeed, if there is something not difficult to find in our society, it is ideas. First because we live in a society where more than 30% of the workforce belongs to the creative class (as Richard Florida already noticed in 2003 in his book *The Rise of the Creative Class*), and therefore there is a great potential for idea creation, and second because the web gives easier access to this diffused wellspring of ideas. The case of the Deepwater Horizon Response website is an example of crowdsourcing and open innovation, an approach pioneered in the 1990s by open-source movements in software development: the kernel of the Linux operating system is the work of a community of more than 10,000 developers.[2] Tapping crowds of creative people to produce massive amounts of ideas is now a practice accessible to everyone. There are indeed more than 1,000 idea marketplaces where organizations can post problems and receive solutions from creative communities. In the areas of engineering and science, probably the best-known such marketplace is Innocentive, which can leverage a community of more than 300,000 solvers. In the area of design and communication, idea competitions posted on Designboom receive typically between 3,000 and 6,000 ideas each.

Mechanisms that enable firms to leverage the creativity of outsiders are nowadays also applied within organizations. In 2005 IBM used its Jam technology to involve 150,000 employees in an intranet-based online brainstorming that produced hundreds of thousands of ideas in just three days. Not all corporations use a similar massive effort at idea generation, but most of them have recently put in place processes to invite employees to generate ideas. I have rarely met companies in the last five years that told me they did not do brainstorming creative sessions.

Getting ideas today, from outside or inside an organization, is increasingly easy and cheap. I do not mean that ideas for new solutions are irrelevant. New solutions are important and necessary. But they are so abundant and easily accessible that they hardly make a difference in competition. Creating one more idea will definitely not provide additional value.[3]

What is scarce instead is the ability to produce visions, to see a meaningful direction in this abundance of options. Actually, ideas and meanings are directly correlated: the more our society generates ideas, the more what really makes a difference is the ability to make sense of this complexity and to propose a new meaning. The examples we include in this chapter, especially in the last section illustrating innovation in several industries, show that whereas every company keeps generating new solutions, there are only a few that are capable of generating new meanings; and these are the ones that win in the marketplace.

What drives them to generate new meanings? There are four possible drivers that you should check to understand whether it is time for an innovation of meaning: a misalignment with the market, a commoditization, a new technological opportunity, a lost focus in your organization. Let's explore them closely.

STUCK IN AN OLD MEANING

"Some French Guy Has My Car" is the title of a 2015 article in *Time* by Joel Stein about the new sharing economy.[4] Its argument is that nowadays people prefer to rent things instead of buying them. Take for example mobility. The car industry is still stuck in the old myth that people want to own a car. But the scenario has radically changed. Why should one own a car nowadays? In western countries 80% of the people live in urban areas, where public transportation is a better option.[5] Or people fly from one city center

DRIVER	SYMPTOM	QUESTIONS TO ASK YOURSELF	OUTCOME OF INNOVATION OF MEANING
People	Misalignment People's lives change, but an industry is still stuck in old interpretations	Is there a change in people's lives? Are customers unaffectionate toward products in our industry, notwithstanding continuous innovations?	New Alignment Capture what people are really searching for (latent aspirations)
Competition	Undifferentiation All competitors focus on the same performance	When was the last time a new meaning emerged in your industry? How long has the industry been competing on the same performance parameter?	New Delighters Stand apart from the competition
Technology	Technology Substitution A new technology is emerging, but until now it is simply substituting an old one to improve an existing performance	Is a new technology emerging?	Technology Epiphany Capture the untapped value of a new technology
Organization	Lost/Unfocused Your organization has lost its purpose or offers too many meanings	What is the meaning of your product? How long ago did you explicitly question it? Have new key people joined your organization?	Focus Provide a direction, a clear value to customers, energize the organization, and build leadership

Figure 3.1
When is innovation of meaning relevant?

to another. So their car sits idle most of the time. And when a car is the only way to get somewhere, still most of its seats stay empty. Does this underutilization pay back the cost in terms of purchasing, insurance, maintenance, parking spaces at home and at work?

Meanwhile new things have happened in people's lives: they have mobile phones in their hands that enable them to instantly search for a ride or rent a car, exactly when needed, where needed, and the kind of car they need. On the other hand there are lots of people interested in rounding up their income by profiting from their underutilized cars, underutilized parking lots, underutilized time when moving around alone.

Most car manufacturers, still stuck in the vision that people want to own a car, have lost touch with these changes in people's lives, with their aspirations. They still compete on who sells more cars, but sales are flat and profitability is as low as ever.[6] Other players have instead captured this shift in what is meaningful for people, and have proposed a new vision: moving around in someone else's car. Take for example the growing business of car-sharing services, such as Zipcar: with a mobile application one can instantly find an available car nearby, rent it for a short ride at a very low cost, and park it in a convenient place. Or one can easily take a lift from drivers belonging to the Uber community. And for longer rides outside cities, one can leverage BlaBlaCar that connects people who need to travel with drivers who have empty seats. Finally, for longer rentals, one can borrow someone else's car through RelayRides, a peer-to-peer car sharing service focused on long-term rentals.

The first major driver of innovation of meaning is a *change in people's lives*. Society changes, and it changes at a fast pace. Often incumbent firms are slower in capturing these transformations. They keep investing in developing better solutions, but their innovations are still driven by an interpretation of meaning that is stuck in the past. The innovation trajectory of the industry therefore becomes *misaligned* with the life trajectory of people. Often this misalignment is unspoken. In fact customers themselves cannot articulate what their aspirations are, since there is no other option in the market yet (marketing frameworks often talk in this case of *latent needs*). They only feel a general sense of malaise, the feeling that the available products are not really meaningful. As soon as a business addresses this misalignment and proposes a new offer that better fits with the new scenario, then it's love at first sight. The old meaning finally looks clearly obsolete, and people move into the new meaning.

In the case of cars, the companies that have addressed the misalignment between owning four wheels and experiencing mobility when needed have created a remarkable business, in spite of the crisis of the industry. Zipcar was acquired in 2013 by Avis for about US $500 million. Uber has raised US $4.9 billion, BlaBlaCar US $110 million, RelayRides US $52 million.

Several other firms have similarly succeeded by capturing changes of meaning in the market, i.e., by addressing the misalignment between the life trajectory of people and the innovation trajectory of an industry. Stein's article in *Time* mentions a long list of companies that thrive by addressing the change toward a sharing economy. Only 20% of people in industrialized countries disagree with the statement "I could happily live without most of the things I own."[7] Why, for example, should one own high-end clothing and accessories that one wears on only a few occasions and that quickly go out of fashion? Renting them is more reasonable. It gives you the opportunity to look different every time and choose the perfect look for a specific occasion and mood. Jennifer Hyman, cofounder of Rent the Runway, which lends high-end women's clothing to its more than 4 million members, says: "Look at *Sex and the City* and the Carrie Bradshaw culture of 'Look how big my closet is and look how much I've spent on shoes.' It would be considered kind of yucky today to do so."[8] Other changes in society support the meaning of experiencing rather than owning: the existence of platforms such as mobile phones that enable accessing things instantaneously, when needed, where needed; the fact that people live in cities, which makes it easy to share; the striving for socialization, which makes renting from others an opportunity to meet new people; the slowing economic growth that has shrunk family budgets; the rising number of freelancers, who are free and willing to round up their wages by renting their underutilized goods and time; and, of course, a growing concern for creating a sustainable economy. Companies that are profiting by addressing this change of meaning are AirBnB, where one can rent real homes and rooms from normal people instead of going to hotels; ParkWhiz that enables you to rent your empty parking spot to a stranger on the fly; crowdfunding and crowdlending services, such as Lending Club, where one get loans from peers instead of going to a bank; Yerdle, which allows people to give away used unwanted stuff in exchange for credits that one can use to get other users' unwanted stuff; SolarCity that enables one to sell to a utility excess electricity generated by a home's solar panels. All of them have not only provided more meaningful solutions but have created significant business success: AirBnB has raised $795 million from investors, ParkWhiz $12 million, Yerdle $10 million, Lending Club $392 million, and Solar City $1 billion.

So the first question you want to ask, to check whether it is time to envision a new meaning, is: Is there a significant change in the market scenario? Is there a feeling of malaise in our customers, who seem increasingly unaffectionate toward products offered by our industry, even in spite of significant innovation in solutions? Is there a segment in the market that is starting to show new behaviors?

DELIGHT

Can you build a business on risk? Definitely yes.

Many organizations face every day an enormous array of risk: financial institutions, manufacturing plants that depend on sophisticated IT systems, corporations that deal with complicated regulations, large construction sites. We live in a world where the chances that something goes wrong are significant. Organizations, especially the largest ones such as banks, have appointed risk managers to control for risk. And for years business consultants have helped these organizations by offering professional risk management services: they have built a profit on their clients' fear of risk.

Most of these risk management services were built with a specific vision: first, risk is a negative factor which needs to be avoided, or at least minimized in terms of the impact and probability of bad events. Second, risk is an operative factor that can compromise the ability of an organization to achieve its strategic objectives.

Within mainstream management culture, risk has always been addressed as something negative, or at least as a challenge to be dealt with. In business schools, risk is part of the curriculum, of course. It is discussed in many courses (strategy, innovation, etc.), but when it comes to practical techniques and tools, risk is often examined in more operational courses (e.g., project management, finance, or accounting) as something to manage by reducing the chances of negative events or mitigating their impacts.

In 2010 Deloitte Australia was facing a significant challenge: risk management was increasingly seen as mainly connected to compliance with regulations and faultless functioning of technology. Risk services were therefore becoming a commodity in the industry of professional services. Indeed, most of Deloitte's competitors repositioned in the lower end of the market by creating more cost-effective solutions to control for compliance, while others discontinued their offerings and incorporated risk services into other product categories such as insurance.

Deloitte, on the contrary, went in a novel direction: to turn risk from just a source of concern into a *source of value*. Deloitte's new vision was that in a world inherently characterized by uncertainty, those who can manage risk better might also be able to capture valuable chances that are inaccessible to others. Hence in 2011 Deloitte launched a new line of risk services, under the slogan "Know the worth of risk," that, alongside traditional compliance, also provided advisory services targeted to the upper levels of their client organizations, such as the CEO and the board. By

changing the meaning of risk from something negative to something positive, Deloitte escaped the race into commoditization. In three years its
revenues from risk services rose by 30% and, thanks to the higher value
provided, profitability rose by 80%, in a market where most competitors
were downsizing.

The Deloitte case unveils a second major driver of innovation of meaning: the definition of new dimensions of delight. When an industry keeps
focusing for a long time on the same meaning (e.g., risk is something to be
avoided), it tends naturally to converge toward a state of *commoditization*:
competitors fight to provide better solutions for the existing meaning, by
increasing the performance or cutting costs; over time, however, as improvements occur, there is a natural saturation (i.e., improvements get smaller
and smaller) so that differences among competitors become marginal (this
phenomenon is determined by what are known as S curves in technological
development). In this context, the winner is the one who identifies a new
performance parameter in a different direction than where competition is,
such as Deloitte did: leveraging risk as a source of value. Kim and Mauborgne call this move a "blue ocean strategy," i.e., a move away from the red
ocean where the crowd of competitors provide commodities, to identify a
new source of value.[9] Analogously Gary Hamel calls this the search for the
white uncontested space. In innovation studies an effective framework to
describe this type of innovation is the model of Noriaki Kano, which states
that within an industry performance parameters change over time from
being delighters (new value sources that make a significant difference in the
market) into linear parameters (existing value sources where most competitors strive for a better performance) into must-haves (value parameters that
are necessary but that do not provide advantage).[10] Innovation of meaning
is the most effective way to identify new *delighting* dimensions and move
into an uncontested blue ocean.

Take for example the case of Vox, a furniture manufacturer in Poland.
The company has recently released a new range of products for bedrooms,
an area of minor innovation in the furniture industry in the last decades.
Indeed, unlike other areas of the home (such as kitchen or bathrooms)
where significant innovations have been proposed lately (with a significant
increase in profit margins), bedrooms still look more or less as they looked
six decades ago. Vox was concerned, however, by major changes in customer demographics, in particular the aging of the European population.

Elderly people spend a significant part of their time, even during the day, in their bedroom, especially when sick. Bedrooms are therefore an important part of people's lives. To escape commoditization, Vox has proposed a new vision: transforming bedrooms into "living bedrooms," a central space of a house where elderly people could meet relatives and friends, socialize with them, and pleasurably spend time, just as usually happens in a living room (and as teenagers do in their own bedrooms). One of the products that came out of this process, for example, is a bed incorporating a large bookshelf (something that typically belongs to the living room), space for visitors to put their shoes, and even a folding screen to watch movies together—a bed whose concept eventually appealed even to younger generations, who place this bed in the main open space of their small apartments. Thanks to this new strategy Vox expanded its business in Europe and overturned the lowering profitability of the bedroom product category.

So the second set of questions you want to ask, to see whether it is time to envision a new meaning, is: How long ago did the dominant meaning in our industry last change? Haw long ago was a new delighting performance proposed? Has competition on the existing meaning reached saturation? Do our offerings and those of our competitors look increasingly similar? Is the profit margin shrinking?

TECHNOLOGY EPIPHANIES

Philips is well known for being at the forefront in the development of new technologies, having introduced several breakthroughs such as the first compact cassette in 1962, the first video cassette recorder in 1972, and the laser disc. Profits from technological advances, however, have not always reflected the technological muscle of the company. One of the main reasons has been the failure to envision and capture the real value of technologies. Philips's strategy was often that of searching for *technological substitutions*. In this strategy, given an existing problem, new technologies substitute for old ones to provide better performance; in other words, technologies are not seen as an opportunity to address new meanings (what people search for), but to improve solutions within an existing meaning. This strategy has informed the development of technological roadmaps (for example from GSM, to 3G, to 4G in telecommunications). Technology substitution strategies often work, but they have a substantial limit: most often a technology may enable new behaviors, new experiences, that are much more meaningful than a mere improvement of the old. To fully capture the value of a technology, one should explore how this technology can facilitate a change of meaning.

In the 1990s Philips activated a new strategy for technology development: to envision how technologies developed by its R&D could be used to generate new meaningful experiences. To this purpose, it decided to more substantially involve its design center, Philips Design, in the exploration of new applications. For example, in the early 2000s Philips was exposed to a wealth of opportunities connected to ambient technologies: LED light sources, ambient and sound control technologies, image projectors, radio-frequency semiconductors such as RFID. In front of these opportunities, in addition to searching for substitutions (e.g., conceiving LEDs merely as substitutes for bulb lamps, to provide better illumination), Philips activated a series of projects led by Philips Design aimed at searching for new meaning. "The idea was to move from how people could give meaning to things, rather than simply pushing our technologies into the market," said Stefano Marzano, then CEO and Chief Creative Director of Philips Design. One of these projects focused on health care.[11] Philips was already a well-established producer of medical imaging systems such as X-ray, ultrasound, computed tomography (CT), and magnetic resonance imaging (MRI). Traditionally, radiologists have been searching for powerful devices to improve the quality of images and reduce an examination's throughput time. Innovation in the imaging industry has been mainly focused therefore on technological substitutions to develop faster devices that could capture more data in less time. In other words innovation had supported a meaning that quality of image comes from speed and power. Philips itself had been leading the development of powerful devices, being first to release a CT scanner capturing 256 images per rotation of the X-ray tube (up from 16 images about a decade earlier), and improving the rotation speed (an indicator of the machine's ability to suppress motion, similar to the shutter speed in a camera) to 0.27 seconds per rotation (from 0.5 seconds per rotation a decade earlier). Marzano instead wanted to explore whether ambient technologies could transform what a "good examination" meant.

The project led to a totally new system, Ambient Experience for Healthcare (AEH), that has created two significant changes in what is meaningful in the imaging industry. First, the quality of an image does not depend only on the power of the equipment, but also on the level of stress of the patient. For example, children tend to have a high level of anxiety when undergoing exams inside CT devices and in most cases need to be sedated to reduce movement, which however compromises their safety and increases the throughput time of the procedure. Second, and even more radical, the level of stress of the patient is affected not only by what happens during the exam but also *before* and *after* the exam, and in particular by the *environment* in which the entire experience occurs. The AEH experience creates a more relaxing ambience by using the "ambient technologies," such as LED sources, projection of video animations, RFID radiofrequency sensors, sound control systems, and switchable glasses. For example, soft warm illumination from LEDs in the hospital rooms promotes feelings of physical and mental well-being and relaxation, both for staff and patients. If the patient is a child, when she enters the hospital she can choose a theme, such as "aquatic" or "nature," and is given a puppet. This latter includes an RFID sensor that is used to automatically start up the theme—a relaxing combination of animation, lighting, and audio—when the patient walks toward the examination room. The theme can also be used in the preparation room to train the child about how to stay still during the examination: a nurse may show a video of a character in the sea and ask the child to hold her breath when the character dives underwater to catch a treasure; when the same sequence is projected during the exam, the child holds her breath at the right moment and stands still for the scan. Children undergoing CAT scanning are even able to do their own clinical scan of a variety of soft toys, through a scaled-down version of the device positioned in the waiting room. This Kitten Scanner helps replace the fear experienced by children with understanding about the procedure they are about to face. In the treatment room there is also two-way visual and audio communication via a camera between patients and staff and/or loved ones waiting nearby, to promote contact and reduce patient feelings of alienation. The result is that as patients are more relaxed, they can be dealt with quicker and are less likely to refuse treatment. This approach has proved to provide a better clinical performance (e.g., a 30–40% reduction in the sedation rate for children under age three, a radiation dosage reduced two- to fourfold) and better efficiency (e.g., a 15–20% improvement in throughput on devices and a reduced number of steps to point a CT scan from six to two). Hospitals using AEH therefore become more efficient and more attractive both to patients and top personnel.

Why was Philips first in recognizing this promising application of ambient technologies? The reason is that competitors were focusing on technological substitutions. They explored the potential of new technological opportunities by extrapolating the existing dominant meaning in the industry, i.e., that the quality and cost of an examination depends on the power of the device. Therefore, they only searched for those technologies that could increase data and speed. Ambient technologies, which were well known in the industry, did not fit into this scope, and were therefore screened off (or used for marginal features: LEDs for examples were used as indicators of functions in the devices). When Philips was exposed to ambient technologies, it followed a different approach. It first questioned the existing meanings and envisioned a new one: the quality and cost of examinations depends on how the patient interacts with the hospital environment before, during, and after the exam. Then, in the light of this new meaning, the value of ambient technologies became more easily recognizable.[12]

The third source of innovation of meaning is therefore technology. When a new technology emerges, an industry often focuses at first on a narrow innovation strategy: *technology substitutions* (see figures 3.2 and 3.3): they use the new technology to *substitute* an old one in order to better address an *existing* meaning. But in reality every new technology usually offers the potential to create novel meaning that transcends existing needs. Companies that succeed in creating such products look for what I call *technology epiphanies*. Indeed, an epiphany is "a meaning that stands in a superior position" and "a perception of the essential nature or meaning of something." A technology epiphany is therefore a new application that is more meaningful to customers. This superior application of a technology is often not visible at first, because it does not satisfy existing needs. Rather it is a quiescent meaning that is revealed only when a company challenges the dominant interpretation of what a product is and creates unsolicited solutions that people are not currently seeking.

Technology is indeed a major driver of innovation of meaning, if properly approached. In my previous book *Design-Driven Innovation*[13] I illustrate several cases of technology epiphanies: with the Wii, Nintendo used MEMS accelerometers to transform the meaning of game consoles from a passive

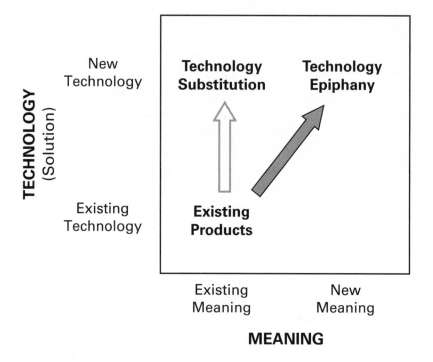

Figure 3.2
Technology epiphanies as a driver of change of meaning.

immersion in a virtual world into an active physical entertainment in the real world, through better socialization. With the iPod, Apple, differently than early manufacturers of MP3 players who saw the new technology as a mean to replace the Walkman as a portable music player (think of the "MP-Man"), used digital audio encoding to access music seamlessly: by discovering and tasting new music on the iTunes Store, buying it with a click, organizing music into personal playlists, and listening to it.

The limits of technological substitutions

Sometimes focusing on substitutions instead of epiphanies may even lead to major downturns. Consider Kodak. Many people think that one of the main reasons for its failure is due to its slow reaction to the emergence of digital photography. But in reality Kodak invested heavily in digital technologies as soon as they emerged. It was among the first to invest in digital media to store photos such as the PhotoCD, with new hardware,

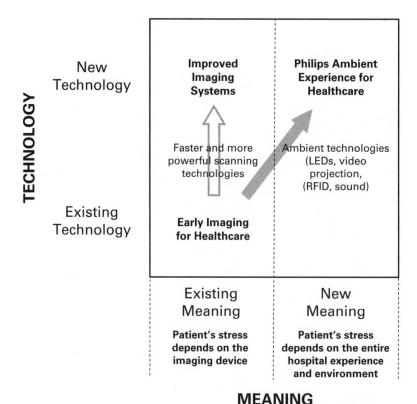

Figure 3.3
The technology epiphany realized by Philips's Ambient Experience for Healthcare in the market for imaging.

software, and an entire infrastructure to support them. And indeed for a while Kodak became the largest producer of CD-ROMs in the world. The problem was that Kodak looked at digital technologies merely as substitutes for chemical-based photography. They would enable a more convenient handling of images, but the experience would remain unchanged: photos would still be the way to "capture the moment," to create memories, that people would later share while sitting in their living room, only now displayed on TVs instead of on paper. What digital technologies did instead was to enable a radical change in the meaning of photography (figure 3.4): from a way to create memories to a way to communicate. Digital images can be easily shared through networks. And they are a much faster way to

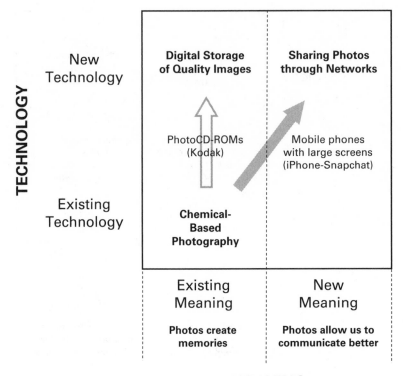

Figure 3.4
The technology epiphany of digital photography, and the failure of Kodak.

communicate where we are and what we are doing than writing texts. In communication, an image is worth a thousands words. Kodak missed this epiphany, which was later captured by producers of smart phones, Apple first, with its daring move to a phone where images could be not only captured but also sent, and especially displayed in the phone-wide screen of the receiver. People nowadays do not simply store photos. They talk through photos, regardless of their quality, and sometimes even regardless of storage, as the success of Snapchat has shown.

Digital epiphanies

Digital technologies have enabled several epiphanies.[14] Think for example about the industry of turn-by-turn navigation. In the late '90s the first navigation portable devices (NPDs) based on GPS systems, such as Garmin USA (leader in the USA) and TomTom (leader in Europe), had a clear meaning: people used them to find the best route to get to a new place they had never been before. With the diffusion of smart phones, new applications appeared in the early 2010s, such as Google Maps or the Maps of Apple. The technology was new, the performance improved substantially compared to NPDs (Google for example integrated the maps with its search engine, providing advice on finding best places in the vicinity of the destination, with reviews and ratings and direct access to telephone numbers), but the meaning remained unchanged: people use a map on their mobile phone to get to unknown places. Waze instead leveraged the mobile technology to radically change the meaning of mobile navigation (see figure 3.5): to get to destinations you already know (e.g., to your office), but in a faster or more effective way. In fact Waze is a social, peer-to-peer navigation app: it uses

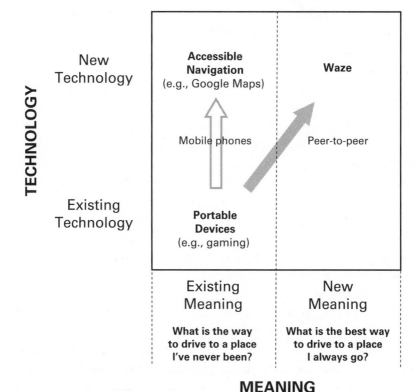

Figure 3.5
The technology epiphany realized by Waze in the market of turn-by-turn navigation.

input from other drivers who are traveling on the same route to provide real-time information on traffic and conditions. As there are often several paths that connect our home to our office, one can use this information to pick the best route in that specific moment. The founders of Waze therefore unveiled a new meaning and value for mobile technology for navigation: not only to conveniently track the route to unknown places (as a substitute for a Garmin navigator), but especially to receive real-time information from peers in order to better reach known places. Their business reward was remarkable: in 2013 Waze was chosen by a community of more than 50 million users,[15] when Google decided to buy it out for more than US $1 billion.[16]

So the third question you want to ask, to see whether it is time to envision a new meaning, is: Are we sure that a new technology that has just emerged can only be used to better perform an existing task? Is there a potential for an epiphany, i.e., does the new technology enable the creation of a new meaningful experience that has even more value for people?

LOST IN TRANSLATION

"You know ... many people in our organization do not know anymore why they are working here ... they do their daily job ... even efficiently ... but they have lost touch with why they are doing what they are doing ... why we create value for the market ... they wake up in the morning and come to the office ... but they do not ask themselves why ... they just do it."

The brand manager of an Italian high-end firm was explaining to me the challenge her corporation was facing. As the firm experienced ten years of success and rapid growth, and the organization grew larger with new management joining, the spirit of the earlier glorious times was lost. Lost was the ability to listen to the market, the joy of creating something unique for people, the awareness of doing something important for the world. Slowly the animated discussions of the early days, when a small corporate team debated on what to offer and why it made sense, faded away to leave space for the new challenge: how to manage a large organization in an efficient manner. The meaning of the business was not a subject of conversation anymore. It was somehow taken for granted. Not reflected upon, not reloaded, not criticized, not updated. The new people who joined the organization received an indication of the strategic direction of the firm, but they were not involved in critical reflections on what was meaningful for them and how this could be integrated into the company's vision. The implication: slowly the meaning was lost in several watered-down interpretations, often even contrasting among themselves. The organization was a machine with a perfect engine that did not know where to go and kept changing direction. Lost in the complex map of competition.

Sometimes organizations have a similar pattern. They slowly turn off any reflection on meaning. They enjoy success, take the why of things for granted, and focus on the how. The consequence is that people get silently lost. The only way to get energy back, to give them back a sense of purpose, to restart creating value, is to reactivate a reflection on meaning. Or better: on a *new* meaning; because no one gets energized by reflecting on the "good old times." People love to be protagonists in the reflection on meaning, and this can only be done by enabling them to steer a new direction, to have a new say on where to go, to feel empathy with others' search for meaning.

So the fourth question you want to ask, to see whether it is time to envision a new meaning, is: When was the last time your organization was explicitly engaged in a critical reflection on the meaning of your business? Do people in your organization know what the meaning of your product or service is? Do they have a clear sense of the purpose of their job? Can they explain why it is important for society? Does your company have a clear focused identity, or is it proposing different meanings to the market? Did new key people recently join your organization?

IS THERE ANY BUSINESS WITHOUT NEW MEANING?

Your second question was: Is innovation of meaning happening in any industry? Is it relevant for my business?

The answer is simple: innovation of meaning is a major driver of value in all industries, and it is probably disrupting your industry at this moment. Why?

First, because any product, any service, anything has meaning. Because they are chosen and experienced by people (either end consumers or people in organizations). There is always a why, a reason why people and organizations use things.

Second, because every industry is overcrowded. In any industry there is an abundance of solutions and ideas, in consumer as well as in business-to-business markets. In both contexts ideas for innovation are pouring in from every side: crowdsourcing, user-generated ideas, massive brainstorming. The problem your clients have is not "please give me one more solution," but "please help me find what is a meaningful direction for me."

Third, because in any industry the speed of change has soared. Therefore you cannot wait for customers to come to you with new needs and requests. You would simply observe the result of new meanings proposed by others. You need to act proactively, otherwise it is too late.

To support these statements, I provide a quick review of cases of innovation of meanings, spanning a broad variety of industries, that have disrupted the dynamics of competition. I include both products and services, consumer and industrial markets. Figure 3.6 displays a quick overview, while in the book's appendix I provide short descriptions of the cases and the changes of meaning they have introduced.

MEANING WHEN YOUR CUSTOMER IS ANOTHER ORGANIZATION

Some special attention should be given to innovation of meaning in business-to-business industries, i.e., when you serve not an end customer but another organization. One might think that meanings are relevant only in end markets, because consumers are more inclined to emotional and symbolic meanings than are industrial clients. Instead, we have already seen examples such as Deloitte's Risk Services or Philips's Ambient Experience for Hospitals in which innovation of meaning is a driver of competitive advantage in business-to-business industries.

Indeed, innovation of meaning is even more relevant in industrial than in consumer markets. The reason is that, if you serve business clients, you may leverage innovation of meaning in three different ways (see figure 3.7).

Creating a new meaning for business clients

Business clients use products and services, and they use them to achieve a purpose, a why. This meaning does not necessarily need to be symbolic or emotional. The why of things can be definitely practical and driven by utility. For example, hospitals have started to use robots for simple

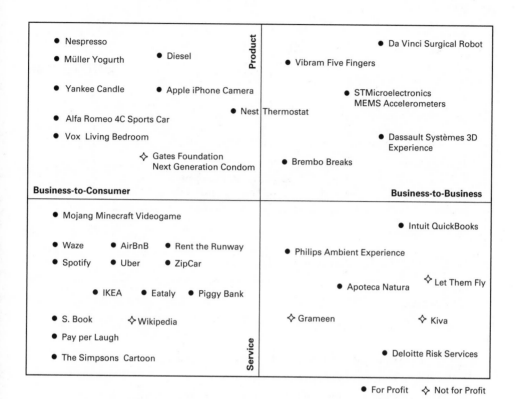

Figure 3.6
Cases of innovation of meaning that have disrupted competition in different industries.

handling operations (e.g., handling and distributing medicines within departments) *because* they want to improve productivity by substituting for human labor.

Given that business clients are exposed to changes in their context, this why (i.e., this meaning) changes as well. And today it changes at an unprecedented speed and depth. For example, the Da Vinci system is a robot that performs surgical operations, such as prostatectomy, with an extremely high precision. This allows expert doctors to conduct complex operations even when they age and start to have shaky hands. Or it can be used remotely through a network connection so that operations can be completed by the most expert doctors even if the patient is geographically distant. The Da Vinci system therefore has changed the meaning of robots for

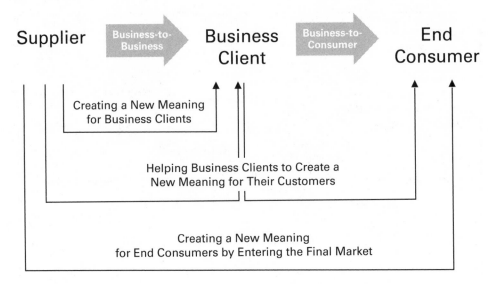

Figure 3.7
Three strategies for innovation of meaning in business-to-business industries.

hospitals. Not to substitute for doctors, but to support them in their profession. The meaning has changed from productivity to quality. Today the Da Vinci system has become the leading prostatectomy procedure.

The perspective of meaning especially invites us to look at the *people* who operate within our client organizations. And these people, who will choose and use a product, have specific purposes and meanings, both utilitarian, symbolic, and emotional. Consider for example the market for accounting applications. Large business clients have specialized units (e.g., finance and accounting) that take care of economic analysis. They have professionally dedicated workers who appreciate the support offered by sophisticated accounting applications. But if our client is a small business, e.g., a carpenter or a hairdresser, then their attitude to accounting is different. There is no professional accountant in these organizations, and doing accounting is definitely not the dream of carpenters and hairdressers. It's just a pain in the neck. This is the reason why Intuit QuickBooks has become the most popular accounting application for small businesses. Because all the other providers said, "Do you want to do accounting? Then use our application." Intuit instead had a different proposition: "You *don't* want to do accounting? Then use our application." Indeed, people in small businesses do not want to do accounting.

Helping a business client to create a new meaning for its end consumers

A business client has its own customers, who are also searching for meaning. You can help your client to innovate this downstream meaning thanks to the components and services you offer. STMicroelectronics, for example, helped Nintendo to create a new meaning for game consoles: from devices that enable teenagers to enter a virtual world, to devices they can use to stay real, to move and socialize better. This change of meaning is possible thanks to a component created by STMicroelectronics: a MEMS accelerometer located in the remote control of the Wii that allows it to track movement.

When STMicroelectronics creates a new component, it searches for new applications by building scenarios of meaning two stages downstream in the supply chain. It imagines how this new component might enable a new experience for the clients of its clients. These scenarios of meaning are built through workshops where engineers and marketers of STM's clients work side by side with STM's engineers and marketers. This of course implies developing new connections with client organizations: instead of interacting only with their purchasing departments, when the component technology is still not mature a supplier needs to working directly with its client's developers and innovators.

This strategy, of helping clients to envision new meaning thanks to the technologies you create, is highly appreciated by industrial clients. Since end consumers are today searching for new meanings, corporations nowadays value those suppliers that support them in their innovation process: who propose not simply new technologies, but also how these technologies can enable new meaningful experiences.

Creating a new meaning for end consumers by entering the final market yourself

Sometimes a supplier that envisions a new meaning for the end consumer may even decide to move downstream in the value chain and propose this new meaning itself. Consider for example Vibram, a supplier of rubber outsoles for footwear producers. In 2005 Vibram envisioned the possibility of changing the meaning of outdoor shoes. Traditionally, the footwear industry focused on creating thicker rubber soles that cushion people's feet from the ground. Vibram proposed a new meaning: using rubber technology to bring feet as close as possible to the ground, mimicking the dynamics of barefoot running. This possibility was so intriguing that Vibram decided to move downstream and produce the entire shoe itself. The shoe is called FiveFingers, since it works as a glove for feet: the sole is thin and flexible and the shoe is contoured to each individual toe. FiveFingers also brought the meaning of fashion and style into the rugged outdoor footwear industry, as the shoes come in bright colors.

BACK HOME AFTER A JOURNEY

This chapter has been a rapid journey. We have been visiting different industries, from peer-to-peer applications in the sharing economy to hospital imaging, from industrial robots to consulting services. This short exploration suggests that in a world overcrowded by ideas, no industry is exempt from innovation of meaning. Clients search for it. And pioneering firms do it. In *this moment* there is certainly someone, a competitor or an organization from an adjacent industry, who is imagining a new meaning for your clients. The point is not *whether* a new meaning is emerging. It is. The point is *how* to create one that is more meaningful.

So let's travel back home now, and get ready to dig into the process of innovation of meaning. Let's go back to our sofa, to our hot chocolate (well, probably it is not hot anymore). We will probably need some candles to get more comfortable.

Yes ... candles ... which used to be the metaphors for the outdated ... which have been derided for years by innovation books with their covers tapestried with light bulbs.

I like to think about candles as the symbol of innovation of meaning. They invite you to take your time and reflect, in contrast to lightbulbs, the symbol of fast ideation. Even candles, whose meaning remained untouched for centuries, are nowadays not immune to innovation of meaning. So when I meet someone who claims: "This story is nice, but it does not work in my industry; there is no space for innovation of meaning here" ... I light up a candle.

Part II   The Principles

Beyond Ideas to Meaning

The grass is always greener on the other side of the fence.

As a scholar, I've always been afraid of being weak on the practical side of things; of fitting the stereotype of the professor who is good at theories and principles but lacks method and tools to implement them. This sense of inferiority has probably led me to engage with firms in consulting projects, trying things, being focused on real outcomes, and to develop frameworks through the inspiration of both theory and practice. But it is never enough. I still keep this feeling that the grass on the other side of the fence, the grass of methods and tools, is greener. So when I was conceiving this book, I thought: "This time I will jump to the other side of the fence; it will be a handbook, a hands-on guide on *how* to create innovations of meaning." And initially I really jumped there. The first draft of the table of contents was focused on the methods we have been using in recent years when working with firms.

But then I felt uncomfortable. I felt I was not practicing what I preach. In the first part of this book I claim that what we miss in our world is not solutions but directions. Not the how but the why. And this happens also in the field of innovation studies. We do not lack methods and tools for innovation; we lack a clear idea of which one to use, when and *why*. In a recent article in the *Harvard Business Review*, Gary Pisano powerfully explains that many companies fail in innovation not because they do not have methods but because they have too many, and they mix and match them without a clear purpose.[1]

I felt I was falling into the trap of providing hands-on solutions for innovation while what are missing, in a world overcrowded by solutions and tools, are the guiding principles that enable each of us to be inspired. To shed light on the why, so that you can then choose the tools that are more meaningful *for you.*

I will still provide methods in the third part of this book (the sense of inferiority toward practice is still persecuting me). Those are the methods that we have applied in projects with firms. There may be other tools, and for sure we want to keep improving and creating new ones. However, before and above those methods lie the principles that inform innovation of meaning. Principles that are valid whatever tool you will use, and that are at the heart of our journey toward creating meaning.

Here we are therefore. With a section on principles.

We will introduce them in terms of their *differences* from innovation of solutions. In fact, innovation of solutions is what we are more familiar with. Many of us have experienced it, probably several times. And it has been the main subject of the innovation discourse in the last decades.

Although this discourse has been extensive in terms of contributions and methods, in its essence it generally sees innovation of solutions as the result of a process of creative problem solving: users have problems or needs, and innovation implies understanding those problems and creating better ideas to solve them.

So what should we do differently when we want to innovate meanings instead of solutions? We will see that there are two fundamental differences in the principles (see figure II.1).

The first concerns the *direction* of the process. Innovation of solutions comes from the *outside in.* It requires us to look first outside our organization, and outside ourselves; when we want to innovate solutions we start by going *out* and observing how users use existing products; then we are advised to "think *outside* the box" in order to be more creative; and even to invite *outsiders* to propose masses of novel ideas. We will see that, instead, innovation of meaning comes from the *inside out.* It's a vision that comes from us and is offered to people. A gift to love because, foremost, *we* love it and we authentically *believe* it will make their lives better. And it could not be otherwise. You can borrow solutions from outsiders, but you cannot borrow visions from outsiders: you cannot wear the eyes of others. You have to see things yourself.

The second fundamental difference concerns the *mindset.* Innovation of solutions typically is built on the art of *ideation.* The more ideas are generated, the better the chance to find a good one. Innovation of meanings

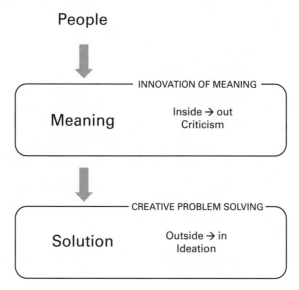

Figure II.1
The principles of innovation of meaning versus creative problem solving.

instead requires the art of *criticism*. In fact, since the process starts from the inside, we need to be sure that what comes from us is meaningful to other people. We need to challenge our old assumptions; to question how we make sense of the environment; to seriously take in new perspectives. Taking a critical stance does not imply being negative but going deeper, searching for the contrasts, creating tensions, discussing differences, reshuffling things to find a new order. Without a critical reflection on what we believe in and what we search for, we would interpret new insights with old lenses. We would see only what we wanted to see.

Both principles, innovation from the inside out and criticism, are a significant departure from the fundaments of creative problem solving. Innovation studies have praised the role of outsiders in innovation, and have described criticism as being marginal or even deleterious. They are not wrong. They just address a different kind of innovation: the search for novel solutions. But when it comes to meaning, these principles are simply turned upside down.

4 Innovation from the Inside Out

Making Gifts

We come with what we might call a beginner's mind.

Tim Brown, CEO, IDEO, 2013

By looking at what users do, we learn how to design a better shopping cart.

David Kelley, founder, IDEO, 1999

[Creative people have] had more experiences or they have thought more about their experiences. Unfortunately, ... a lot of people in our industry don't have enough dots to connect.

Steve Jobs, founder, Apple, 1996

People will never love a product you do not love. If you do not love it yourself they feel it ... they smell it ...

Steve Wozniak, founder, Apple, 2014

Two pairs of sentences. On the left David Kelley and Tim Brown, of IDEO, on the right the two founders of Apple.[1] Sentences pronounced by extremely successful innovators. Yet they say exactly opposite things.

The two leaders of IDEO explain that innovation comes from the *outside in*, i.e., from the outside of an organization, from outside ourselves. Brown in particular says that one of the advantages of IDEO is that, being a design consultancy that does not operate in any specific industry, it may approach its client's problem unencumbered by expertise. Expertise brings with it preconceptions, which bound our ability to think new. *Outsiders*, Brown indicates, do not have these preconceptions. They come with a clean mind. Kelley adds an insight: among all outsiders, users have a key role. Innovation stems mainly from them. Hence we need to start from users and understand their problems. This sentence comes from the popular ABC *Nightline* video "The Deep Dive," in which IDEO illustrates its innovation process through an example: redesigning the shopping cart. In this video the *first* thing the IDEO team does is to leave its offices, go *out* to a local supermarket, and observe closely how users use shopping carts.

The sentences of the founders of Apple go in a different direction. Jobs stresses the importance of *our own* experience. Pondering a problem we inevitably start from what we have lived ourselves. It's our initial precious resource. Hence, the need to *enrich* our own experiences, possibly to make them broader. Wozniak reinforces the point, with a sentence that "mirrors" the sentence of Kelley: "mirrors" in the sense that it is exactly turned the other way around! A necessary condition for customers to love what we do is that *we* love it ourselves. We have to like it in order for others to like it. Definitely not a user-driven approach. Both sentences of the Apple leaders indicate that innovation runs not from the outside in but from the *inside out*; from ourselves to the external world. To create products that people love, we need to start from what *we* love, and we can only find it out *ourselves* through our personal experience, through our own immersion in the world, not through outsiders.

This is a conundrum. Two pairs of successful innovators have been driven by antithetical principles. They seem to live on two different planets. How can we explain this?

THE MYTH OF OUTSIDE-IN INNOVATION

In the last 15 years the dominant explanation in the innovation discourse has been unanimous: the inside-out perspective is wrong. Apple was considered just an exception. Not even a notable one at the beginning, given that Apple's success, when it was just a computer company, was limited to a small segment of passionate "flower children." And Jobs was considered an extemporaneous guru (at the time of the above quotation he was still managing NeXT Inc.). But business … real business was considered another story.

Mainstream innovation discourse indeed took the opposite direction: it promoted a process that unfolds from the outside in. The IDEO shopping cart video has been a blockbuster in business schools for 15 years (I used it myself, as a great compendium of problem solving). To the point that if I asked my students if they had already seen it, I got as a reply: "Please no more! We have discussed this video three times already." (It's interesting to notice that this video of IDEO, which is a design firm, is by far more popular in business schools than in design schools. It looks like IDEO has hit the right nerve, finally finding the right language to talk to business people about design.) Anyway, IDEO has definitely not been alone in this perspective. They have been probably the most representative and effective thinkers; but they have been joined by many others.

Take for example *open innovation* and *crowdsourcing*, which have attracted the most attention for more than a decade.[2] They praise the role of outsiders in finding new solutions. "No matter who you are, most of the smartest people work for someone else," said Bill Joy, the cofounder of Sun Microsystems, to counteract Microsoft's striving to attract the smartest minds around.[3] And Larry Huston, VP for Innovation and Knowledge at Procter & Gamble, added: "For everyone of our 7,500 P&G researchers there are 200 scientists or engineers elsewhere in other parts of the world who are just as good—a total of perhaps 1.5 million people whose talents we could potentially use."[4] There are good reasons for this perspective: nowadays problems are so complex that we cannot master all possible competences in-house; meanwhile involving outsiders has become easier, especially thanks to web technologies.

The assumption that innovation *does not come from myself but better comes from others* has also permeated what happens within organizations. In this case "from others" should be read as "from the team." Rewind the IDEO shopping cart video. It's Friday and the project is completed. The ABC reporter explains: "It is day five, and David Kelley has no idea of what the final cart looks like. Only the team does." What a difference from the maniacal attention of Steve Jobs to the details of Apple's projects as they were unfolding!

Finally, even when it comes to us, to our own creative process, the advice has been to jump *outside* of who we are. "Think outside of the box" has been the chorus of the innovation songs.

The verse has been that innovation should be user-centered. Users know what the problems of use are better than anyone else.[5] And sometimes they even know the solutions, as Erik Von Hippel has masterfully shown.[6] So *user-centered* innovation, or even user-*driven* innovation, have been the major refrain that few have dared to question. The classroom walls in business schools have been echoing with this: don't start from yourself, from your experience; don't trust your gut and, most of all, do not design for yourself.

So slowly we, scholars and practitioners of innovation, have been building a myth: innovation comes from the outside in. It illustrates the typical nature of myths: uncritically supported; definitely indisputable. The discussion within the innovation debate has become close to monotone: outside-in innovation has been praised as always right, whatever context we are in and whatever strategy we are pursuing. No voice is heard from outside the choir. And those who dare to question this assumption are attacked as outlandish. In 2010 I wrote an article for the *Harvard Business Review* online magazine, titled "User-Centered Innovation Is Not Sustainable," observing that user-centered innovation has not helped bring us into a more sustainable world. I do not want here to dig into this argument.[7] But what struck me was the tone of many comments posted on the website. Aside from a few deep reflections, in favor or in opposition, many reactions could be summarized like this: "How dare you? Do not touch user-centered innovation!"

SHAKING A MYTH

Yet we need to touch it. And the community has indeed started to wonder whether it is really true that an inside-out process is always wrong. The dazzling sequence of successes of the iPod, iTunes, iPhone, MacBook Air, and iPad, joined with the empathy after the loss of Steve Jobs, has instilled doubts into the rocklike certainty of the innovation discourse. Apple cannot be considered an outlandish exception anymore. And Apple is not even alone in its inside-out approach; other successful organizations we have already encountered in this book follow a similar direction: Nest, Yankee Candles, Philips, AirBnB, Deloitte, STMicroelectronics. And many others that we will encounter later.

So how do we resolve this conundrum? Who is right and who is wrong? Brown or Jobs? Kelley or Wozniak?

The point is that both pairs of sentences opening this chapter are right. They simply refer to two different types of innovation. Outside-in processes are extremely effective for finding new solutions. Inside-out processes for finding new meaning.

Or, put differently, when it comes to innovation of meanings, the myth of outside-in innovation does not work. We need to take exactly the opposite direction: from the inside out. This has three reasons, which we will elaborate in depth. First, meanings are interpretations, and *interpretations cannot be outsourced*; they can only come from us. Second, our own interpretations are *precious*; people will never love something we do not love ourselves. Third, we have the *responsibility* to drive the world in the direction that we believe makes more sense; this is good for people, for business, and for us; if we abdicate, what is our role in this world?

In discussing these reasons, I will purposely stress the differences between outside-in and inside-out processes. Not only to make the point clearer, but also because the differences are indeed profound. To balance this, one might point out that outside-in processes do still involve our internal organization, and that open innovation and user-centered innovation eventually ask us to decide what to do. These are true. But what is different in the two approaches, 180 degrees different, is the *direction* of the process. Innovation of solutions requires *starting* from outsiders and *then* moving to us. Innovation of meaning requires *starting* from ourselves and *then* involving outsiders. This different sequence implies that the two processes, when implemented, are deeply different.

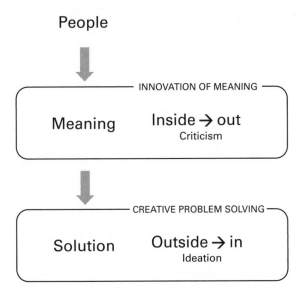

Figure 4.1
The first principle of innovation of meaning: innovation from the inside out.

SEEING IS NOT INTERPRETING

We see but we do not see: we use our eyes, but our gaze is glancing, frivolously con-
sidering its object. We see the signs, but not their meanings.
Alexandra Horowitz[8]

"Ha ha ha ha! ... five hundred dollars!," Steve Ballmer, then Microsoft's
CEO, exploded in one of his epic laughs. "That's the most expensive phone
in the world ... and it does not have a keyboard, which makes it not a
very good email machine." It was January 2007 and Steve Jobs had just
announced the iPhone at the Macworld Conference. Microsoft meanwhile
was commercializing its own mobile solutions. "Right now we are selling
millions and millions and millions of phones a year," continued Ballmer to
the journalist. "Apple is selling zero phones a year ... they have the most
expensive phone by far ever in the marketplace."[9]

Maybe he laughed too loudly. But he was not alone in his feelings.
Several experts at that time predicted the iPhone would be a failure.[10] In a
way, Ballmer was right. $500 for a phone was way too much. And an email
machine without a keyboard wasn't a good solution either. The point is
that the iPhone was not only a new solution. It was a *new meaning*, a new
why. Eventually, people did not buy it because it was just a phone, nor
because it was an email machine. The iPhone for them was a personal companion, to entertain themselves and their friends.

Ballmer's laugh epitomizes a key challenge: when a new meaning is proposed, recognizing its value is not easy. He had a great idea in front of him.
It was even more than an idea: it was a finished product. He *saw* it. Yet he
(and many others) totally *missed its meaning*. Why?

In her fascinating book *On Looking: Eleven Walks with Expert Eyes*, Alexandra Horowitz, a behavioral psychologist, wonders why we miss things that
happen in front of us.[11] For example, we miss a lot of things that happen
while we walk around a block.

Horowitz explains that we naturally get used to things around us, especially when we walk on paths that we have already seen before and we
know well. Slowly we come not to care for what is around. We take it for
granted.

But Horowitz adds something more interesting: we also miss a lot of
things when we are purposely attentive and concentrated. Attention is a

powerful mechanism. It helps us to focus carefully on something, by filtering out something else that we deem unnecessary. We see a car coming when we cross a street because meanwhile we filter out a million different stimuli and sensations. The hum of fluorescent lights of billboards, the movements of children playing on a nearby playground, the shape of clouds in the sky, the background roar of a lawnmower, the fragrance of blossoming cherry trees, the tensions we are holding in our jaw. This mechanism of attention, which is so helpful because it enables us to capture important things, like an approaching car, brings with it a companion, however: inattention to everything else. We are attentive only to what we *want* to see.

And, in reality, we see even less. Sometimes, even if we *want* to see something, we do not have the capability to detect it. For example, even if we want to see ultraviolet light, or hear ultrasound, we can't. Our eyes and ears have not been created with these capabilities. We need special tools for this. So, eventually, we see what we *want* to see and what we *can* see.

This challenge affects not only our everyday life, let's say when we walk around our block. It affects also our ability to change. In a context like the one we are in today, filled with millions of signs and information, we naturally tend to take in a limited number of stimuli. This enables us to survive and focus on the moment. But unfortunately it often prevents us from detecting the weak traces of the new.

Most thinkers on creativity propose a way to overcome this challenge: to look at the world with new eyes; to jump "outside of the box," i.e., outside of the framework that usually drives our search for insights. In this perspective, outsiders have the advantage of being already outside of the box. They are "as clean as a sheet," unaware of the solution heuristics that dominate a domain. "We come with what we might call a beginner's mind," says Tim Brown in the sentence at the opening of this chapter; or, using another metaphor, with a child's mind.[12]

This might be valid for finding new solutions. But when it comes to innovation of meanings this advice is hardly effective. No one is, or will ever be, a beginner vis-à-vis meanings. Early in my studies I met an R&D manager of a global corporation. He was quite experienced, having worked for his organization for a long time. His firm had a long glorious history of innovation and design, but the brand was now losing its glitter and touch with customers. He therefore engaged his team to find a new meaning for a new generation of the company's products. I was there when he was reflecting on which path to take in the project. Before him there were two directions. One was outside-in: first meeting outsiders, collecting insights, and then using these insights internally to decide what to do. The other direction was inside-out: first conducting an internal workshop in which his team could propose new visions, and then checking with external experts whether these visions made sense. I asked: "What are you inclined to do?" He replied: "We had better begin by meeting people from outside of our context. If we start from generating visions ourselves I'm afraid we will come up with the same things that have been circulating in our organization in the last few years." It sounded reasonable. So his innovation team started by meeting outside experts, most of whom they had never met before, who brought in several new stimuli. However, when after these meetings the team proposed possible meanings, the same old ideas still came out, to the dismay of the executive. It was as if encountering the outsiders was useless. The team had been exposed to fresh insights, but nothing changed. Why?

The involvement of outsiders early on in a project, or the observation of users, is based on a fundamental assumption: that the most difficult thing is to *see* something, but once we see it, we can easily *recognize* it. So, if outsiders bring us ideas from outside our cognitive frame, we can recognize the value of their ideas. Or, if we observe customers, we can recognize unexpected behaviors.

This holds true for solutions, not for meanings. In fact, *solutions can be easily put on a scale*: we can judge which solution is better and which is worse, in terms of what a product is meant for. Let's illustrate this with a simple example. Figure 4.2 shows what happens when we search for solutions. Let's imagine we produce balls, and that, currently, users say that they prefer larger balls; in other words, "larger balls are meaningful." This entails a scale of judgment, based on size. Innovation will therefore aim at creating solutions and technologies that enable us to produce larger balls; once we have found these solutions (see the options depicted in the left side of the figure), we can screen them according to their size. Thanks to the scale, every time we invent a new ball, we can easily recognize its value; eventually we pick the best one we have created, i.e., the largest one. In other words, *with solutions, seeing is enough*. We know what we are looking for (in this case, a larger ball), and we can use an *optimization* attitude. This

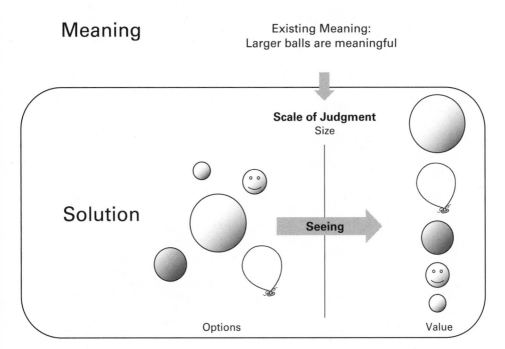

Figure 4.2
Seeing and optimizing in creative problem solving.

is the framework Ballmer had in mind when answering the journalist's question about the iPhone. Until that moment, phones were meant to be … phones (devices to make calls), or email machines. Not devices to entertain. The scale of judgment for innovative solutions therefore involved battery life or speed of typing. In the context of this existing meaning, a solution with a longer battery life would have been difficult to find, but easy to recognize: it would have topped the scale. The iPhone definitely did not top the scale in those dimensions.

But, as said before, the iPhone was an innovation of meaning, not just a new solution. And new meanings are different than new solutions. They cannot be put on a scale.

The reason is simple: the "scale" of judgment *is* the meaning, which is what we want to *change*. Meanings are what enable us to distinguish between what is good and what is bad. So, at the moment when we search for *new* meanings, when we are questioning our traditional parameters of judgment, there is no reference, no scale. Figure 4.3 illustrates this. Let's

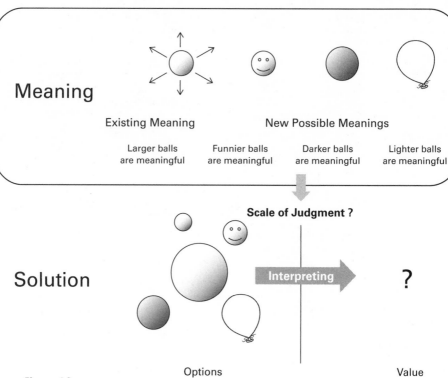

Figure 4.3
Interpreting in innovation of meaning.

imagine we now want to move beyond "larger balls are meaningful" and search for new meanings. We can envision several new possibilities, for example patterned balls are meaningful, darker balls are meaningful, light balls are meaningful, funny balls are meaningful, bright balls are meaningful, and so on. Imagining new meaningful propositions is not a big deal. But recognizing their value is much more difficult. If someone proposes a new ball saying: "This ball is smaller than what we currently offer, but it has a funny face pictured on it; people will love it," this insight will escape us, because it acts on a *new* dimension: fun instead of size. We cannot put size and fun on the same scale. We need to make interpretations: will a fun ball be meaningful to people? Will they love it, instead of a larger ball? This was the problem faced by Ballmer, and by many others at that time. The iPhone changed the meaning, i.e., the scale of values. It was worse on the existing scales of value that were dominating the market at that time.

It took more battery power and typing time. But in reality, it proposed new dimensions, such us entertainment, or pleasurable software interfaces, that could be more meaningful to people. Ballmer saw the solutions, not the meaning.

New meanings, in other words, are *interpretations*, not optimizations. They are interpretations of what people *will* love.

So, you may wonder: why don't we just ask users? Or why don't we go and observe people using existing products?

Well, user analysis would provide a definitive answer if all the users' insights pointed in the same direction. Unfortunately, in our sophisticated and rapidly changing world, the signals that we get from the market rarely all go in the same direction. And if they do, it simply means one thing: it's too late, because someone else has already established a new meaning. In 2012, five years *after* the iPhone was launched, customers unanimously acknowledged that "an entertaining phone is better than an email machine," and that a touchscreen is better than a physical keyboard. This, however, was not the picture in 2007 *before* the iPhone was presented. Before an innovation of meaning occurs, user observation would produce a very complicated picture that we would *still need to interpret*. In particular we typically observe two things from users:

- a *dominant behavior*, i.e., an existing meaning that is currently searched for by users;
- a *rich multitude of weak signals*, novel behaviors, small insights, new customers, all pointing in different directions. They may contain some seeds of a new meaning, but they all look similarly interesting and at the same time arbitrary.

Any marketing or trend analysis tool based on statistics, i.e., that has the advantage of not being biased by our interpretation, would unfortunately only capture the first of these two things, i.e., the existing meaning. The qualitative methods based on behavioral *pattern* recognition (such as ethnography) would produce a similar outcome.

To envision a new meaning, we need to focus on the second thing: the multitude of weak signals pointing in different directions. Which implies that eventually we will still need to make our own interpretation.

So, even if we start from users, the point still remains: *when it comes to new meaning, we can't avoid making our own interpretations.* Whichever method we use to understand users, we need to make several interpretations: which users to address; what to ask for, or when to observe them, and where; which signals to focus on and which to disregard; how to make sense of them.

Even worse, users are often quite bad predictors of novel meanings. They may be good at making us understand what they currently love, but not what they *might* love. Several studies have proved that customers hardly help in creating radical innovations. The well-known and respected studies of Clayton Christensen at Harvard Business School have shown this, both theoretically and empirically, in an extremely compelling way.[13] When it comes to the creation of breakthrough meaning, several cases are also illustrated in my previous book *Design-Driven Innovation*.[14] More recently, I've had the pleasure of further elaborating this critique of user-centered innovation with Don Norman. Don, one of the founding fathers of human-centered design,[15] came to the same conclusion: radical innovation does not come from users.[16]

In any case, regardless of whether users are good or not for radical innovation, eventually we still need to do our own interpretation of their insights. We can't avoid it.

The same holds if we consider other kinds of outsiders (experts in other fields, suppliers, researchers, trend analysts, etc.). We could ask for their interpretations of what customers would love. But, again, *before* an innovation of meaning occurs and becomes dominant, their interpretations would point in many different directions, all similarly interesting and arbitrary. So we would still need to interpret their interpretations ourselves.

The bottom line is that when it comes to innovation of meaning, *seeing is not enough*. As powerfully indicated in the epigraph by Alexandra Horowitz: "We see but we do not see. ... We see the signs, but not their meanings." We need to interpret what we see. And we can only do it ourselves. *Novel interpretations cannot be borrowed from others*. We can even see a particular user doing something new, or listen to an expert's unique interpretation; but, in the complexity of today's context, we still have to judge whether this detail that we see or listen to is relevant or marginal, good or bad.

This does not mean that users and other experts are irrelevant for innovation. They are still essential. But which is the most effective way to involve them? And especially, when? Should we start from the outsiders and then develop our interpretation, or first envision our interpretation and then check with outsiders to see if it makes sense? In other words, should we move from the outside in, or from the inside out?

The problem with a process that moves from the outside in is that it is simply deceitful. We believe that we start from the outsiders, but in reality when we meet them we already have our own preinterpretations. We already have our own personal hypothesis about what could be meaningful to people. Because meanings are based on values and beliefs, and no human is without them. Hans-Georg Gadamer, a German philosopher of hermeneutics (the philosophy of meaning and interpretation), clearly explains in his book *Truth and Method* that we, as human beings immersed in today's world, have our own historical grounding: our experiences, our culture, our situation that can't be escaped.[17] No one can leave her immediate situation in the present by merely adopting an attitude.[18] The dream of the naive mind and heart, when it comes to meanings, is a naive myth itself. Everyone has her own interpretation of what phones are meant for. Everyone inevitably senses the changes in the environment and slowly and silently develops her own personal hypotheses about new future directions. The team of the project I mentioned earlier kept proposing the same old ideas, even after meeting the outsiders, because its members entered into the project already having an inner sense of direction for where to go. They had implicit hypotheses. So, eventually, even if they were exposed to several insights, they recognized only those stimuli that best fitted with these silent hypotheses: they interpreted only what they wanted and were able to interpret.

We can try to pretend that these values are not there, to pretend that we are beginners, as we do when we search for solutions. But it's impossible. Values can't be faked. They can't be washed out.

So what did Alexandra Horowitz do to address this dilemma? She took walks with eleven experts to see new things. But she did it in a peculiar direction: by moving from the inside out. *Before* walking around the block with the experts, she took a walk around the block herself.

MAKING SHADOWS

If we are blinded by darkness, we are also blinded by light. When too much light falls on everything, a special terror results.
Annie Dillard[19]

"I began by walking around the block by myself. I wanted to record what I saw *before* I was schooled by my walking companions."[20] Why does

Horowitz move from the inside out? Or, put in the context of innovation of meaning: why is it better to start from ourselves in proposing a new vision, a new meaning? Why, before being exposed to insights of others, do we need to expose ourselves *first*?

Starting from ourselves has several advantages. The first is logical and pragmatic. We do not learn in absolute terms. We learn from differences, from comparisons. To see things, we need contrast. Light alone does not enable us to see anything: we need the shadow. When we start from ourselves, we create the shadow, something against which to contrast the light of the insights that will come from outsiders.

In any case this term of comparison, when it comes to meaning, is *already* inside us: as said above, we have our silent hypotheses about new meanings that people will love. By looking inside before meeting outsiders, we simply make these hypotheses explicit. With the essential benefit that, in the effort to express and formalize our hypotheses, we make them grow, shape them better, and turn our silent confused grayish hypotheses into a background that is darker, ready for the light. It will be easier then to capture the small wrinkles in the landscape, the weak signals in the scenario, the serendipities. Also, by exposing our hypotheses, we make them visible to ourselves, and to others in our team: it will be more difficult then to lie, take shortcuts, or pretend that we did not see things that go in a different direction, because we have set a baseline for what is different.

Also, by taking out what we have inside, we create inner space to accommodate new thoughts. Early on in my study I witnessed an interesting event. The innovation team of a large corporation was engaged in a project to create new product meanings for consumers. They were halfway through the project: the team had already formulated possible directions and had met outsiders to see if these directions made sense. As the new vision became clearer, the project leader realized that, in assembling his multidisciplinary team, he had neglected to involve a key marketing manager of the firm. Never mind. Things were still unsettled, so he was still in time to get this person's insights and commitment. The team leader invited him to a coming two-day workshop, where the task was to further finalize the new meaning and translate it into product concepts.

Of course, the first thing on the agenda was to illustrate to the marketing manager the project direction, the new meaning that the team had crafted early on, so he could jump on board. This was not an easy task, though. I noticed the puzzled face of the manager. He gave interesting comments and feedback on specific details, but I felt that he could not embrace the core of the vision. He was not judging whether the direction was right or not; he simply could not understand it. But he went on and worked with engagement the entire first day. Every now and then, however, his discomfort surfaced in the form of disagreements on marginal details of the concepts. The morning of the second day the tensions were higher and the conversation started to become harsher and unproductive. Until he burst into "Please, let me say what *my* vision is!" In the crescendo of the soundtrack, the emphasis was on "my". The statement was so peremptory that the team fell into total silence. As people were in disarray and thinking what to do, he simply went on without waiting for their agreement on changing the agenda. For the next fifteen minutes he pictured his scenario, the meanings that in his view customers were searching for. They did not clearly match the current direction of the project. I saw the team leader growing anxious and the others moving nervously in their chairs.

But then, after he completed his description, he came out with an unexpected statement: "And now that I've said my things … now I'm ready to listen." In an instant the tension dissolved. I noticed the relief of everyone: the team, the leader, and the marketing manager. It was as if he had something inside that he needed to take out before starting to take new things in. Like when we have a fight with our partner, and we keep discussing small details unproductively for hours without touching the core of the matter. Until finally one of the two throws out a big inner discomfort, and puts it on the table. That is the moment when the real conversation starts … and so it was in this project. From that moment on, the marketing manager embraced the new direction better, and the team incorporated some relevant criticism from him. The new meaning and product concepts that resulted from the workshop were definitely more robust than they had been at the beginning of day one.

What happened is that the marketing manager simply needed to follow the same path of the team: start from himself. The workshop's agenda was from the outside in: first point was illustrating the team vision *to him*. But he needed to move from the inside out; first point in the agenda: "let's start from what *I* think people could love."

THE GIFT MAKER

Who pays any attention
to the syntax of things
will never wholly kiss you
E. E. Cummings[21]

Now, I hope that I have not passed on a misleading message. I have illustrated that, when it comes to meaning, everyone already has preliminary hypotheses that they can't escape, a kind of silent preinterpretation about what could be meaningful to people. I do not mean, however, that these inklings of hypotheses are *negative* preconceptions that we want to fight. We do not take them out simply to clean ourselves and create an inner empty space for new insights. Our starting hypotheses have *positive* value. We need them.[22]

Let's go back to the comment of Steve Wozniak: "People will never love a product that you do not love. If you do not love it yourself, they feel it … they smell it."

In the world of user-centered innovation, this sentence would be considered blasphemy. We design for users, not for ourselves. Why should users like something we like?

Quite so. Wozniak, however, is saying something different. Let's delve into his reflection more carefully. He does not mean: users will like what we like; but: users will *not* like what we do *not* like. In other words, it's a *necessary* but *not sufficient* condition: we have to propose something we love. Which does not mean people will love it for sure. Something else will be needed (which we will discuss in the next chapter). But our own love is the necessary foundation, the minimal starting point.

Wozniak is touching a nerve. Every one of us is a user of products. And we know that we hardly fall in love with products that have been designed just because we users want them. We smell when things have been created just to conquer our love. We smell the lack of genuine love from the givers. In the absence of other, more meaningful options, we will likely buy these products, which may have a great performance and be very useful. But we do not fall in love. Which implies that, as soon as we find a product with a better performance, we simply switch. And we keep switching until we stumble into something meaningful that really makes us fall in love.

To fall in love, we need to see the love, genuine love. And we often see it in the care taken for the details. In the *discovery* of something whose value we grasp only *after* we see it. When we say, "Wow … I did not expect this. How nice!"

Think about the experience of buying a Nest thermostat. You take it home, unpack it, and see this round device that stares at you like HAL 9000 in Kubrick's movie *2001: A Space Odyssey*. You smile … Hal … the first computer with genuine human emotions … a good introduction for a thermostat. Still, you feel nervous. "Will I be able to disassemble my old thermostat and substitute this new one without the help of an expert? Will it be a DIY nightmare? What will my children think if I fail and eventually call for assistance?" And while all these thoughts of an unconfident father occupy your mind, you come through the surprises. First, the package contains a Philips head screwdriver, including four different heads, and … "Oh! by the way … it has a cool design. It's even better than normal screwdrivers. Is Nest going to enter the tool industry? They should! Anyway, I'll keep it in my daily backpack … you never know." Then you discover that the installation guide provides blue stickers prelabeled with letters (W1, Y1, etc.) that you can attach to the wires of your old thermostat before disassembling them from the wall, so that you are sure that the right wire goes into the right port of the Nest thermostat … a masterpiece in understanding what is really meaningful to people. "Good. My children will believe I'm a great electrician."

We smell the same love in the maniacal attention of Apple to its product details: the right curves of the MacBook Air; the fonts of iOS. We smell the fragrance of firms that start from what their designers and managers love. We smell the surprise of the unnecessary that suddenly becomes necessary because someone unveils it to us.

Another caveat surfaces if we examine Wozniak's sentence carefully. He does not claim: "You have to design things for yourself." He still invites us to design for others. But we should be driven by *what we'd love people to love*.

Let me explain using a metaphor. Designing meaningful products is like making gifts. There is a profound difference between a gift done to conquer and a gift done with genuine love. At his 32nd birthday famous novelist John Green produced a short clip inspired by an unexpected and improbable gift, a funny adulterated portrait of Gary Busey's family. In the video Green sizes the opportunity to explain why and how we should create things: "Make gifts for people—and work hard on making those gifts in the hope that those people will notice and like the gifts."[23]

When we make a gift, *we* think about what the receiver would love. We do not ask her (sometimes this may happen, with the likely consequence that she will use it, not love it); and we shouldn't make the gift just because we have to (this unfortunately happens more frequently, with the definite consequence that she will pile our gift up in the remote cabinet of unexciting gifts, or recycle it as a gift to others). We make it because we feel pleasure ourselves in making it. So, *the gift is for her* (not for ourselves), *but the act of making the gift is for us*. When this happens, we create meaning. People will smell it even before seeing it.

CARING

When you get what you want
but not what you need
Coldplay, "Fix You"[24]

In their famous 2005 song "Fix You," Coldplay go through some of the hardest things that may happen in life. "You try your best, but you don't succeed … you lose something you can't replace … you love someone but it goes to waste." Among those hard things, there is one that always hit my guts when I listen to the lyrics: "you get what you want, but not what you need." Enchanting. Surprising. Scary. And terribly true. Getting what we want is one of the worst things that may happen in life, if what we want is not good for our life.

These few words capture the essence of innovation of meaning. In the previous section we said that giving people simply what they want will hardly make them fall in love. Here we are adding something more: it's not just that people will not love it. It's that giving them what they want could indeed be *bad* for them. Unless it is good and meaningful.

Every time we offer something to people, a product, a service, we have an impact on their lives. We do a moral act.

Now, in the context of innovation of solutions, in problem solving, we might ignore this moral dimension. In fact, we work on existing parameters of value, on an existing why. We do not judge whether these parameters are good or bad. We just focus on finding better solutions along them. If radiologists want more powerful CAT scanners so they can have better images, we search for solutions and technologies that make CAT scanners more powerful. In essence, we reinforce the existing morality.[25]

But when we want to innovate the meaning of things, we can't escape this moral dimension. Because what we innovate is the parameter of value itself, the why. We change the criteria for judging what is good. What if quality of health care imaging came not from the power of the machine (the old value parameter), but from making patients more relaxed so they do not move during the scanning (a new value parameter)? When Philips designed the Ambient Experience for Healthcare, described in chapter 3, it was faced with this question. Which is a moral question, about what is good for people (the radiologist and the patient).

Who should decide then what is good? Eventually, the customers of course.

But who should make the proposal, offer new options, given that, as Coldplay say, what people want is not necessarily good for them? Well, there is no escape. It can only be us.

"Fix You" was written when the father of Gwyneth Paltrow, former wife of the band singer, passed away. The connection of the lyrics with fatherhood (or more generally parenthood) is not incidental. A parent has a momentous role in a child's life: to support her in her search for meaning. And how is this best done? How does he really care? He does not just start from the child, from what she wants; he starts from himself, from a deep reflection on what he believes could be good for the child. If the child wants candies, maybe he can propose something as tasty, but healthier.

Stefano Marzano, former CEO and Chief Creative Director of Philips Design, and one of the main creators of the Ambient Experience for Healthcare, uses a similar metaphor to explain why the process of innovation of meaning should start from the inside out: "Users do not always know what they want. … We *propose* new visions instead of simply following market wants. I use the metaphor of the good father: he is not one who gives his children what they want, but what is more meaningful. *A father pursues a vision.*"[26]

Even if radiologists were asking for more powerful scanners, Philips proposed that better images could be achieved by improving the hospital environment and the patient experience, especially for children. Eventually, it turned out that radiologists loved the new system, because working in an environment where children were less scared of the exams gratified the staff and made the exam procedure smoother and faster.

Marzano tells us something important. It is not true that if we move from the inside out, if we start from what *we* believe is meaningful, we do not care for the user; it does not mean that we are being paternalistic and arrogant ("I know what's best for you better than you know"). Not at all. If we start from ourselves, from our vision, we deploy an *even deeper care* for the user; or, better, for the *person* who is the user. Like a good father, we care. And we have responsibilities toward this person. She indeed wishes us to propose a meaningful option. Then she will decide. For a child, a father with a caring vision is much better than a father without a vision.[27]

If we think about this deeply, this is the great thing about innovation of meaning: it gives us a chance to turn the world in a direction that we (who else otherwise?) find more meaningful. To put forward our vision for a better world. Gary Hamel recently wrote an article titled "Innovation *Starts* with the Heart, Not the Head" (italics added by me). He says: "If you want to innovate, *you* need to be inspired, your *colleagues* need to be inspired, and ultimately, your *customers* need to be inspired. ... The best innovations—both socially and economically—come from the pursuit of ideals that are noble and timeless: joy, wisdom, beauty, truth, equality, community, sustainability and, most of all, love. These are the things we live for, and the innovations that really make a difference are the ones that are life-enhancing. And that's why the heart of innovation is a desire to *re-enchant* the world."[28]

Our vision is the mysterious energy that makes us wake up every morning, take a long commute, go to work, and feel good. It's the "why" discussed by Simon Sinek in his bestseller *Start with Why*.[29] The why that connects who we are with who our customers are. Human with human.

Maria Popova, a writer whose blog BrainPickings hosts inspiring reflections and theories on the search for meaning in life, put it in a powerful way: "To create wealth is not to give people what they want, but to help them figure out what *to want* by making sense of what is *worth having*. There is a moral element to the marketable deliverable. ... If we didn't invest so much of ourselves in what we do—which includes what *we* ourselves believe, what *we* wish existed, and what direction *we* want to move the world in—then why bother doing it at all?"[30]

WHAT WE'D LOVE PEOPLE TO LOVE

So in this chapter we have learned that innovation of meaning, unlike innovation of solutions, comes from the inside out. We need to start from our hypotheses, from *what we'd love people to love*. Why? First, because in any case these hypotheses are there and, if not exposed, would silently lead us to interpret what we want to interpret. Second, because people will never love a gift we do not love. And third, because we have a responsibility to propose what we believe is more meaningful.

A process of innovation of meaning therefore starts from our own organization, and from the question: *What would we love people to love?*

Which is different from simply "What do we love?" We are envisioning what *customers* would love.

And it's different from simply "What do customers love?" It starts from what *we* would love them to love. It's a meeting between what we believe is meaningful and what they believe is meaningful.

And it's different from "What *are we capable of making* for people to love?" It does not start from our core competences. We are not talking here of resource-based strategies that offer customers what we are good at.[31] We are talking of a *new* vision that we would love to pursue. We probably need to *change* our core competence to achieve it.

And it's different from "What would we love people to love *in the future?*" It's not a forecast, nor a trend analysis (is it still possible to talk

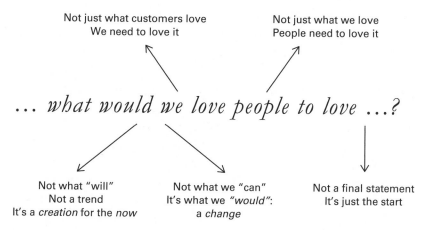

Figure 4.4

about trends in this unpredictable and multifaceted world where several things coexist?). It's about the *now*. Because change is happening now, and people are searching for new meanings now (and competitors are acting on it now).

And it's different from *"This is* what we would love people to love!" It's not a final statement. It is a wonder. It is just the start of a reflective process. There is a long journey to go through. These preliminary hypotheses are the raw ingredients that will be fused with others, challenged, and framed into a new interpretation of product meaning. What we will deliver at the end of the process will be significantly different from what we started from.

Yet nothing would emerge without these essential ingredients. They are precious. *Innovation of meaning does not need naive minds. It needs visionary minds.* Minds filled with hypotheses and wishes. Hans-Georg Gadamer, the philosopher of hermeneutics we introduced before, celebrates the importance of our preunderstanding, of our "horizon." According to Gadamer, "a 'horizon' is a range of vision that includes everything seen from a particular vantage point. A person with no horizon does not see far enough and overvalues what is nearest at hand, whereas to have a horizon means being able to see beyond what is close at hand."[32] The new interpretation will eventually come as a fusion of different horizons (our own and the horizons of others we will meet along the way). But if there is nothing to fuse, no ingredient to melt, there is no new interpretation.

Perhaps the most inspiring metaphor on the importance of starting from us, from our preliminary hypotheses, is the metaphor of the painting. Alexandra Horowitz masterfully renders it in the conclusion of her book *On Looking.* She is at the end of her journey, after she has walked around the block with eleven experts. She thinks back to the role of her preinterpretations, developed in the first walk she took herself, alone, *before* meeting the outsiders. "My initial walk now felt like the imprimatura for an oil painting: the very first layer of paint on a canvas."[33] The new layers (the new interpretations that come from meeting outsiders) are then added on top, but they do not totally cancel or cover this base layer. In many paintings, even the heavier ones, the imprimatura still shines through gaps in the new layers. However, now it assumes a totally new meaning. "The meaning of the gaps changes because the context around them has changed. The bit left unpainted is now surrounded by

smears of pinks and reds that form the nose or ear or the eye of the subject of the portrait; the unpainted bit becomes the nostril, or the inner ear,
or the corner of the eye—and will never be just a base layer again." Our
initial ingredients are there, we can perhaps still sense their flavor. But the
final preparation, where the ingredients are mixed and melted, has its
own taste.

The point now is how to paint new layers on top of this imprimatura, so
that the final result is a meaningful painting that people would love. For
this, we need a second principle. Let's turn the page, then.

5 The Art of Criticism

The Quest for a Deeper Vision

"How are we going to make money?" asked Steve Ballmer, Microsoft's legendary top executive. "Let me tell you why it's not going to work."[1]

It was summer 1999. In front of him, in his small meeting room in Red West, were four employees, some of them newly hired. They had proposed an idea that could radically change Microsoft's approach to the business of videogames: to build a new console, independent of Windows.

Ideas for the digital game industry were not new at Microsoft. The firm had been exploring several options for years. For example it had launched a software tool, Direct X, that enabled game developers to create games for the PC. And it had even assembled an internal department to design games for computers. All these solutions aimed at sustaining the existing vision of the company: people should do things through the PC, i.e., through Windows. Including playing videogames. This strategy, so far, had scarcely been successful. The PC, indeed, was a limiting factor for gaming. For teenagers, playing games on Windows meant a slow experience, sometimes frustrating (PCs are prone to crashes), mostly solitary (you played alone against the computer, your face stuck to a small monitor). You even had to wait minutes for the computer to bootstrap before starting to play. For game developers it meant a cap to their creativity: PCs enabled only a limited kind of games (typically, strategy or shooting) that needed to run on multiple hardware platforms whose life cycle was extremely short. The focus on technical complexity diverted their focus from the creative side of game design.

While Microsoft was trying to understand how to deal with this challenge, these four employees came out with a bold proposal: gaming as high art; and the artists, in their view, were the game developers. In their vision, Microsoft would provide game developers with the most powerful canvas to freely express their art in creating games without compromises, so that technology would not be a constraint anymore. And indeed the Xbox became "the first console to emphatically celebrate the importance of the people who make the games."[2]

This proposal, however, had a radical implication: instead of a general-purpose Windows-based platform, it required a game-specific platform, explicitly designed for game artists, which Windows was not. Their vision moved totally outside of Microsoft's current direction.

Pushing teenagers far from PCs! Far from Windows! Ballmer had opened the meeting by ribbing the four poor employees with a loud sarcastic monologue: "I know! I know! [Your idea] is the greatest fucking thing in the world! It's going to make billions! It's the greatest thing ever! It's gong to do this, it's going to do that!" Then he turned serious, picked up a pen and walked over to the whiteboard. Like a professor in front of young students, he asked them to give numbers. His questions were relentless. At the end of the analysis he pronounced judgment: "You're off by $100." One of the team members recalls: "He showed us we were pretty stupid."[3]

Still, they did not give up on their vision.

Two years later their bold fragmentary proposal became a product that radically changed Microsoft's vision for the videogame industry: the Xbox. And, yes ... it made billions.

I'm not passionate about videogames, but the story of the Xbox has puzzled and fascinated me. An impressive transformation. Microsoft, the giant until then focused only on software, with a strong hold on business clients and productivity applications, embraced a novel proposal made of hardware, young consumers, and entertainment. Even more surprisingly, the product that eventually came out, the Xbox, had an operating system that was incompatible with Windows, the mythical, unquestionable and untouchable core asset of Microsoft. How was this possible? How did it happen that this outlandish vision, which questioned "what is good" in Microsoft, was not knocked down as soon as it came out? Not even when top executives were still not seeing its value and tried to kill it?

Innovation of meaning is founded on two principles. The first was introduced in the previous chapter: innovation of meaning comes from the inside out (indeed, the Xbox too, with its new meaning of being a "canvas" for artist-developers, came from the initial vision of four passionate renegades inside Microsoft's organization). But this is just the beginning, the raw ingredient. How to be sure that these initial hypotheses will eventually be meaningful to people? How to avoid being stuck in our own assumptions? How to take in others' visions without killing them? How to complement our interpretation with others' interpretations and turn blurred early insights into value for people and business?

The story of the Xbox, and other cases that we will explore in this chapter, will tell us that innovation of meaning requires a second ingredient: the art of *criticism*.

I understand that the word "criticism" may scare you. As a matter of fact, in the last 15 years dominant innovation theories have demonized criticism, banning it as detrimental. Which might be true in the context of innovation of solutions. But we will see that, when it comes to searching for new meaning, things are exactly the opposite: more than ideation, we need criticism.

A special kind of criticism, though. Not the negative destructive criticism chronicled and outlawed by classic innovation studies. But the capability to stop and reflect by going deeper; to question our assumptions and the assumptions of other; to make different perspectives clash in order to find a novel, more robust interpretation. This kind of criticism is the engine that provides energy to the entire process. It's the mechanism that turns the blurred internal hypotheses we start with into a final robust vision that people love.

Criticism is an art. An art that unfortunately we rarely nurture. Let's explore how to practice this art through a few stories. One step at the time. First discussing another myth of creative problem solving: ideation.

THE MYTH OF IDEATION

To recover our presence in the world, we must revisit our myths, both individual and collective; we must subject them to criticism … to cure the ideas that we use to interpret life.
Umberto Galimberti[4]

"Ping!" the bell chimes. It's a special bell. A kind of bicycle bell, laced on the wrist of Peter Skillman, an IDEO designer. Peter is introducing the brainstorming session filmed in the popular ABC *Nightline* video "The Deep Dive," which I talked about in chapter 4. In day one of the workshop, the

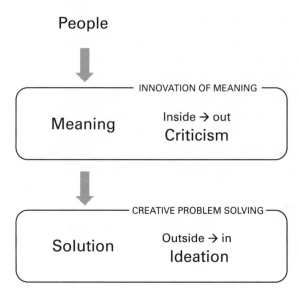

Figure 5.1
The second principle of innovation of meaning: criticism.

team has collected insights on how users use shopping carts. Now, in day two, it is going to engage in the creation of ideas. On the walls, signs remind participants of the basic rules of brainstorming: "encourage wild ideas," for example, or "defer judgment." Skillman rings the bell on his wrist and explains, "The hardest thing for people to do is to *restrain themselves from criticizing an idea*. So if anybody starts to nail an idea, they get the bell."

This is the second time I have mentioned IDEO in discussing the myths of innovation thinking. You may start to believe that I have an allergy or aversion to IDEO. I don't.

Actually, I believe they are smart and inspiring. I've been using their thinking and this video in my classes, to explain what creative problem solving is. Their process and the way they illustrate it are extremely effective. Simply, they focus on innovation of solutions, a different kind of innovation from the one we address here.

The reason I refer to IDEO is because we learn from differences. We need a foil, a term of comparison, to understand what the process of innovation of meaning is. And IDEO, with its focus on creative problem solving and its influence on innovation thinking, is the perfect foil. Perfect also because, being smart and clever people, they know that advances only come through critical reflection. And this chapter *is* about critical reflection.

Criticism. The enemy of the bell laced on the wrist of Peter Skillman. The enemy of ideation.

Ideation has been indeed the second myth of innovation studies in recent decades. Next to the myth of outside-in innovation, but even more powerful. Ideation really took the main spotlight, if we look at the recurring subject on the covers of innovation books: the light bulb (well, we need to admit that the cover designs of innovation books are not really creative). To the point that "to innovate" for many spelled "to find ideas." We can see it for example in the widespread diffusion of brainstorming as an innovation tool.

More generally, our entire culture in recent decades has praised ideation and banned criticism. Figure 5.2 charts the frequency of the word "ideation" in books published after World War II. We can notice a steep,

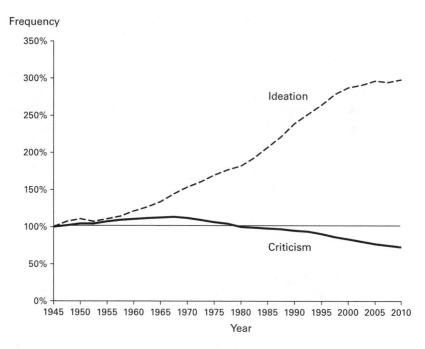

Figure 5.2
Frequency of the words *ideation* and *criticism* in books published after World War II. (Base frequency starting in 1945.) Source: Google Books Ngram Viewer.

constant increase (with a plateauing in recent years: maybe an early sign that the myth is wearing out?). "Criticism," instead, has diminished its presence in our cultures and discourses (apart from a growth in the late 1960s, indeed a period of intense social revolutions and change in cultural meanings).

This increased attention to ideation was much needed, especially within the world of management. But, as in the case of outside-in innovation, it slowly turned into an unquestionable myth, based on two untouchable assumptions: (1) the most *difficult* thing to find in innovation is a good idea, and (2) the *more* ideas we have, the more likely we will find a good one. This myth is now teetering.

First, because of its own success. In chapter 3 we showed that, thanks also to the recent impressive increase in the creative capabilities of people and organizations, we live in a world awash with ideas. So the more successful and widespread this myth has become, the more the first assumption has evaporated: what is difficult to find, in our creative, complex and connected society, is not a good idea but, rather, the capability to *make sense* of this wealth of opportunities: to find a good vision, a good interpretation, a good meaning.

And when it comes to making sense of things, the second assumption also evaporates. Having several ideas is good if we can then easily put them on a *scale* to recognize their value. This scale exists when we search for solutions (remember the diagram in figure 4.2, with balls, smiles, etc.?). But not when we search for new meanings. Because what we want to create *is* the scale, a new scale of judgment. In innovation of meaning we cannot "defer" judgment. Judgment is part of the *creation* process. It is what we create: a new way of making sense of things.[5]

CREATIVE CRITICISM

> *Find more pleasure in intelligent dissent than in passive agreement, for, if you value intelligence as you should, the former implies a deeper agreement than the latter.*
> Bertrand Russell[6]

Ideation therefore is not the core factor in innovation of meaning. We do not need more ideas. We need better interpretations, and criticism is the way to get there.

What criticism is

Although criticism often carries a sense of negativity, in reality it has no particular negative or positive disposition. Rather, it indicates *the practice of going deeper* in interpreting things. A movie critic does not necessarily produce a negative critique. She simply helps us understand better the content of an artwork. Some critiques can be positive, some negative, some both. But a good critique is always deep. It strives to unveil what lies *underneath the surface of things*. How? By taking a particular *stance*, a side.

Criticism is the practice of going deeper by *clashing together* different perspectives. Clashing not to destroy, not to show who is right and who is wrong nor to win a battle of opinions. Clashing to develop a richer and more robust interpretation. It's *emphasizing the differences* between diverse perspectives to *find the underlying connections*. In the awareness that, if two people interpret things differently and these people are both good and smart, there should be a reason for this difference. Maybe there is something underneath, a *new* great opportunity whose wholeness they cannot grasp individually; because each person, from her particular perspective, can only see *one side*; and most often she does not even fully grasp the merit of her own side until she goes through criticism. Criticism enables us to find this deeper new interpretation.

Why we need criticism: challenging the "inside"

Innovation of meaning needs criticism for two reasons. First, because innovation of meaning comes from the *inside out*. In chapter 4, we showed that the process of innovation of meaning necessarily starts from ourselves, from "what we'd love people to love." One reason for this is that no one is a clean sheet vis-à-vis meanings. We have our silent hypotheses about what could be meaningful to people. We each have our "side."

But, if we start from our side, we need to be sure that we do not get stuck there. Criticism helps us avoid this. By exposing our initial proposal to critical reflection, we enable ourselves and others to go deeper, in *search of the assumptions underlying our hypotheses*. Assumptions which often we were not even aware of. They may come from our past experience and we might take them for granted.

The four Microsoft renegades in front of Steve Ballmer, who proposed the vision of "game design as a high art," initially thought that game developers should not pay royalties. Sony and Nintendo charged developers a fee of $7 per game. But in the renegades' new vision, the developers were artists, not clients. A no-royalty policy would therefore have attracted the best game creators. But early criticism (from others in Microsoft and from outside experts) unveiled a different perspective: the best developers would in fact have preferred to pay, because royalties were a way to screen out the amateurs from the business. If game development were to become an art, it would require deep commitment and mastery of the art. And royalties were considered by the artists themselves to be one of the ways to ensure commitment and mastery.[7] The Xbox team realized they had a wrong assumption (which probably came from Microsoft's previous experience in the PC game business, where developers do not pay royalties); they refined their interpretation and decided that royalties were important (happily for Steve Ballmer's financial estimate). The vision of game design as high art was still there, twisted in a richer and deeper way.

So the first reason for criticism is to avoid being stuck in our own framework of interpretation. Criticism is a way to *challenge* our own cognitive frame, which is often implicit and built on past experiences. It's a way to shake us out, make assumptions explicit, and get rid of a past that might be not be meaningful anymore: to "*cure* the ideas that we use to interpret life," as Galimberti put it. In psychological theories of organizational *change*, criticism is indicated as a powerful way to help people unfreeze old schemes and create inner space to move forward toward different organizational arrangements.[8]

Why we need criticism: creating new meaning

There is, however, a second, more important reason why we need criticism: it enables us not only to move beyond the past, but also to *create the new*.

When we propose a new vision, we simply start from inklings of hypotheses. Our initial proposal is blurred, vague. Just a *sense of direction*, whose value and implications are mostly unclear. Not only to others; even more to ourselves.

When the four renegades of Microsoft came out with the vision of "game development as high art," they did not have a clear understanding of what this meant. They did not even have a common interpretation. Two of them believed deep down that Windows could still be the core of the platform, while the others were equally ready to leave Windows behind. When they first met, they only shared a malaise at the current Microsoft approach to gaming, and a similar sense of direction: game developers should face fewer technological limitations.

This initial fuzziness is normal. Visions do not pop up clear and complete. When we set out our hypotheses, we are just at the beginning. These hypotheses are just infants. We need to make them grow if we are to create more deeply. We need to turn these inklings of hypotheses into new meaningful visions that are robust, rich, and that people would love.

Here is where criticism plays its core role: criticism brings us into a journey, a *quest*, to create a novel, more powerful meaning. A quest where, by making different perspectives clash, we go deeper in the search for the underlying connections, a new understanding, a new interpretation. It's a process of *innovation* in which envisioning and judging happen *simultaneously*. Our initial hypotheses were just the striking of a match, a means to start the conversation. After that, the new interpretation is envisioned

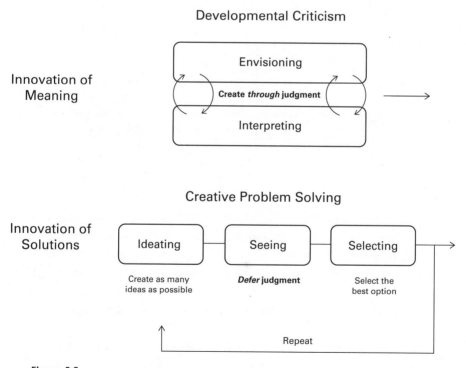

Figure 5.3
Innovation of solutions creates by deferring judgment. Innovation of meaning creates through judgment.

through judging. And if we do it several times, carefully and relentlessly, adding new perspectives along the way, then the final meaning has a great chance to flow into people's hearts.

What we are talking about here, therefore, is criticism in its ultimate essence: a criticism aimed not only at *challenging* the past, but most of all at *creating* the new.

It's a delicate process, though. To be handled with care. Because it is based on the creation of *tensions*. The wrong kind of criticism would simply kill the infant. It would destroy the potential of a great vision. Especially if the vision is bold and radically new, which usually implies it is also weak. So how should we do it? How should we embark on this quest for a deeper interpretation? How to combine creativity and criticism (apparently an oxymoron)? How did the vision of the Xbox survive Ballmer's reaction and launch Microsoft into a new world?

To answer these questions, let's travel back in time for a moment. To Paris, nineteenth century.

CRITICISM THAT CHANGES THE WORLD

Nothing could be more interesting than the talks we had with their perpetual clashes of opinion. Your mind was held in suspense all the time, you spurred the other on to sincere, disinterested inquiry and were spurred yourself, you laid in a stock of enthusiasm that kept you going for weeks on end until you could give final form to the idea you had in mind. You always went home afterwards better steeled for the fray, with a new sense of purpose and clearer head.
Claude Monet[9]

"You are crazy!" exclaimed Sisley when he saw Renoir's painting. "The idea of making trees blue and the ground purple!"[10] They were painting open-air, in the forest of Fontainebleau, south of Paris. It was 1864. Alfred Sisley and Auguste Renoir used to meet there together with Claude Monet and Frédéric Bazille. The four are nowadays known as the main founders of impressionism. But at that time they were unnoticed young painters, in their early twenties.

At that time the artistic discourse was dominated by the Académie des Beaux-Arts, a state-sponsored agency whose mission was to nurture the arts and to discern what was good work and what was not. And "what was good" in that moment was mostly classicism, with its mythological subjects. Paintings were typically created in studios, using careful drawings, clear lines, and soft tones. In 1863 a painting by Édouard Manet, *Déjeuner sur l'herbe*, went against this tradition. It portrayed a contemporary subject: two bourgeois men, fully dressed, and a fully nude woman having lunch in the woods. It was drawn using a sketchlike handling and sharp color contrasts. The painting was rejected at the art Salon that was held yearly in Paris, and it was ridiculed by journalists as obscene, crude, and unfinished.

In this context, Monet, Renoir, Sisley, and Bazille came to know each other as students in a studio in Paris. They were still at the beginnings of their careers as painters, and their early attempts had little in common with their later impressionist works. But they shared a sense of alienation from the artistic establishment and liked to explore more realistic painting. They enjoyed mocking their teacher's preference for classical, idealized forms. In response, the teacher disparaged their exercises, and soon labeled Monet the class rebel. Indeed, Claude Monet was the most undisciplined, daring, and therefore charismatic among the four. It was Monet who invited his classmates to Fontainebleau to paint "en plein air," a practice not supported by the Académie. And that is where Renoir did his unconventional experiment: painting the trees blue and the ground purple. At school, they were taught to use dark colors (bitumen and tobacco juice) to paint shadows. But Renoir wanted to capture what his eyes saw. "I tried to render the light on the trees, in the shadows, and on the ground as it really appeared to me," remembered Renoir.[11] And what really appeared to him was … blue and purple. He ventured to disclose his experiment to Sisley, who was his closest companion among the four. Renoir found it easier to share his outlandish attempt in the intimate context of a pair. Sisley's first reaction was astonishment. But then he started similar experiments on his own, and eventually he adopted the innovation. The pair then passed the idea on to Bazille and Monet when they met at night at the inn, and it became another little step in their journey toward the creation of a painting revolution. A journey fueled by the practice of criticism.

Michael P. Farrell, a professor of sociology at the University at Buffalo, has studied the collaborative dynamics of the impressionists, and of other groups that have created breakthrough innovations in art, science, politics. His book *Collaborative Circles*, in addition of being one of the most inspiring books I have come across in recent years,[12] is a precious source of information on how criticism drives innovative people. His chapter on the impressionists is the quintessential story of the practice of criticism.

Impressionism (like other radical innovations in the meaning of things) was not the result of pleasurable quick brainstorming sessions where people patted each other shoulders. It was the outcome of long constructive confrontations among its creators. And it can't be otherwise when you are gestating something really new. People cannot sit tight when you are challenging myths, not even your closest peers. You necessarily arouse reactions.

The style of interaction described here between Renoir and Sisley ("You are crazy!") was among the kindest possible. As Farrell explains, "the *intimacy of the dyad* was more conductive to taking risks and opening up to one another," to daring "forbidden" things. Sisley was for Renoir a kind of *sparring partner*:[13] someone trusted, whom he could show a *half-baked hunch* to without being killed. Still, a sparring partner doesn't pat you; he replies with a hard punch. Not because he wants to knock you down, but because he wants to make you stronger. You need it. Otherwise, when you meet a more muscular boxer, you risk being smashed. Same for breakthrough ideas. You need frank feedback,[14] an initial criticism as honest as it can be. Otherwise your outlandish half-baked idea will be killed when it meets harsher criticism.

And indeed, *later interactions were more difficult.* When they met as a quartet at night at the inn, the dialogue was more heated. But this more "abrasive dialogue with the whole group led to clarifications of the idea. ... Working as pairs during the day, and discussing their work at night, the men began to develop the ideas that became the foundation of their shared vision."[15]

In the following years their team further expanded, forming a circle that included other painters (Camille Pissarro, Édouard Manet, Edgar Degas, Paul Cézanne, for example) and thinkers from different fields: novelists, poets, sculptors, musicians, of whom probably the most famous was Émile Zola, a journalist and writer. They established a routine of weekly meetings. Every Thursday night they met at Café Guerbois in Paris. In these largest group discussions, criticism was even more intense. "Unlike paired collaborations," writes Farrell, "the interactions in the café were boisterous and combative." But, as explained powerfully by Monet in his quote that opens this section, these acrimonious confrontations were an essential part in building new visions. They helped the individuals to go deeper, understand better the implications of their own personal ideas, and build a more powerful vision.

Members of the circle spontaneously took different roles in the dynamics of the discussions. Pissarro for example was effective in negotiating *consensus*. He played in the middle, finding a synthesis for a coherent vision. Other important members instead played at the *boundaries*, at the extremes. On one side, there were the most incremental and conservative painters, such as Degas. He was closer to established dogmas of art, and he was sometimes accused of watering down the principles of the circle. On the other side, there were the most radical and outlandish members, such as Cézanne. He was the most rebellious and deliberately provocative against the establishment. These *boundary markers* had a crucial role. "Group members often can express their dislikes more clearly than their likes," writes Farrell. "It is through clarifying what they see is wrong with the work and behavior of the boundary markers that the group begins to reach consensus about their values."[16] "Their exchanges could be characterized as confrontational, sarcastic, and witty, but only rarely they were destructive."[17] Not all the experiments were accepted, of course. Some stirred negative reactions and were eventually spurned. For example, in an experiment they tried to scrape paint onto the canvas with a palette knife, but this technique was eventually abandoned.

Eventually, through this relentless and engaged work of *clashing* and *fusing* different perspectives, the group reached a consensus toward the creation of the revolutionary vision of impressionism. In terms of subjects, they discarded historical, religious, and mythological themes in favor of everyday modern life and landscapes. "What need is there to go back through history, to seek refuge in legend"? wrote Castagnary, a contemporary art critic. "Beauty is in front of the eyes, not inside the brain."[18] It was a *breakthrough new meaning*, a new why to paint. To capture this beauty that appeared in front of their eyes, they needed a new technique. They therefore abandoned the precise, mild, idealized lines that are produced by the mind in studio paintings, in search of methods that enabled them to capture the moment in the real light. This meant to paint in open air, quickly, focusing on what the eye saw rather than the mind. "When you go out to paint," said Monet, "try to forget what objects you have before you, a tree, a house, a field or whatever. Merely think here is a little square of blue, here an oblong of pink, here a streak of yellow, and paint it just as it looks to you, the exact color and shape."[19] They started to use short commalike brushstrokes, juxtaposing sharp contrasting colors, which for example brought a shimmering life to water. They could even rapidly paint many views of the same scene, therefore capturing the changes in light during the day.

Meanwhile, their paintings were still repeatedly rejected by the jury of the Salon. But the circle moved on, energized by their internal clashes in the search for a new vision, and further reinforced by the external opposition. They were growing stronger. Until they organized themselves and built their own exhibitions. The rest of the story ... is in contemporary museums and the most expensive art auctions.

RADICAL CIRCLES

I met a group of people who challenged me, supported me, and changed my life. ... It was the best time in my life.
Jonathan "Seamus" Blackley[20]

Farrell narrates many other stories in which breakthrough innovations are forged by the art of criticism. For example the Inklings, a group of writers in the 1930s and 1940s who created a radically new stream of mythopoeic novels based on imaginative Nordic myths, such as *The Hobbit* and *The Lord of the Rings* by J. R. R. Tolkien, or *The Lion, the Witch and the Wardrobe* by C. S. Lewis. Or the early history of psychoanalysis, with Sigmund Freud and Wilhelm Fleiss. In these stories Farrell shows how successful novel visions are built through a *"constructive sympathetic style of critical interaction."*[21] What is most interesting is that this interaction, this art of criticism, does not depend as much on a particular technique as on meeting the right *people*. The point is not *how* to practice criticism, but *with whom*.

In this perspective, I'm not in the realm of theories of "critical thinking" that focus on how *individuals* can think more critically by *themselves*. Of course, having a mind trained to think critically is important. And visionary leaders often develop new interpretations by acting self-critically. However, when a scenario is complex and difficult to interpret, a reflective process in which a single person artificially creates "sides" in her mind is hardly effective by itself. One needs to create tensions with the help of others. To encounter those "sides" in real life, embodied in other people.[22]

In particular, Farrell shows that all these breakthrough transformations in the world of art and science were ignited by a small circle of thinkers. And, indeed, we may find a similar dynamic within the world of business. The story of the Xbox impressively mirrors the story of the impressionists. "The Xbox was conceived of and championed by a small group of passionate, creative individuals ... Microsoft, the great giant, allowed itself to be drawn into this project by a group of relatively junior employees," says Seamus Blackley, a major protagonist of the conception of the Xbox vision.[23] As colorfully illustrated by the initial reaction of Steve Ballmer, the Xbox was not the result of top-down directions. But neither did it come from a bottom-up process of diffused ideation. It was mainly driven by a small circle of renegades, who previously had had no formal mutual relations but came to know each other through informal social connections. Inflamed by their passion for gaming, and by a sense of the opportunity that Microsoft was not seizing, they voluntarily started to think about how Microsoft could more effectively have a role in that business and react to Sony PlayStation's threat, even before Microsoft's top management started to address it. This small circle was centered on four people.

Jonathan "Seamus" Blackley was a new hire who had joined Microsoft on 9 February 1999. He had significant previous experience, however, in digital game technologies, including a major failure: he had led the development of *Trespasser* for Dreamworks, a videogame connected to the movie *Jurassic Park*, meant to be played on personal computers. *Trespasser* was an ambitious project in terms of performance and simulation of reality, but it failed because its elaboration requirements were too demanding for PCs. When Blackely joined Microsoft after his career debacle, for a new restart in software development, he brought not only his innate passion for games and his strong technical experience in game development, but also his personal view that computers (and their operating systems) were not good for gamers. An outlandish vision that definitely was not in line with the existing trajectory of Microsoft. An outgoing character, Blackley was a major engine behind the creation of the team of renegades who started to work on the Xbox, and the only one who stayed until the market launch of the product.

Kevin Bachus was a former product marketing manager for DirectX, the Microsoft software tool that enabled game designers to develop games for the PC. He had significant experience within Microsoft's organization and a very good knowledge of the game industry. He made a major contribution in developing the first preliminary business plan for the Xbox. An introvert, he shared Blackely's extreme intention to move away from the PC: from his perspective, games could not be played on normal operating systems; they required a dedicated platform. Although he had not known Blackley before, the two became close friends during the project, until Bachus left Microsoft in 2001.

Ted Hase was formerly a manager in the Developers Relations Group of Microsoft, i.e., he took care of relationships with developers of games for the PC. He had good knowledge of Microsoft's organizational dynamics and helped the renegades to secure early political support from top executives. Concerning the Xbox he had a milder perspective. Although he shared Blackley's and Bachus's belief in the need to create a new product, he still considered the PC as an interesting platform, since it enabled developers to develop games without paying royalties. Already in 1998 he had personally reflected on a concept for Microsoft based on a low-cost computer, with everything stripped out of its operating system except what was needed to run games, i.e., a kind of simplified Windows focused on games. An outgoing character, he left the team of renegades in the fall of 1999, after the team assumed a formal structure, to go back and focus completely on his previous job.

Otto Berkes was formerly a DirectX programming whiz with a strong technical expertise (especially in graphics). He also started to think in 1998 about creating a version of Windows for entertainment. An introvert, during the journey he became very close to Ted Hase, with whom he shared a milder perspective of a stripped-down Windows focused on gaming (a "Windows Entertainment Platform"), to be used on normal PCs. Similarly to Hase, he went back to his former job in the fall 1999.

Other people joined the circle later with more supportive roles (e.g., Ed Fries, the VP of Games created by Microsoft). Blackley, Bachus, Hase, and Berkes, however, were the ones initially directly engaged in the creation of the Xbox vision. None of them had a top executive role. None of them had been appointed to this task. They voluntarily came together as they discovered that they shared the same interest and a vague intuition: that there was an opportunity for Microsoft to become a major player in the video-game industry, and that this opportunity could be seized only by rethinking some myths of the Redmond giant. This group of renegades managed to transform this vague intuition into a breakthrough vision, a clear direction, and to convince Microsoft's top executives and organization that this direction was promising, although it contrasted the company's existing strategy.

They formed what I call a *radical circle*, i.e., a primary group of individuals who tightly collaborate outside of formal organizational schemes.

"Radical" because it promotes a *radically new vision*, typically in contrast with the existing direction of a firm.

"Circle" because it is a small *stable* group, and it is not open to anyone. Like any circle, it is "by invitation only." The invitation is extended only to those who share the same will: to create a new direction, a new meaning.

A radical circle is an effective path toward the creation of a breakthrough vision because it brings together *key resources*. Resources that are needed to make our initial hypothesis grow, to transform bits and pieces of intuition into a powerful vision.

I'm not talking here only of economic resources and social capital. These are important of course, since one needs budget and contacts to conduct experiments in the quest phase of a new vision.[24] And a circle consisting of more people can have greater access to economic and social resources than a single individual. But these were not the only nor the most relevant resources that the circle pulled together. The most precious things were intangible: affinitive *encouragement* and developmental *criticism*.

Affinitive encouragement
What! You too? I thought that no one but myself …
C. S. Lewis[25]

When one explores breakthrough directions that go against the dominant existing trajectory, one often meets derision and skepticism, as in the case of the reaction of Steve Ballmer. Most often, an outlandish proposal is not understood at first (not even by those who propose it). This is normal. Definitely, a breakthrough exploration will be punctuated by failures.

Encouragement helps one endure the frustration and disappointment that necessarily build along the path. And the members of a radical circle are a major source of encouragement, as recounted by those who had the lucky chance to be part of one: "Alone among unsympathetic companions," said C. S. Lewis, a member of the Inklings, "I hold certain views and standards timidly, half ashamed to avow them and half doubtful if they can after all be right. Put back among my friends and in half an hour—in ten minutes—these same views and standards become once more indisputable. *The opinion of this little circle ... outweighs that of a thousand outsiders.*"[26] And Tolkien, in turn, wrote about Lewis, "The unpayable debt I owe to him was ... sheer *encouragement.* He was for long my only audience. Only from him did I ever get the idea that my stuff could be more than a private hobby."[27]

The same things happened in the case of the Xbox: "[We] were so driven and convinced by the power of our idea that even the setbacks that rose in our path served only to strengthen our conviction," said Jonathan Blackley.[28]

I refer here to a special kind of encouragement: *affinitive.* I do not mean the encouragement that you can get from friends, relatives, or generic colleagues. They may tell us we are good, give us a pat on the shoulder. Instead, the encouragement provided by a radical circle comes from discovering that someone else is trying a *similar direction.* Which means that she really *believes* in it, to the point of putting herself at stake. When we discover this affinity, we suddenly feel that we are not alone. That maybe what we are trying is not totally crazy. Especially if the other person is someone we respect, we esteem.[29] Sigmund Freud once wrote to his sparring partner Wilhelm Fliess, who sustained him through a decade of professional frustration and isolation: "It is primary through your *example* that intellectually I gained the strength to trust my judgment, even when I am left alone ... and like you, to face with lofty humility all the difficulties that the future may bring."[30] This kind of *affinitive* encouragement is extremely powerful, even if the feedback we get is not a pat on our shoulder, but, as in the case of Sisley, a *critical* reply. We get the strength to resist pressure to conform; we dare to try radical forbidden experiments. Farrell writes about the Inklings: "In 1925 [Tolkien] showed [an epic poem] to an old mentor, who advised him to drop it. The rebuff reinforced his decision to keep the work secret. But after discovering that Lewis *shared* his interest in 'Northernness' and epic poetry, ... Tolkien gave Lewis one of the *unfinished* poems to read."[31]

Developmental criticism

My dear Tolkien, … I quite honestly say that it is ages since I have had an evening of such delight … so much for the first flush. Detailed criticisms (including grumbles at individual lines) will follow.

C. S. Lewis[32]

This quote recounts the reaction of Lewis to Tolkien's unfinished poem. His first words provide encouragement. Then Lewis announces his criticism to come. Criticism is indeed the second, even more important, resource. A radical circle is the healthier environment for the constructive sympathetic style of critical interaction that is necessary to make a vision grow. This critical feedback comes because its members have expertise and knowledge (they are not beginners). Simply, their knowledge and way of interpreting complement ours. We have seen that in the case of the Xbox the four team members had backgrounds that spanned from marketing to technology to business. Some of them were aware of what is meaningful for young gamers, some for developers, some for people within Microsoft's organization. They provided the other members of the circle an *informed engaged audience* with different perspectives that are essential for discussing a new vision. It was not only a matter of complementary kinds of expertise, which is typical of multidisciplinary teams. Before complementing each other to design technical solutions, we need to share the direction. The radical circle, indeed, gives critical feedback *on the direction*, on the meaning, not only on the solution. Its members do not work on different things; they work on the same: on creating a breakthrough vision. Criticism is the dynamic that enables transforming initial individual intuitions into a new robust shared interpretation that will stand much harsher and doubtful criticism when shared with the larger organization and external players. *Individuals get killed by criticism. Circles instead get energy from it.* The power of this critical quest was enormous for the Xbox team. It enabled them to transform their blurred initial insights into a robust vision that eventually stood the much harsher and doubtful criticism of the larger organization (of which an example is Steve Ballmer's comment that opens this chapter).

Instrumental intimacy: trust and the common enemy

A radical circle provides a healthy environment in which to get the *encouragement* to do outlandish experiments and the precious *critical* feedback to develop. It replicates the typical research dynamics that are necessary to transform intuitions into real outputs, but in a *protected* context. Or, as Farrell more precisely puts it, in a context of "instrumental intimacy."

At the foundation of this healthy environment, where criticism becomes a source of creation, there is *trust*. In three ways.

Trust to *talk*, otherwise we would hardly share *half-baked* thoughts.[33]

Trust to *do*, otherwise we would hardly dare to try *forbidden* experiments.

Trust to *listen*, otherwise we would hardly really take in the developmental feedback from the one who is *criticizing* us (this last is the most difficult trust: our sparring partner is punching us and creating pain, and we need to trust that she is not doing this because she wants to knock us down, but because she wants to make us stronger).

This trust does not come for free, of course. How do we create it? Theories on trust explain that trust occurs when we rely on another person to have an expected behavior, and one that will not harm us.[34] This expectation about the behavior of the other person may be grounded on different things: a relationship that dates back in time, for example. But the stories of successful radical circles tell that this is not always the case. The four young impressionists-to-be just met at school. The four renegades of Microsoft *did not have previous formal organizational connections*, and Blackley, the main driver of the quartet, had been hired just a month before they started to collaborate spontaneously.

In a radical circle, trust comes from a totally different source: *a common will*. The will to change, to build a breakthrough new vision. To be precise, this does not imply that a radical circle comes together because they share a vision. The shared vision is the *output* of the process. At the beginning, of course, it is still not there. As Renoir put it, "We were full of good intentions, but yet we were groping in the dark."[35] What builds trust is the "good intentions." We can trust criticism from others because we are all full of the same *will* to change for the better.

This "will to change" comes typically from a shared sense of malaise about the current situation. The impressionists felt this way toward classicism and indoor studio painting. The four Microsoft renegades toward Redmond's approach to the videogame business and toward the threat of Sony with its PlayStation 2. They all had a passion for videogames and had autonomously started to imagine possible new strategies to enter the business in a different way. Hase and Berkes had independently imagined a stripped-down version of Windows specifically tailored for playing games. Blackley had previous experience in the industry, and as he joined Microsoft (in an area that was not targeted to games), he spontaneously started to think about how the corporation could do something more meaningful in this arena. When Sony announced the PlayStation 2, the renegades' malaise grew and they felt the urge to act. Through informal, unplanned relationships they came to know each other and appreciated the fact that someone else had similar feelings of malaise. What glued them together was *not a common vision.* Their initial intuitions moved in different directions (Blackley and Bachus toward a more radical departure from PCs, Hase and Berkes toward a specialization of Windows). What drove trust at the beginning was the awareness that they all shared a common hot cause, *a common enemy.* Actually two: Sony and, more audaciously, Windows. Sony, of course, because of the PlayStation 2. Windows because it drove the existing vision of Microsoft: playing games on a general-purpose platform such as the PC, which was unsuited to games. Similarly to the radical artistic circles described by Farrell, at the beginning they found it *easier to talk about what they disliked than what they liked.* For example, this sharing of the common enemy was reflected in the code name they picked for the project in their early interaction: Project Midway. Indeed, it was a project of a US company against the Japanese empire of Sony, Nintendo, and Sega; and it was midway between a general-purpose PC and a game console.

Sometimes, as in the examples I discuss above, the sense of malaise surfaces in an undeniable way. We feel uncomfortable with the existing situation. Sometimes the malaise is milder, just a sense of *wonder:* we struggle to understand the existing myths, to capture the meaning of current norms ("why can't we paint open-air"?). Bernard Lonergan, a Canadian philosopher, shows that wonder is often a powerful driver that generates inner tensions: we *want* to understand. And we *tend to glue better with people who share similar wonders, rather than with people who have similar answers.* "Wonderment … is the unifying basis for the possibility of collaborative inquiry. Wonder gives rise to a sense of being bothered by something one does not understand, … the *tension of inquiry* … the *pure desire to know.*"[36]

Voluntarism, "by invitation only"

You gather in groups because you believe in the same things and you would rather die of hunger than retract.

Pierre-Auguste Renoir[37]

The shared sense of malaise is the basis of trust. It's the igniting spark that activates the dynamics of criticism, to "tell, do and listen." Discovering that others share our malaise is a powerful drive. The "same things" mentioned by Renoir in his quote above are the "same enemy," and the same "will" to move away from it. A radical circle has a tacit rule: "If you are here, working in this circle, is because you dislike something in the status quo and want to find a new direction. If you don't, it's fine, but please leave." We work in a circle and, when confronted by criticism, we engage even further rather than retract, because we know that criticism comes from others who share our malaise and will to change. If this ingredient is not there at the beginning, critical dynamics will never start. The members will simply bring destructive criticism, or, even worse in my opinion, they will be apathetic and navigate in silence. Then it's really better to leave.

Here arises a first important observation: most radical circles come together *voluntarily*. No one asked the four Microsoft renegades to work together. They just started in, driven by the same sense of malaise about Microsoft's existing path into the gaming business, and a will to propose something new, to change it. Of course voluntarism is not always possible within organizations. We will see in chapter 7 how we can instill voluntarism into group dynamics. Within an organization, there is always someone who, earlier than others, feels a sense of malaise with the current situation, or simply has an unexpressed will to change. And there are many more of them than we think. They are typically silent. But when they enter a context of instrumental intimacy, these people open up.

And here arises a second important observation. Members of a radical circle are hardly outspoken revolutionaries. *Their purpose is not to destroy*. It is to help their organization grow. The impressionists were not just rebels. They wanted to *succeed* and be accepted into the world of art for their innovations. For this reason, I'm inclined to trust people who have an unspoken and humble will to change more than I would trust the bold integralist contrarians. The latter often cross the line into destructive rebellion, like Cézanne for the impressionists (especially when their own vision, eventually, does not succeed). Microsoft had already had an earlier circle that tried to revolutionize its approach to gaming. It happened in 1994, after Sony released the PlayStation 1. The circle was nicknamed the Beasty Boys and was led by Alex St. John, who had a key role in the development of DirectX. St. John was outspokenly rebellious and belligerent. He did not just feel a sense of malaise; he became destructive and sarcastic. Eventually, having burnt many bridges within the organization, he had to leave[38] and Microsoft stayed where it was.

This also implies that one becomes part of a radical circle "by invitation only." We accept others and are accepted if we share a common malaise and a common will to change, a will to challenge and be challenged in a critical constructive way. Absent these conditions, we are not invited to attend, and, if we are already in, we are invited to leave.

A radical circle is therefore completely different from an open community. An open community assembles itself around a vision. Since the value of the community depends on the number of participants, its doors are essentially open to anyone. Its entry barriers are low. And its exit barriers are low: often, when you leave an open community, no one even realizes.

But who generated the vision that brought this large community together? Not the community itself. Because vision generation requires the delicate dynamics of developmental criticism, of "instrumental intimacy," which only happens in a radical circle. In fact, people gather in a circle through a careful and vigilant process of mutual recognition: about sharing the same malaise, the same will to change, the same constructive orientation. There are entry barriers (and also exit barriers, as Renoir's sentence points out). A vision behind a large open community has always been developed first by a radical circle of people who came together by invitation only (figure 5.4).[39]

A radical circle is also significantly different from a traditional formal team. A team (such as a product development team or a concept development team) does not come together voluntarily. It is usually assembled by executives on purpose, on the basis of its members' competences, skills, and decision power. Initially they might not share the same sense of malaise and will to change. And in fact, traditional group theories within organization sciences look at the early phases of team formation as critical: given that the team does not come together voluntarily but rather is assembled,

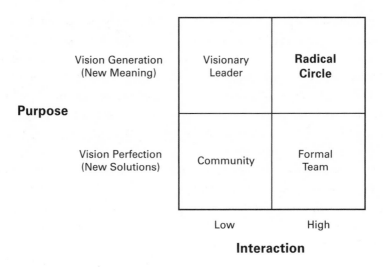

Figure 5.4
Organizational configurations for innovation.

agreement on a common direction can be quite problematic.[40] A formal team thus may be effective for creating ideas when the vision is already there (as in brainstorming, where the focus is clearly defined), and for execution. It works great for solving problems and developing solutions. But it is less effective in the early phases of innovation of meanings.[41]

A radical circle is therefore extremely effective in the early quest necessary to generate a robust deep vision (figure 5.4). It overcomes the limits of the traditional model of the lonely "visionary leader," which is extremely rare (if it ever really existed), random, and risky in complex environments, because of its lack of critical confrontation. In a way, a radical circle acts as an empowered visionary leader.[42] Its members are as one in terms of intent, will, drive. But they also enjoy the strong clashes, tensions, criticism, and insights that a lonely person cannot experience. A circle provides the additional resources (affinitive encouragement, developmental criticism, and of course economic and social resources) that are necessary to create meaningful visions.

INSIDE-OUT CRITICISM

We have seen that innovation of meaning is based on the art of *criticism*. An art that, more than depending on specific tools and techniques, depends on *who* we collaborate with. Criticism needs "sides." And to have these sides, we need people with different perspectives who are willing for their preliminary hypotheses to *clash* and *fuse* into a breakthrough vision. We have also seen that this process has to start from ourselves, from the *inside out*.

Figure 5.5 combines these two principles (inside-out and criticism) into a coherent actionable process.

Being an inside-out process, it starts from *us*, as individuals. We begin by exposing our own individual preliminary hypotheses. They will become the meat of the process, the basic ingredients to be clashed. This is why a "beginner's mind" is useless in innovation of meaning: without anything to clash, there is nothing to start with, nothing to fuse. We will see in chapter 6 how this first exercise can be conducted critically (or better, self-critically).

Then the process moves slowly to the *outside*, in order to be sure that we are not stuck in our own assumptions. We need criticism from others, but in a careful way, because our initial hypotheses are still weak and unclear, even to ourselves, especially the most outlandish ones. So we need to open up *gradually*.

The best way is to start working in *pairs*, with a sparring partner. A pair is the most delicate way to practice the art of criticism. We have seen in the story of the impressionists that the most daring experiments where first tried and shared in the small intimacy of pairs. Renoir with Sisley and

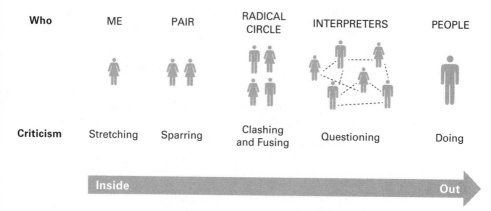

Figure 5.5
The inside-out process of innovation of meaning, based on the art of criticism.

Monet with Bazille. And similarly, the four renegades of Microsoft first shared their half-baked hypothesis within pairs. Blackley felt more comfortable with Bachus, because he shared the tendency toward a radical departure from PCs. Hase was closer to Berkes because they had the same initial hypothesis of developing a specialized version of Windows. Pair interaction was precious for strengthening these merely sketched initial visions through a protected conversation. "We started with nothing more than a slide presentation," said Blackley. He had a strong foothold in the game industry but was weaker on the business side. Interaction with Bachus, with his background as a product marketing manager, enabled him to strengthen the economic sustainability of his initial hypothesis. "When I saw the proposal," says Bachus, "I refocused it. I said 'Let's think about what kind of consumers we're building this for, and how to get game publishers onboard.'" In the course of the project Blackley and Bachus become so close and complementary that they were dubbed Laurel and Hardy. "Bachus was the yin and Blackley the yang," said the director of the Game Developers Conference.[43]

Next, after we have made our hypotheses clearer and stronger, we can take *harsher* criticism from a *larger circle*. The analogy is with what happened to the impressionists during the night meetings at the inn in Fontainebleau, or to the four renegades of Microsoft. Larger discussions will probably be more acrimonious. In fact, we start confronting our own hypotheses (and those of our own sparring partner, who is closest to us) with those of others who have a will to change, but not necessarily in the same direction. It is during this discussion that the real process of clashing and fusing occurs. The raw material, the initial hypotheses, have been already deepened and strengthened by the pairs; they will hardly succumb ("you would rather die of hunger than retract"). They will likely be fused into a new, more powerful interpretation.

The following step of the critical process implies opening up further, this time to real outsiders, i.e., people *outside our organization*. First, to *interpreters*, i.e., experts from far-flung fields who address our strategic context but from different perspectives. In the case of the impressionists, this happened for example at the meetings at the Café Guerbois, when they discussed their ideas with writers, sculptors, musicians. Interpreters us help reflect even deeper on the implications of our emerging vision. Second, to *users*, who are those we hope will eventually love our proposal.

The impressionists eventually organized their own exhibition when their paintings were still not accepted at the official Salon. The Microsoft renegades met experts (such as providers of hardware technologies) and users (especially developers). Outsiders, of course, can help us learn a lot, *once we have a new framework* through which to interpret their feedback and insights. Their involvement late in the process is prompted by a profoundly different purpose than that of open innovation and crowdsourcing tools. Outsiders in innovation of meanings are *carefully identified*. Their main role is *not only to provide insights*; rather, it's to *challenge* the innovative direction that we propose and make it stronger and deeper. Here what outsiders have to bring are good *questions* rather than good ideas. In other words, they contribute to *criticism*, not to ideation.

LOVE IS NOT ABOUT SELECTING OPTIONS

> *He wasn't exactly sure when it had happened. Or even when it started. It may have been the morning when he'd seen Kristen holding Katie after Josh had fallen in the river, or the rainy afternoon when he'd driven her home, or even during the day they had spent at the beach. All he knew for sure was that right here and now, he was falling hard for this woman.*
> Nicholas Sparks[44]

The purpose of going through a process based on inside-out criticism is to create a vision that is powerful, robust, and, especially, meaningful: something for people to love.

Classic theories of problem solving assume that the process of finding novel solutions goes in a sequence that I illustrated in figure 5.3: we generate (or insource) ideas, then we judge ideas, then we select. This can be iterated several times until we come to an optimal or at least satisfying option. Ideation and judgment in any case are clearly separated. "Defer judgment" when you create ideas was written on the walls of IDEO's brainstorming room. And eventually, select. Also in management culture, judgment and selection occur separately from ideation. A team of innovators would generate ideas, then these ideas would be presented to a board of executives who would judge and select.

This may work for solutions. But not for creating meaningful visions to love. We do not fall in love through a process of selecting options. Speed dating is about … dating. Love is another story. One find herself or himself in love through a process (short or long) in which there is no moment of selection, no pondering of options. At a given moment, along the way, that person is simply ... inevitable.

Once again, the metaphor of love, chary as we are to refer to such a delicate subject, helps us better comprehend why forging meaningful visions substantially differs from creating solutions. These differences are summarized in table 5.1, and in particular the contrast between ideation and criticism.

The first difference is that ideation is about *quantity*, whereas innovation of meaning is about *depth*. In a world awash with opportunities, we do not develop better meaning by tossing in truckloads of interpretations; this would simply increase the confusion, the entropy. We instead need to go deeper.

Solutions may either be *right* (better) *or wrong* (worse). We screen them. Interpretations have a different nature: they most often have an inch of truth *and* an inch of falseness. In other words, there is an inkling of truth in any preliminary hypothesis that trusted pairs put forward. We just need to find it! How? By going deeper, through criticism. The way to get to a novel meaningful interpretation therefore is not by having another one, but by going deeper with a few good perspectives, *clashing* them, *fusing* them. Like the imprimatura of the painting mentioned by Alexandra Horowitz (see the end of chapter 4 in this book): every layer brings a bit of color, one on top of the other. The final painting is a meaningful fusion of layers.

Table 5.1
Differences between Ideation and Criticism

Ideation	Art of Criticism
Quantity of insights	Depth of insights
Communities	Intimacy
Seeing	Interpreting
Scale and screen	Clash and fuse
Defer judgment	Create through judgment
Naivete	Having a horizon
Neutrality	Taking sides
Playfulness	Engagement
Designers create, managers judge	Designers also judge, managers also create
Select the best option	No need to select; the new is inescapable

This implies that while in innovation of solution creativity *anticipates* judgment, in innovation of meaning creativity *occurs through* judgment. They happen together. It is the act of *criticism*, of clashing and fusing, that enables us to *create* a new painting.

The consequence is that while in traditional problem solving ideas come from the bottom of the organization and judgment comes from the top, here *judgment also has to come from the bottom*. Or better, from anyone who participates in the creation. Because creation occurs *through* criticism. Actually, the dynamics of creative circles shows that the first judgment, and the first endorsement, most likely come from peers.

So when we have an inspiration for a new vision, we shouldn't be tempted to knock at the door of busy top executives expecting to be listened to and get an endorsement (and being regularly frustrated because, of course, our vague intuition, which was not yet clear even to ourselves, was not understood by the top executives). We do better to search for other peers to share our weak initial intuition with and to leverage their judgment and interpretation. When our hypothesis for a new vision becomes more grounded and shared, we can knock on the doors of the top executives, expect to be listened to, and withstand their doubts.

Unfortunately, finding peers who are good sparring partners and provide effective creative criticism is often as difficult as ringing the bell of a CEO's office. Many creative people are not trained and not used to the art of criticism (indeed, they have been repeatedly told that criticism is bad). So we need to search carefully around us, and cherish our peers who are good in providing frank critical feedback. They are precious in the journey toward the development of a new vision.

The most notable implication of this process of going deeper is that *the act of selecting dissolves*. Along the way, we cannot say exactly when and where, the vision that is building up comes to appear inevitable. Maybe, retrospectively, we can point to a specific moment: the combination of two perspectives during a workshop, a comment from an interpreter, a feedback from a lead user, a chat in the canteen. Most likely it has simply happened through a combination of all of this. But for sure, we see the love in those who created it and those who are exposed to it. No need to select.

And if love is not there, it means it is still too early: we need to dig deeper, understand what does not work. We add new layers of paint, through envisioning and criticizing. New clashes and new fusions. Until the meaning surfaces.

And then, you can't go back anymore. In several projects we participated in, we have noticed that at a given moment the team looks back and almost cannot recognize its earlier beliefs. "How could we think that this was meaningful?" No need to select, no need to convince anyone about the change. They have already changed.

The funny thing is that often the final vision incorporates ideas that had already been explored in the organization beforehand. Someone could complain: "These solutions were already here before you started. They had been around for months." It happens. Some specific painting techniques of the impressionists had been used earlier. For example, the idea of avoiding dark colors for shadows was already diffused among minor artists who painted landscapes. It was suggested to Renoir by Narcisse Virgilio Díaz de la Peña, an established painter.[45] Many technologies incorporated in the Xbox had been explored within Microsoft before. And many ideas in the Nest thermostat had already surfaced in the industry and in idea competitions.

But there are two main differences between earlier scattered ideas and the final vision. First, these specific solutions were confused among a myriad of other options. Now, instead, there is a *direction*. Second, and even more important, now we see the *meaning*. We do not simply see the signs. We have a new interpretation that puts individual scattered solutions in a new light. What appeared to be a meaningless bunch of ideas now seems an inevitable scenario.

The person we meet and love does not come to life while we fall in love. She was already there. And probably we had already met her. But through the process of falling in love, her meaning blossoms, and her value becomes inescapable.

Part III   The Process

Methods and Tools

In part II of this book we have discussed the two principles of innovation of meaning: innovation from the inside out and criticism. As these two principles are exactly the opposite of the principles for innovation of solutions, the process of innovation of meanings is necessarily different from classic problem solving. The purpose of this third part of the book is to illustrate this process for creating new, meaningful experiences.

The methods and tools that I will share here are just "how we do it" when we collaborate with organizations. They come from almost a decade of experience on innovation of meaning.

It has been a long journey. First, we studied companies that had successfully done it in the past. Then we assembled the best of what we learned into a viable process that could be replicated in different contexts, industries, and cultures. Finally, we experimented with this process in several projects with a variety of organizations. We have been lucky, because along the way we have met managers who were willing to try a new path, especially when we were still at the beginning of our exploration. Over the years the process has changed from the initial blueprint. We have learned, and, I feel, improved significantly. And we are still engaged in making this process increasingly effective. So what I share here is just a work in progress. Quite advanced, of course, but still in a perennial dynamic of improvement.

I'm also aware that there could be several ways to implement the two principles introduced earlier. Here I illustrate what we have been doing so far. I hope that others will try different avenues, expand the range of available methods, and share their findings.[1]

So what does this process look like? Its basic articulation was introduced at the end of chapter 5 (see figure III.1).

First, we saw that innovation of meaning has to start from us (i.e., the inside-out principle). The process therefore is structured along a sequence of steps of which the first is to ask individuals to expose their preliminary hypotheses.

The process then opens up progressively to criticism from others. Initially within our own organization: a sparring partner who can provide trusted feedback; and then a circle of other people engaged in the same process, but who may have envisioned preliminary directions that differ from our own. Subsequently, we can receive criticism from outside our organization. From interpreters (experts in other fields who address the same customer base), and from customers themselves.

As we move from the inside to the outside, our own preliminary vision gets merged with the vision of others, in a process in which criticism gets progressively more intense. Through this process of clashing and fusing, we build a deep vision that is more likely to be meaningful, powerful, and feasible.

The next three chapters will move into the details of these steps. In particular: chapter 6 focuses on the first phase, in which each individual

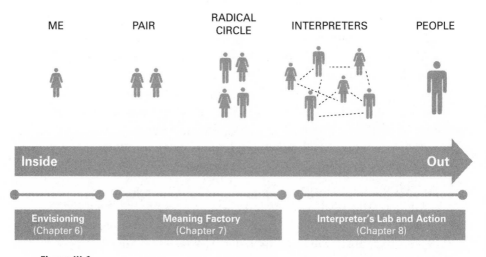

Figure III.1
The process of innovation of meaning and the structure of part III of the book.

envisions possible new meanings. The purpose is to expose her own preliminary hypotheses about what she would love people to love. Chapter 7 illustrates the two following internal steps: the work in pairs and within radical circles. Most of this work, in our process, occurs within a two- to three-day workshop that we call the meaning factory. Chapter 8 concentrates on the interaction with interpreters. At the core of this step there is a meeting that we call the interpreter's lab. We will see how to select the interpreters, brief them, interact with them during this meeting, and summarize the results to inform the following steps. As far as interaction with users is concerned, this step has been so intensively explored by other innovation studies in recent years that I will not dig deeply into it in this book. There are already good tools and methods on how to conduct ethnographic analysis, market testing, focus groups, especially using the most advanced digital technologies. I will refer to good material that you can consult in this regard, and that we use ourselves and find effective.

In this last part of the book I will use a different tone compared to the previous pages. In the earlier sections I used the language of stories to support our reflections. Now I move to the simple format of methods and process: brief, clean, with examples. For each phase I will schematically illustrate (figure III.2):

- the *purpose* of the phase,
- how the *new meaning evolves* (how it emerges and take shapes through the different phases),
- what the basic *questions* are that each phase addresses,
- which *methods* and *thinking frames* we can use to answer those questions.

Not all details are discussed, of course. Every project has its own story and context, and every organization has its own mission, capability, culture. What I illustrate here is just an alloy of different experiences. A coherent summary of the several processes we have experienced, which in reality had countless variations. The process presented here therefore needs to be framed to your specific situation. In our collaborations we always start from a basic framework that we tailor for a particular project. Indeed, a standard innovation process would simply harm any organization. And, I confess,

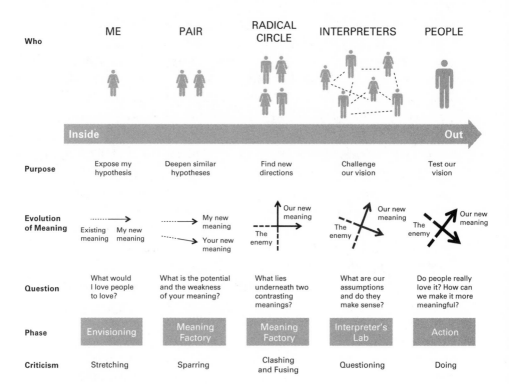

Figure III.2
Overview of the process.

after a while we would also rapidly get bored, lose our energy and our innovation drive. So let's see how this process looks, and then, if you'd like to
move on, remember to make it *yours*. And, if you like, please reflect with us,
because we are always keen to improve our understanding of how to create
new meanings.

6 Envisioning

From Me to People

The process of innovation of meaning moves from the inside out. It starts from us.

Actually, in its first phase, the right pronoun is "me," because we begin by working individually.

As discussed in chapter 4, everyone within an organization harbors a sense of what could be meaningful to customers. Everyone nurtures hypotheses. They may be explicit, but most often implicit, in our mind and in our heart. If we do not expose them, they will in any case sway our interpretations when we listen to others. Better, then, to take them out. First, because by exposing our hypotheses we reduce the risk of being stuck in our own assumptions. Second, because our hypotheses are the precious raw ingredient to fuel the entire process. The ingredient that will be then critically melted and fused with others along the way.

The purpose of the envisioning phase is therefore to expose our individual hypotheses. We do this by addressing this question: "What would I love people to love?"

It looks like an obvious question. Yet we rarely raise it. Because we are busy with our daily tasks, or we take it for granted. Maybe we answered it once when we started our job. And then we left it aside.

Meanwhile the context changes, and the answer we gave a while ago is probably no longer valid. We also change as persons: we have a new understanding of the context, of the business, of how we would like to contribute to improving the world around us.

The phase of envisioning creates a space in which to raise this question again. It asks us to elicit what has been silently boiling inside for a while. It provides a formal and legitimate context for thinking about what we

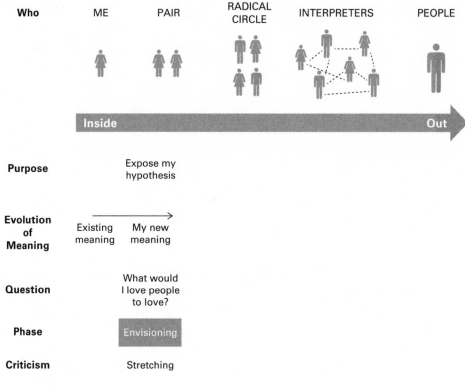

Figure 6.1
The phase of envisioning.

would love people to love. This chapter illustrates who should envision, and how.

WHO

Not everyone can become a great artist. But a great artist can come from anywhere.
Anton Ego, *Ratatouille*

The process of innovation of meaning starts from individuals within our organization. But who are these individuals? Who should be engaged at the beginning, to envision what could be meaningful to people?

One could suggest involving as many people as possible, on the assumption that the more proposals we generate, the better it is. However, as discussed in chapter 5, this may work for solutions but it doesn't for meanings. Innovation of meaning comes from a process of critical reflection, where we need to go *deep* in our interpretations. We need good raw material and then need to inquire in depth. A massive number of proposals would not help us to interpret better. It would just make the scenario more confused.

"Not everyone can become a great artist," says restaurant critic Anton Ego in the movie *Ratatouille*. The same is true for innovation of meaning: in a given moment in time, not everyone has harbored new interesting ways of making sense of our context. However, as Anton indicates, a great interpretation "can come from anywhere." Which suggests that individuals who harbor interesting hypotheses may lie in unexpected pockets of our organization. We therefore need to *identify* those individuals, *carefully*. A good approach is to start with around fifteen people. Boxes 6.1 and 6.2 provide guidelines on how to identify them. This is just an initial group. Along the way, others will join as the new meaning evolves.

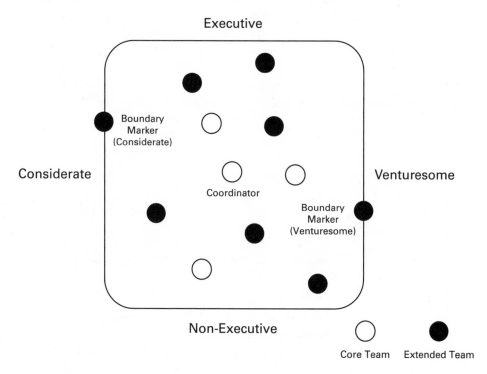

Figure 6.2
The blend of individuals.

Box 6.1

Who: the common characteristics

Each individual involved in the phase of envisioning needs to have three characteristics:

1. *They likely feel a sense of discomfort with the existing situation.*

We need individuals who are more exposed to the dynamics of meaning. This may be due to their profession, their role in the organization, their personal attitude and private life, or because they are immersed in new contexts. These individuals are likely to be first in perceiving a sense of malaise about the existing trajectory of our business and industry. They express these kinds of feelings:

- "I feel we are *misaligned with the life of our customers*, notwithstanding our continuous innovation. That there is a change in their life but our industry is still stuck in old interpretations." This feeling may occur in some individuals in touch with the life of customers and the evolution of society.

- "I feel that our product is becoming *undifferentiated*. That our industry is competing on the same performance parameter, and all products look alike." This feeling may occur in some individuals in touch with the dynamics of competition.

- "I feel that we have a great new technology in front of us, but we are *not really capturing its full potential*." This feeling may occur in some individuals in touch with new technological opportunities and with suppliers of advanced technologies.

- "I feel that our organization has *lost its sense of purpose*." This feeling may occur in individuals who are in touch with the culture and identity of our internal organization or with how we communicate to third parties and create brand identity.

(For more details on the symptoms of lack of meaning, see chapter 3.)

2. *They likely have a will to change and interesting hypotheses on where to go.*

We need *engaged* individuals, who have a personal drive, and who believe that, through their work, they may contribute to creating a better world. In addition to discomfort, they are more likely to have developed their own hypotheses of what customers could love. In other words, individuals who likely harbor new *gifts* for customers.

(For more details on innovation as a gift, see chapter 4.)

3. *They enjoy reflecting on the why of things.*

We need individuals who like to reflect, to ponder why there are certain dynamics in society, to understand what lies behind the malaise of some customers. Individuals who are not necessarily wellsprings of ideas, but who appreciate going deeper, taking in critiques and give constructive feedback.

(For more details on the art of criticism, see chapter 5.)

Box 6.2
Who: the blend

What also matters is the assortment of individuals (see figure 6.2). We need *heterogeneity*. Differences in their background, and especially in their inclinations, ensure the tensions that are necessary for the art of criticism.

1. *Considerate vs. venturesome.*

A considerate individual is thoughtful about the implications of a radical transformation. She may be more aligned with the existing direction, although she still harbors a will to change. A venturesome individual is tempted by outlandish forbidden directions. She often expresses a radical inclination, although still within the scope of making the organization grow (i.e., a venturesome person is not a destructive rebel). A good piece of advice is to pick one extreme considerate individual and one extreme venturesome individual. These "extremes" act as *boundary markers* (beyond whom there are people who are too considerate or too venturesome). Typically, these two boundary markers are the people who later, during mutual interactions, will contribute more in terms of creating tensions and helping the entire group to go deeper.

(For more details on the role of boundary markers see chapter 5.)

2. *Executives vs. non-executives.*

Individuals who have a sense of discomfort, a will to change, hypotheses on where to go, and who enjoy reflecting can be at any level in the organization. Paraphrasing Anton Ego's pronouncement from the movie *Ratatouille*: A great interpretation of new meanings can come from anywhere. In particular, from the top or from the bottom of our organization. We cannot restrict ourselves to just one category: only executives (in the classic perspective that vision comes from the top) or only non-executives (in the recent view that innovation should come from the bottom). *We need both.* Involving only executives would land the reflection in the territory of formal decision making, and would bring only one type of (corporate) culture. In addition, not all executives, at a given moment, treasure the characteristics of box 6.1. In this initial phase, we need to bring the process of search for new meaning outside of formal systems (which have been designed for the existing meaning) and to cut across organizational levels by bringing perspectives from anyone who has a new sense of direction. At the same time, involving only non-executives (and letting top executives wait for their proposals) would generate disappointing results. In fact, in any case, a top executive harbors hidden assumptions and hypotheses that would inevitably act as filters when others present their vision. She will never capture a new meaning by just looking at a final presentation. As discussed in chapter 5, judgment occurs *during* creation, not later. A *key top executive*

Box 6.2 (continued)

needs to participate from the beginning. She needs to expose what she would love people to love; to judge and be judged. By engaging the critical process and making explicit her inklings of direction, she creates inner space for taking in from others new interpretations that she alone could never see. In any case, developing a new vision is a key task for any top executive. So here we simply make this task more effective and integrated into the organization. Luckily, this approach enables efficient involvement of busy top executives only at key moments. The payback is that the process flows faster: there is no need for selection of options and approval, because judgment has already occurred progressively along the way: the new meaning will simply be inevitable.

(For more details on creating through judging, see chapter 5.)

3. *Multifunctional.*
Of course, the classic principle that multidisciplinary andmultifunctional teams favor innovation still holds in innovation of meaning. We need to ensure perspectives from different departments of the organization: marketing, R&D, strategy, design, branding, operations, etc.

4. *Core vs. extended.*
Among the team members, we need to appoint a restricted group (a *core team*) who will have the role of summarizing the critical reflections in a shared integrated vision. Individuals in the core team have a more intense involvement in between meetings. Among them, a coordinator can be the focal point for facilitating the process.

In the choice of the individuals, the *mix* (considerate and venturesome, experienced and new, top executives and non-executives, from different departments) should ensure a *variety* of possible directions and especially the *tensions* that are necessary to fuel a process based on the art of criticism. Their *common characteristics*, on the other hand, ensure the fundamental prerequisite for the dynamics of criticism: trust. Indeed, notwithstanding their heterogeneity, all individuals in the group should share a sense of *malaise*, a *will* to change, and an appreciation for *critical* reflection.

THE QUESTION

Each individual envisions new meanings by addressing this question: "What would I love people to love?" This question has been introduced in

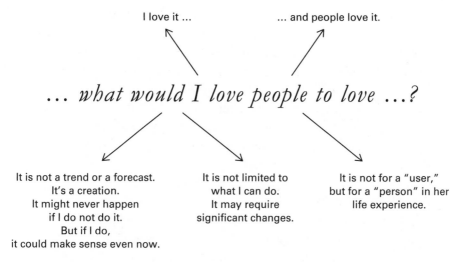

I love it ...   ... and people love it.

... what would I love people to love ...?

It is not a trend or a forecast.   It is not limited to   It is not for a "user,"
It's a creation.   what I can do.   but for a "person" in her
It might never happen   It may require   life experience.
if I do not do it.   significant changes.
But if I do,
it could make sense even now.

Figure 6.3
The question to address when envisioning new meanings.

chapter 4, and its implications are here summarized in figure 6.3. "People" means the target customers whom we want to address. And, of course, since there might be different kinds of people and different contexts, we may need to reiterate this question for each archetype of customer.

How to address this question? How to envision what I would love people to love? Radically new meanings are found through developmental criticism. In this phase, in which we start from individuals, this entails practicing *self-criticism*. We will illustrate four ways to stimulate self-criticism:

- Stretching between *solutions* and *meanings* (or, in other words, between *users* and *people*),
- Stretching between *existing* and *new* meanings,
- Working autonomously,
- Taking time.

STRETCHING (1): FROM SOLUTIONS TO MEANINGS

Starting right away by envisioning a new meaning can be challenging. Meanings are often abstract concepts. They invisibly undergird what customers do. We need something practical to start our reflections. This "something practical" can take the form of an inkling of a solution.

You might be surprised that I suggest starting from solutions. Until now, in fact, we have always kept our conversation at the level of meanings, not solutions. However, individuals are often more used to the practical language of products and services than to that of meanings. Envisioning an inkling of a solution can therefore be a good icebreaker. Provided that we use it just to jump-start the process. But then we need to move deeper, and reflect on what meaning underpins this solution. We need to investigate, and expose, our assumptions on *why* people would love it. We need to stretch from solutions to meanings.

The experience of life

To support stretching from solutions to meanings, we can pass through an intermediate step: the experience of life. Consider the diagram of figure 6.4. A product, a service, is just a part of a broader experience; a sliver in the life of people. Take beds for example. A bed is a piece of furniture, of course. But, in people's perspective, it's one of the many things they consider when thinking about their health (especially about their back). A bed contributes to their "fitness experience," an experience that also involves other product categories, such as training devices, health care, and food.

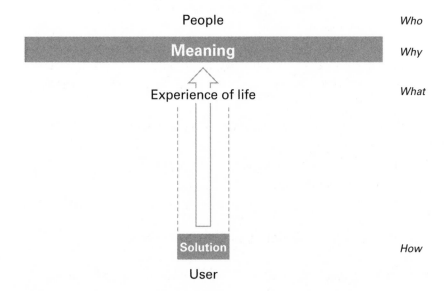

Figure 6.4
Stretching from solutions to meaning: a solution is just a sliver that contributes to a broader experience of life. And a user is just a small slice of a person.

Theodor Levitt, and more recently Clayton Christensen and Anthony Ulwick, express a similar concept with the term "jobs to be done":[1] *customers* use a product to *perform* a *job*. The principle here is analogous: to step back from the solution and move closer to the purpose of things. Instead of using the term "job," I find the term "experience of life" more inspiring, since it is closer to how *people* think and feel. Indeed, people hardly think in terms of jobs and performance, but in terms of what happens in their lives (the experience). In addition, we stretch here even deeper: from what is happening to why. We move one step further, from the experience to its meaning.

To stretch up from solutions to meanings, we can therefore take three steps, passing through people's experience of life:

We can start by just expressing the solution we have in mind. This is the how: a new product, service, business model, way of communicating, etc.

Then we step back and reflect on the underpinning experience of life. This is the what: what is the broader task (the job to be done) that the customer would be trying to achieve? What experience would this solution contribute to?

Then we go even deeper, and reflect on the underpinning meaning. This is the why: why is the customer doing it? Why would this experience be meaningful to her? Why should she love it?

To support this stretching, we can also use the following sentence: I would love "*a* [solution] *that enables me to* [experience] *because* [meaning ...]" (see figure 6.5). In this case "me" is the *customer*. Writing in the first person helps build empathy with the person whose life we'd like to make

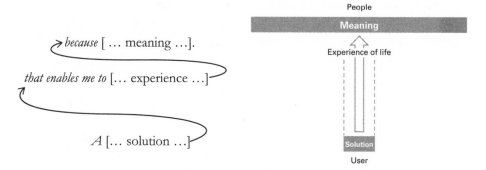

Figure 6.5
A sentence that helps us to stretch from solutions to meanings.

more meaningful. It helps us to think and feel like her. The focus is on the last part of the sentence (the meaning). The first part (the solution and the experience) is just an excuse to start the reflection.

Then we can move in the opposite direction: we frame the meaning and the experience better, and we envision a specific solution that would fulfill the meaning.

Box 6.3 illustrates these three steps of stretching in the case of Vox, a furniture manufacturer. Of course the concept holds for any kind of market, including business-to-business (see figure 6.6 for shorter examples; many other cases are reported in the appendix to this book). Consider for instance the market for industrial robots. A customer may be a VP of Operations who is redefining her firm's manufacturing strategy. When she considers buying a robot, she does not simply see a fast machine. Rather, she sees one of the several things that can transform her plant from a cost center into a source of business innovation. Perhaps she wants to create bespoke products for her consumers, and a flexible robot may help in this regard. A robot, for her, is part of the "creating bespoke products" experience, which also involves other product categories such as product design services, confer-ences, education in industrial engineering, and management consultants. This experience becomes meaningful to her if bespoke products become a source of business model innovation, which would also raise her reputation and strategic role within the executive team.

New meanings and new life experiences

A solution can be part of *several* experiences of life. Take food for example. It can be seen both as part of "how I get fit" or "how I socialize with others through cooking" (see figure 6.7). Although all of this happens simultane-ously, over time an industry often tends to take a prevalent perspective. Slowly, one perspective becomes dominant. Innovation of meaning there-fore may happen in two ways:

A change of meaning within the same experience. For example, premade salads and hemp granola address the same experience of getting fit. But hemp, rich in proteins, captures a change of what being "fit" means to people: from being lean and clean to being healthy and strong.

A change of experience of life. For example, the popular Slow Food movement considers eating as an "agricultural act": eating is just the last phase of farming. "When we eat an apple," say the founders of Slow Food

Box 6.3
Solutions, experiences, and meanings: Vox

Vox is a furniture manufacturer in Poland founded and chaired by Piotr Voelkel. In 2011 Voelkel was concerned about major changes in customer demographics, in particular the aging of the European population. How could Vox address this scenario? He felt that this context brought opportunities that could not be captured by merely improving existing products, but rather by a novel interpretation of what furniture is.

To create this new meaning he started by triggering the critical capabilities of individuals in his organization. He asked 19 individuals (including himself) to reflect on how Vox could design a new offering for a market where the population was aging. He laid out the scenario, then asked them to reflect individually for a month and come up with one or more proposals in terms of products or services or business models. He granted each of them full autonomy on how to conduct these reflections: whether based on quantitative market data (some individuals were picked because they had already conducted explicit research on the subject), or through daily observation of people, or by pulling together insights from different sources. However, he gave them a strict requirement to help them stretch their minds: each solution should consist of a new meaning, i.e., it should be based on new value parameters rather than on improving existing ones. During the month, these individuals autonomously envisioned a total of 90 proposals, seven of them by Voelkel himself. The following are examples of their early hypotheses, formulated with the sentence of figure 6.5.

Solution	*A* cabinet with soft LED lights illuminating the pathways and corridors in the night,
Experience	*that enables me to* walk in the darkness when I wake up,
Meaning	*because* I wish to live in a safe home without being an annoyance for my family.

Solution	*A* bed equipped with simple fitness devices (e.g., elastic bands affixed to the bed frame),
Experience	*that enables me to* stay fit by doing simple training exercises, even when I'm in bed,
Meaning	*because* I wish to remain active, even if I need to spend a lot of time in my bedroom.

Solution	*A* modular table with adjustable size and height, and with drawers to keep tools at easy reach,
Experience	*that enables me to* do activities with others: cooking, painting, or playing,
Meaning	*because* I wish a home that fosters socialization, where visitors gladly come (especially my grandchild).

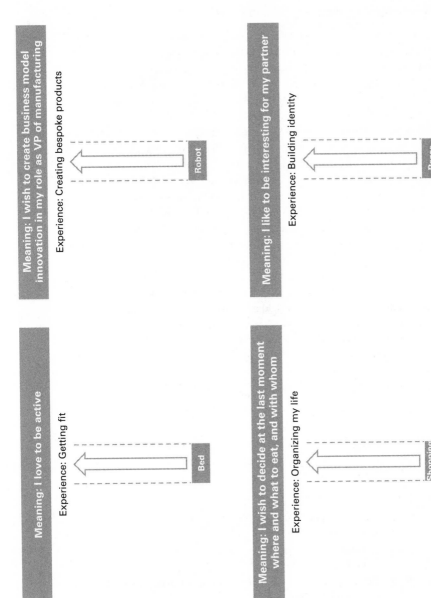

Figure 6.6

Examples of solutions, experiences, and meanings.

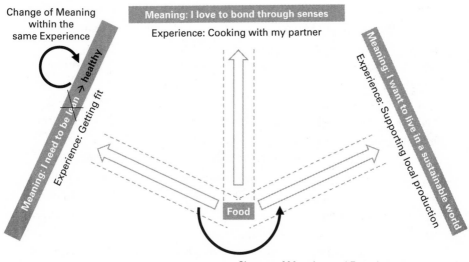

Figure 6.7
A product is part of several experiences of life. Here we have an example in food. Innovation of food's meaning can occur within the same experience (e.g., a change of
what "being fit" means) or by giving prominence to a new experience (e.g., from getting fit to supporting local food production).

provocatively, "we eat the entire supply chain, including the farmer
who has produced the apple." By buying a rare cheese from a remote
valley in the Alps, we can help "endangered food species" to survive in
the global markets dominated by standard food producers. From this
perspective, food is seen within a *new* experience of life: "how I support
local production and food biodiversity."

From users to people

An important consideration: stretching up to the level of meaning implies
stepping back from *users* and looking at *people*, which is not the same. Consider for example the shopping cart created by IDEO in the ABC *Nightline*
video "The Deep Dive." The IDEO team gets *close* to *users*, and observes how
they use *existing* shopping carts. This provides insights on their *existing*
behaviors. Actually, it even further *supports* those behaviors. For example,
the team eventually creates a large modular cart featuring small removable
baskets. The solution is inspired by the behavior of professional shoppers,

who use their cumbersome cart as a stationary hub, then move rapidly around the supermarket to pick what they need. This idea never took off in real markets. Meanwhile, a different kind of cart became popular: the rolling shopping basket (i.e., a large plastic basket on wheels that customers pull). This solution is midway between the two traditional options: a large cart and a small basket.[2] Why did it succeed over IDEO's large modular cart? Because *people's lives* have changed since large carts were invented. They have become extremely unpredictable. When I was a child, my mother went shopping once a week (on Saturdays), because she had a clear picture of what would happen in the coming seven days: a very regular schedule, with my father, my brother, my mother, and I eating lunch and dinner at home. Nowadays, most people do not know where and with whom they will eat tomorrow night. They can't plan the grocery needs of an entire week. Rather, they shop more frequently and buy less on each occasion. In this new scenario, large carts are meaningless. A half-sized cart, instead, is good both for people (who can move rapidly in the supermarket) and for storeowners (who wish to sell more than a traditional small basket can carry).

With its focus on the user, the team missed the person behind the user. By stepping close to existing use, they improved the existing experience, but they missed the changes in the big picture: the deep transformations in people's lives. A shopping cart is not just a cart; it is part of shopping, which is part of an even broader experience: "How do I organize my life, so that I have groceries at home when I need them?" We will never capture how people give meaning to this experience by going to supermarkets and watching them use existing carts. Better to step back and consider the person who shops, how she organizes her life. Which we better capture by looking at her agenda than by watching her pulling carts.

STRETCHING (2): FROM EXISTING TO NEW

The second stretching exercise is to describe not only the *new* meaning but also the *existing* one. In other words, we want clarify what is really *changing*. This change of meaning, illustrated in figure 6.8 with an arrow, is called a "Direction."

Making the change explicit has several benefits. First, as said in chapter 4, we *understand better* through differences and comparisons. In order to

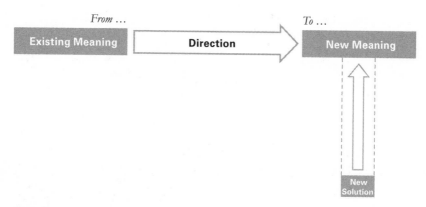

Figure 6.8
Stretching between existing and new meaning.

capture the essence of the new, we need to compare it with the old. Second, we spotlight the truly novel content of our proposal, with an invitation to stretch more into *innovative* directions. Third, we empower our self-criticism, since we expose our assumptions on why the existing situation is not meaningful. Finally, we pave the way for the art of criticism that will follow, when we will involve others. In fact, as seen in chapter 4, it will be easier to converge first on what we dislike than on what we like. Defining the "from" will create a ground on which to start a critical conversation.

Figure 6.9 summarizes both stretching exercises (from solutions to meanings, and from existing to new) in a simple form. The form also contains a space where we can accommodate an image (drawing, photo, metaphor, etc.) that visually represents the new meaning. This will be useful later when the hypothesis is shared with others. Figure 6.10 reports on the project of Vox on furniture for elderly people.

AUTONOMY

This first phase of the process should be conducted by individuals on their own. This may seem a weird prescription, given that most studies suggest that innovation is facilitated by collaboration. And, of course, later in the process (as soon as the next phase, in fact) we do collaborate. But at the beginning, when we have to present our preliminary hypotheses, we work better autonomously. Why?

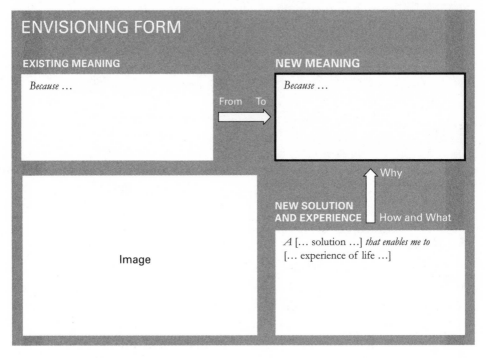

Figure 6.9
The envisioning form.

Autonomous reflection is important to enable everyone to first dig deep into her own insights, without watering them down. By working individually, we also have the freedom to perform the task according to our own background and attitude. For example, box 6.4 illustrates possible tools to support the creation of new meanings. This is just a list, and there are probably several others available. We can pick them and combine them following our personal style of reflection or the type of information we start with. Honestly, there is no best tool.[3] And there should not be, because heterogeneity is an important asset. The more the 15–20 individuals of our group use methods that differ from each other, the more likely they will propose different directions.

Of course, working autonomously does not mean that we do not talk to others. Sharing our reflections with others may be extremely helpful. What matters is that in this initial phase we take full responsibility for our proposal, without negotiation or compromise. People we talk to can provide

Figure 6.10
Envisioning forms in the case of Vox.

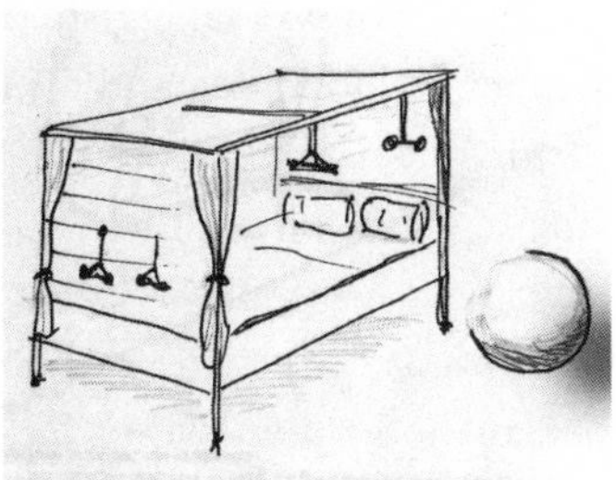

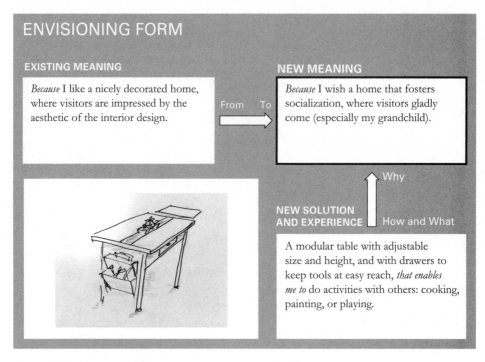

Figure 6.10 (continued)

insights, stimuli, comments, but the proposal at this stage has to come from us. The tensions and clashes will occur later in the process.

TAKE TIME

Long ago, in an indeterminate village in China, a wealthy man commissioned a renowned artist to paint his beloved horse. The years passed and the man, who had paid in advance, wondered why it was taking so long. Finally, old and furious, he went to the painter's studio to demand his picture. After a discussion, the artist grasped his brush and, in the time of twenty heartbeats, he painted an extraordinary picture of the horse. As the old man turned to leave, enraged by how quickly the portrait was executed, he saw the back of the studio. There lay thousands of sketches of horses, drawings and attempts that the artists had made in preparation for his masterpiece. Then the man understood the struggles, and the value of the result.

Box 6.4
Reflecting on meanings autonomously

Many methods may support us in the task of envisioning new meanings. We can use one or combine several: starting from the tool that is closer to our background, next trying something new, then comparing the insights.

Eliciting	A simple but powerful method is to look inside and just take out what we'd love people to love. Indeed, we are immersed in society, and in the market. Over time, silently, we develop a new sense of direction (especially if our profile matches those illustrated in box 6.1). We have probably been storing our reflections in our emotional and intellectual secret cabinet, since there was no arena in which to discuss them. Now the occasion has come to take out what we have been silently and implicitly elaborating in the past few months. In our experience, this is the most effective way to start.
Sharing	A good practice is to share our early reflections with someone we trust and esteem. In this early phase our hypothesis depends only on us, so we do not need to negotiate with others or to converge. Simply, the articulation of our inkling of vision to others stimulates us to go deeper. Their comments and insights can also help us reflect.
Making	Another powerful mechanism is to make our reflections tangible. A practical representation of a meaning can be a sketch of a new product solution. But we can also simulate other tangible representations. For example, imagine we would want to promote the new meaning through an industry-focused magazine: what would its cover look like? Or imagine we want to organize a conference around the new meaning: what would the title and agenda of the conference be, or its brochure?
Qualitative unstructured analysis	Observing people is of course a good practice also when reflecting on meaning. Our attention, however, should not be on the user but on the person. We should observe how she goes through the experience of life (of which using a product is just a small sliver). A similar method is to use empathy, i.e., to put us in someone else's shoes and try the experience ourselves.[4]
Qualitative structured analysis	There are plenty of frameworks that can help us reflect on new possible meanings. Examples are the strategy canvas and four-action framework; jobs-to-be-done and the customer-centered innovation map; the value proposition canvas; the Kano model; empathy maps; discovery-driven innovation; the customer experience and customer journey mapping; inside-the-box innovation.[5]
Quantitative sources	Of course, studies and reports providing quantitative data are always useful. Data mining techniques may also help in this regard. The advice, however, is to avoid spending too much time on collecting quantitative information at this early stage. Just try to see if quantitative data and reports are already available (they probably are). The focus, as always, should not be on solutions and users, but on the people in their experience of life.

This story, based on the novel *Twenty Heartbeats* of Dennis Haseley,[6] invokes an important dimension often forgotten in creative processes: the value of time. Especially when it comes to the creation of new visions. Innovation of meaning is based on reflection rather than ideation. We do not need numerous proposals. In many projects we have conducted, individuals envision three or four (but even one or two may be fine). And filling in an envisioning form as in figure 6.9 may really take twenty heartbeats. What matters is that they have been reflected upon. Innovation of meaning requires *depth* rather than quantity. And depth requires *time*.

Not time in terms of working hours. But time in terms of calendar time. We need time to let thoughts rest; to take a distance from our proposals, let them sediment, and reconsider them later with a fresh perspective.

The example of Vox shows that there were no quick ideation sessions, such as brainstorming, to envision new meanings. Rather, Piotr Voelkel gave the individuals one month to reflect, in parallel with their normal work activities. Full-time commitment was not necessary, since it was a matter of bringing out hypotheses that these individuals held inside themselves. But giving them one month enabled each person to put these insights in order, make them explicit, let them rest a few days, reflect, reconsider them critically with new interpretations and add new ones, so that nothing was left to the extemporaneity of the moment. This was relevant especially to protect the most innovative and outlandish hypotheses, which are typically weak because they are more blurred and confused, even to those who propose them. In a quick session those outlandish hypotheses would be dismissed. Giving people one month to reflect also meant enabling them to work on those outlandish directions to make them a little stronger and see them better before disclosing them to others.

In order to reflect and critically reconsider our hypotheses, we can apply different methods illustrated in box 6.4 iteratively. We can start by eliciting the intuitions we have inside, and filling in an envisioning form. After a while, we can go back and explore a hypothesis by using a tool among those we feel more comfortable with (for example people observation). Does it fully support our intuition or not? Why? As a result, we may modify the form or propose a totally different one. Then again we can iterate, talking to someone we trust. We can share our vision, reflect, modify, let it rest. After a while, we can reconsider our insights once more using another tool. For example, we can try a method for structured analysis (e.g., the "jobs to be done" tool), and see whether it further supports our direction or provides different insights. And so on.

Box 6.5 illustrates the power of time in a historical example: Raphael and the meaning of the Madonna. It shows his struggles and reflections in creating a new meaning. This example spans six years of work, since it marks one of the greatest cultural revolutions in history: the transition from the Middle Ages to the modern world. We do not need so much. *One month* for autonomous self reflection is more than enough. It's 720 hours, considering that our mind keeps reflecting, especially when we sleep; or it's 30 morning

---

Box 6.5

The power of time for self-reflection: Raphael and the "Madonna as a woman"

Raphael (Raffaello Sanzio, 1483–1520) is a major artist of the Renaissance. His art, together with other masters of his time (for example Michelangelo and Leonardo Da Vinci), marks a historical revolution: the end of the Middle Ages and the beginning of the modern world. Culturally, this revolution is a transition from the symbolism of the Middle Ages, where society had a strong grounding in religion, to a new era with humans at the center, with their mind and beauty. Among his several masterpieces (including for example the frescos in the "Raphael Rooms" of the Vatican), most notable are a series of portraits of the Madonna and infant Jesus. These paintings are outstanding examples of the change of meaning occurring at that time: from "the Madonna is a religious symbol" (in the Middle Ages) to "the Madonna is a woman" (in the humanistic perspective). A new meaning that was earlier considered outlandish, even blasphemous.

Below I introduce this innovation of meaning by comparing two paintings: the medieval *Madonna of the Large Eyes* (1260) and Raphael's *Madonna del Cardellino* (1505–1506). The focus of this example is on how Raphael got to this masterpiece. Through a series of earlier paintings we can easily observe his relentless process of self-reflection on the new meaning "the Madonna is a woman." I report here just a few examples of paintings (whose images can easily be found on the web). Here we can see his first attempts, his reflections, his later modifications, on what it means to be a woman and to be a child, rather than being a symbol. We can almost read his mind: how slowly, over six years, he got rid of his own preconceptions and frameworks. Of course, Raphael painted many more versions than I report here, which you can enjoy admiring and positioning in his self-reflective path toward a momentous change of meaning.

Box 6.5 (continued)

Old meaning (Middle Ages): the Madonna is a religious symbol	New meaning (Renaissance): the Madonna is a woman
Old solution (Middle Ages): *Madonna of the Large Eyes* (1260)[7] (see figure 6.11)	New solution (Renaissance): *Madonna del Cardellino* (Raphael 1505–1506)[8] (see figure 6.12)
The Madonna stands on an abstract golden background	The Madonna stands on a real natural background
She wears a halo (nimbus) and a veil	She has no halo and no veil
Her figure is "flat"; no shadows, light, or perspective	Her figure is a curved body, marked by shadows, light, and perspective
She and Jesus have fixed, inexpressive faces	She and Jesus have human emotions
She is holding Jesus with just one finger (Jesus is weightless)	She has eased Jesus down on the ground; he has weight
The characters are misproportioned, according to their religious importance	The characters have correct reciprocal proportions, according to their ages and distance from the observer
The characters do not interact with each other	The characters interact and are engaged in human activities

The self-critical path of Raphael:

Madonna Solly (1500–1504)[9]	Most of the new solutions appear already in this painting. However, the Madonna still wears a veil and hold Jesus with just one finger. Jesus seems to have an unnatural lightness. We can hardly see the background of the painting.
Madonna del Granduca (1505)[10]	Now the Madonna holds Jesus with both full hands (Jesus has weight).
Piccola Madonna Cowper (1505)[11]	Now the characters stands on a clear natural background. The Madonna has no veil or halo.
Madonna del Prato (1506)[12]	Now the Madonna has eased down Jesus on the ground.
Madonna del Cardellino (1506)	Now the proportions among the characters are correct (John the Baptist stands next to Jesus; they are both children, but John is six month older and actually looks bigger). They are engaged in childish activities (they play with a goldfinch).

Figure 6.11
Master of Tressa, *Madonna of the Large Eyes*, c. 1260. Photo: Museo dell'Opera Metropolitana, Siena, Italy. Scala/Art Resource, NY.

showers (for those who find it easier to reflect with a fresh mind and warm water pouring on their neck). Definitely much more than a two-hour brainstorming session (with no shower).

EXPOSING OUR WILL, WITH SELF-CRITICISM

In chapter 5 we saw how innovation of meaning comes from an inside-out process of "creation through judgment," a process where we envision

Figure 6.12
Raphael, *Madonna with the Goldfinch* (*Madonna del Cardellino*), 1506. Photo: Scala/
Ministero per i Beni e le Attività culturali / Art Resource, NY.

possibilities through criticism. This process starts from us. We autonomously envision new possibilities. This is a process of self-reflection and self-
criticism, initially done alone. We make hypotheses, than take a distance,
and after a while we *deliberately* reflect on what we have been doing. This
process of reflection-on-action is the core of many innovative designs.[13]
Figure 6.13 summarizes this phase of the process.

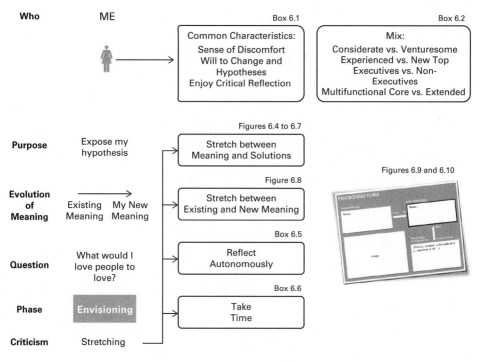

Figure 6.13
Map of chapter 6.

7 The Meaning Factory

Insiders' Criticism

The purpose of the first phase of the process was to envision initial hypotheses. A group of individuals, working autonomously, have asked themselves, "What would I love people to love?" These initial hypotheses are the precious ingredients to start with.

Just to start, however. We want to be sure that we are not stuck in our own assumptions. We need to create novel robust interpretations. Now therefore is the time to dig deeper, through the art of criticism.

Chapter 6 already took us into the practice of criticism. Self-criticism, to be precise, since the task was conducted autonomously. Now we welcome criticism from others. This chapter, in particular, examines how to harness the art of criticism by collaborating with insiders, i.e., others within our organization (next chapter will focus on the role of outsiders). These *insiders* are the same individuals introduced in chapter 6: they have envisioned, autonomously, the initial meanings. Now they can mutually compare their hypotheses.

Collaboration with insiders may occur in two ways (figure 7.1).

First, between *pairs*, i.e., between two individuals who had previously worked autonomously. The first criticism aims at going *deeper*: we want to better understand the implications of each hypothesis (implications that are often unclear even to those who proposed them). Especially, we want to nurture the most unorthodox directions, which are probably weaker but potentially powerful. This kind of criticism therefore needs to proceed with care. It blossoms in the protected intimacy of two trusted peers, i.e., two individuals who share *similar* directions. So similar that it is easier to spot one another's discrepancies. And make their vision more robust. The question to address here is "What is the potential and the weakness of *your* preliminary hypothesis?"

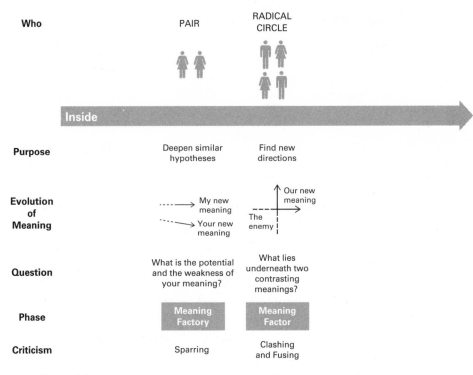

Figure 7.1
The meaning factory.

Second, among the entire *group*. The second phase of criticism aims at finding *new* directions: we want to compare and combine *different* hypotheses to search for new unprecedented interpretations. To this purpose, the pairs assemble into a larger group, which acts as a *radical circle* (see chapter 5). By clashing together the work of different pairs, we look beyond their apparent contrast in search of something new, a novel meaning that underpins both of them. Contrasts and tensions are therefore favored for the sake of innovation. Criticism becomes more abrasive. The question here is: "What does lie underneath two contrasting meanings?"

The work of pairs therefore focuses on the *differences* between *similar* hypotheses, in order to make them *stronger*. The work of the radical circle, by contrast, focuses on the *common* ground underpinning *different* hypotheses, in order to find *new* meaning. This chapter illustrates how to work in pairs and radical circles in a two-day intense meeting that we call a meaning factory.

WHO

The meaning factory is conducted by the individuals who participated in the phase of envisioning (see boxes 6.1 and 6.2 for their characteristics and blend). They have previously generated hypotheses for new visions. Now they can (figure 7.2):

- *Share* these hypotheses. This can be done before the meeting of the meaning factory occurs (see box 7.1 for a description of this step);
- *Cluster* the hypotheses in order to spot similarities and differences (see box 7.2 for a description of this step);
- *Spar* over similar directions, to make them stronger;
- *Clash and fuse* different directions, to find new ones.

The next sections dig deeper into the third and fourth steps.

SPARRING

> *If two men agree on everything, you may be sure that one of them is doing the thinking.*
> Lyndon B. Johnson

Once all directions have been identified, it's time to dig deeper. The purpose is to identify the potential and the weakness behind relevant directions. The best approach is to work in pairs, i.e., splitting the group into couples

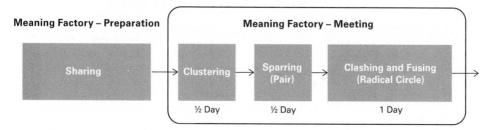

Figure 7.2
Steps in the meaning factory.

Box 7.1
Sharing

The first step of a meaning factory is to share the hypotheses that have been envisioned earlier. This task can be conducted at either of two moments: in preparation for the meeting, and as the first step of the two-day meeting. Let's first examine what happens before the meeting.

Collect the hypotheses	One week before the meeting, each individual sends to the coordinator her hypotheses for new meanings, i.e., her visions about "What I would love people to love." This can be done by emailing the envisioning forms introduced in figure 6.9. Each individual can send as many forms she wants, although a good practice is to come up with a few hypotheses (two or three) that have been carefully reflected upon.
Share the hypotheses	The coordinator gathers the hypotheses and make them available to the entire group.
Chew over	Each individual, in preparation for the meeting, examines the hypotheses of the other participants, by addressing the following questions: 1. What lies behind each hypothesis? A participant has proposed a solution and a meaning, but do I see a different potential? Can this same meaning by achieved with a better solution? Or does this same solution hide a more powerful meaning? Could I stretch the same solution toward a different customer experience, or a different direction? 2. Which one of the several hypotheses is closest to mine? Which participant is going in a direction that most aligns with mine? Whom would I like to pair with during the meeting? 3. After seeing all the hypotheses, would I reframe mine? How? Or are there any new hypotheses that came to my mind? 4. After seeing all the hypotheses, which of my hypotheses is the most unique and promising? If I had to pick one to present at the meeting, which would I pick?

Box 7.2

Clustering

The meaning factory is organized around a two-day intense meeting. The meeting starts with necessary introductions (of challenge, topic, participants) and warm-up (a reflection on personal meaning from the participants; for example, a memory from childhood, a personal passion, something meaningful they wear, describing themselves through an object). Then the first task is to cluster the individual hypotheses they have envisioned in preparation for the meeting. This task is conducted in a plenary session and may last around three hours: we want to give space to reflections stimulated by each hypothesis.

1. Present	Each individual presents the most unique and interesting hypothesis among those she has envisioned. The form describing this hypothesis is posted. Next to its form we mark a "direction" (i.e., a large arrow indicating the *change* of meaning: from ... to ...). The direction has the purpose of emphasizing the focus on meaning (figure 7.3).
2. Enrich	Other participants may enrich the hypothesis that has just been presented. Maybe they see a different, more powerful meaning in it. If so, a new direction indicating a change of meaning is posted next to this hypothesis. Or they find a more powerful way to articulate the same meaning. In this case the form and the direction that have just been presented can be modified or reworded.
3. Map out	The next participant presents her hypothesis. If this is similar (in terms of meaning) to another proposal already presented, her form is posted next to the same direction. Otherwise we create a new direction.
4. Expand	Once every participant has presented her most interesting hypothesis, we have a map with several hypotheses, clustered around possible directions of change of meaning. Then we can focus on the remaining hypotheses that participants still hold in their hands. First, we can ask if any of these hypotheses goes in a direction that is till not on the map. If so, we ask the person to present it, and we add a new direction.
5. Fill in	When the forms that are still in the hand of the participants do not point to new directions, then we can ask participants to simply position the residual hypotheses next to the directions that have been already presented. This way, each possible change of meaning is associated with several instances (solutions) that will become useful later.

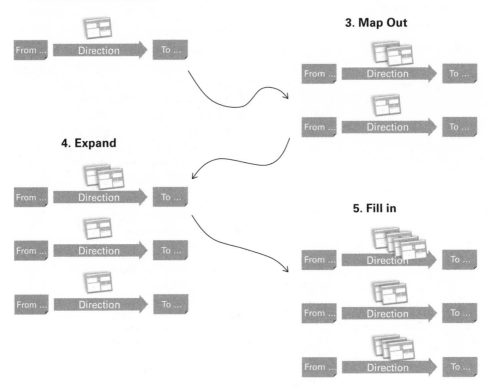

Figure 7.3
Clustering.

who share similar directions. In fact, as discussed in chapter 5 with the stories of the Xbox team and the impressionists, a pair is the most delicate way to start practicing the art of criticism. Working with a trusted peer who shares our sense of direction creates a healthy context of instrumental intimacy, where half-baked hypotheses can be explored more deeply and strengthened without the risk of being killed. The protected dynamics of pairs invites people to dare. Dare to *talk* about their unclear and confused insights, even if these are not totally supported by facts. Dare to *do*, to try forbidden directions. Dare to *listen*, openly and honestly, to the frank feedback from someone who is criticizing us.

Pairing

First, we need to form the pairs. To this purpose, we can use a simple match-ing mechanism: pairing those who envisioned a *similar* direction. After the hypotheses have been presented, we can ask every participant to indicate which direction she would like to explore among those posted. If a direc-tion gets an even number of preferences, the pairs are easily formed. If it gets uneven preferences, one of the participants indicates a second option, and so on, until all pairs are created.

Working as sparring partners

A pair work on the same direction. Yet before the meeting the two peers had probably envisioned different interpretations of that direction. Their purpose now is to come up with one common proposal, which embraces their own autonomous interpretations and therefore is deeper and more reflected upon.

Practically, their task is to produce one common envisioning form that summarizes their reflection (like the one they have already used individually; see figure 6.9): an existing meaning, a new meaning, and a solution.

During the task, they initially focus on the (slight) misalignments among their original interpretations. In fact, by focusing on their differ-ences, they create the tensions that enable them to go deeper. By challeng-ing each other, they work as sparring partners, who put the potential and weakness of their hypotheses through a stress test to make them more robust. The purpose here is to be critical. Being supportive (or even worse, passive) is unfruitful. The two peers need to *engage* in a committed critical *discussion,* not just a conversation; the more intense the debate, the better. Tension here is a positive resource. They can play safely because, funda-mentally, they are going in the same direction, so they can trust each other.

First, one peer plays the role of the challenger and the other that of the defender. The challenger discusses the hypothesis proposed by the defender: she expresses what she likes, what she is doubtful about, and finally she takes an empty form and reformulates the hypotheses of the defender in her own words. Then the defender *inquires* about the changes the chal-lenger made in her reformulation: why she used different language or proposed different solutions.

Note that paying attention to *language* in critical reflections is important. Initially, when visions are confused, words are imprecise. It is through the search for the right words that one often develops a deeper understanding of a meaning.

Then they switch roles: the defender becomes the challenger, and vice versa. The purpose is to unveil hidden potentials that each one of them individually could not see, spot the weak assumptions, and especially clarify their proposals.

Finally, they fill in a common envisioning form together that expresses the richness of their interpretations. This new form will indicate the direction (from the existing meaning to the new meaning—as reinterpreted by the pair), and a solution. This solution is the most representative and interesting among those they have personally envisioned or that have been proposed by others during the initial sharing session. We call this an "exemplar" solution, because it is the best practical example of how their change of meaning could turn into a new product or service.

Each pair eventually presents its common vision to the other participants of the meaning factory. Similarly to what happened at the beginning of the meeting, the others provide feedback, especially about implications that the pair did not capture in its discussion. This sharing will probably be rapid, since there are likely only about 8 to 10 forms to be presented (one for each pair).

CLASHING AND FUSING

I love argument. I love debate. I don't expect anyone just to sit there and agree with me—that's not their job.
Margaret Thatcher[1]

Pairs shared a similar direction. The purpose of their collaboration was to dig deeper in that direction and come up with an interpretation that is clearer and more robust. The next step (which typically occurs in the second day of the meaning factory) concerns instead directions that are significantly *different* from each other. Its purpose is to uncover what lies behind contrasting meanings, in order to find new interpretations that none of the participants, individually, could envision. We dig deeper, but in doing so we also dive into *unexplored* spaces.

For this step we need to involve the entire group of 15–20 participants, who act as a radical circle. They work through a process of *clashing* and *fusing*. Clashing implies creating tensions, to explicitly compare different directions. While a pair was a locus of instrumental intimacy, a radical circle is a locus of confrontation. Criticism now will be acrimonious. But the raw material, the directions crafted by the pairs, will hardly succumb, because the previous collaboration among sparring partners made them stronger.

Clashing is not done for the purpose of *selecting* which direction is right and which is wrong, but for the purpose of *fusing* them into something new. Fusing implies understanding *why* directions differ; what lies behind them. If others had envisioned different directions, and they have even discussed these already in pairs, they have probably captured insights that escaped us. In other words, directions that apparently contrast may under-pin an even more interesting scenario. Note that fusing does not imply finding a halfway synthesis between two different directions. It's not a com-promise, but a move deeper into one direction: "I criticize your direction by first creating a tension and then integrating mine into yours, and vice versa. We do not meet in the middle, but deeper in your direction or deeper in mine." A process that Hegel calls *Aufheben* or sublation.[2]

As always, we need to handle criticism with care, in order to transform the tensions into creative energy. The art of criticism in a radical circle is favored by the following practices:

* Focus on delighters,
* Create in quartets, challenge in circles,
* Converge on the enemy first,
* Use metaphors.

Delighters

In front of us, when we start working as a circle, we have the 8–10 direc-tions envisioned by the pairs. One could think to contrast all of them simultaneously. But this would be a too complex task. In reality, even if a product has several different dimensions, what makes it stand out, in terms of meanings, is a few value parameters. We just need to focus on the *delighters*, i.e., those few dimensions that will most likely make a difference for customers.[3]

To this purpose, the clashing and fusion of different directions is much more effective if we proceed by selecting only two, which we consider the two most delighting directions. The work of the circle will therefore produce diagrams as in figure 7.4, which we call scenarios.

A scenario of meaning simply consists of four quadrants, created by clashing two directions (from ... to ...) that are significantly different from each other.

The quadrant on the bottom left indicates the existing meaning. This represents the "enemy," i.e., the meaning that we all want to change.

The quadrants on the bottom right and on the top left indicate what would happen if only one direction were to change. This is what each pair has envisioned in the previous step.

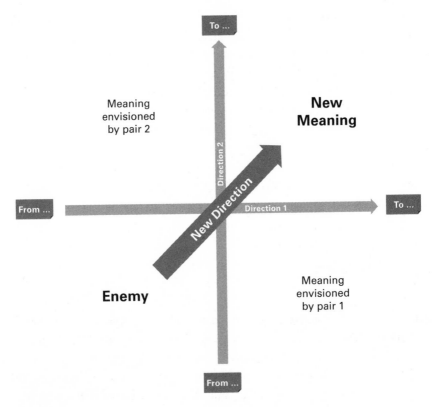

Figure 7.4
A scenario of meaning.

The quadrant on the top right is the new meaning, which comes by fusing the two dimensions. This is what we are looking for.

Take the example of Vox (figure 7.4). After individuals and pairs had autonomously developed their hypotheses, there were significantly different directions on the table. Two of them were particularly interesting.

One suggested transforming bedrooms *from* places to simply rest *into* active places where people could train (e.g., creating beds with little devices that elderly people could use for doing simple exercises). This sounded like a relevant delighting dimension, since bedrooms have been an area of little innovation in the furniture industry in the last decades; and elderly people spend a significant part of their time there, even during the day, especially when sick.

A second direction proposed to transform furniture *from* being decorative and functional *to* being a vehicle for socialization with family and relatives (for example, tables that easily transformed into surfaces to cook, paint, or play together). This also looked like a promising delighter. In fact, data on European demographics show that the number of elderly people is growing and the birthrate of infants is decreasing. Grandparents are now competing to access their only grandchild; so an inviting home where a child enjoys staying with her grandparents looks like a promising picture.

The new meaning came by combining these two unrelated directions: a new active role for bedrooms, and furniture as a mean of socialization. The resulting new scenario was called the "living bedroom": a home where the bed becomes a central space of socialization. The bedroom, where elderly people are often compelled to stay, becomes the equivalent of the living room (or vice versa, the bed moves into the living room thanks to a functional and aesthetic design that fits with the language of daily living). Here elderly people can meet relatives and friends, socialize with them, and pleasurably spend time, just as normally happens in a living room (and as teenagers do in their own bedrooms). One of the products that came out of this process is a bed incorporating a large bookshelf (something that typically belongs in the living room), several folding surfaces, space for visitors' shoes, and even a roll-up screen for watching movies together.

Another example is provided by Alfa Romeo. This car brand has a legendary history (it was the first car to win a formula one race and produced

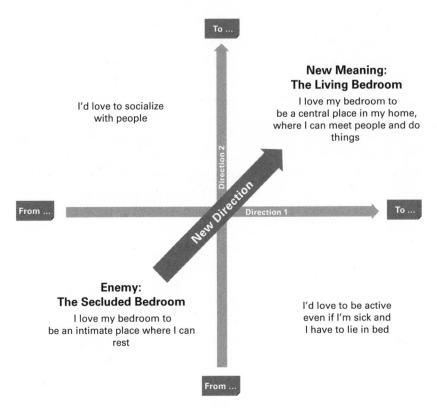

Figure 7.5
Scenario of meaning in the case of Vox.

famed cars such as the Duetto convertible driven by Dustin Hoffman in the movie *The Graduate*) but has recently struggled in the intense global competition of premium car brands, where German manufacturers dominate. To face this context, Alfa has engaged in an innovation project in which a radical circle of about 20 individuals has proposed several possible directions. One direction proposed moving *from* the dominant vision that people buy premium cars to show their wealth (e.g., a vision of cars as luxury goods) *to* a new vision of "premium cars as excitement goods," i.e., cars that people buy to express their passion for driving regardless of their wealth. Another direction proposed moving *from* a perspective where value comes from engine power and top speed, *to* a vision where value comes from the agility of the car and its responsiveness to the driver's commands. By combining these two unrelated directions, the team envisioned an interesting overlapping space where Alfa builds cars for passionate drivers rather then expensive machines. In this new vision, exclusiveness comes from competent drivers being able to enjoy a light responsive car that is not overburdened by unnecessary features. An instantiation of this new strategy is the Alfa Romeo 4C sports car, launched in 2013. The 4C is not heftily expensive like many sports cars, and Alfa's innovation efforts have not been directed to increasing engine power (the 4C is equipped with a small 1750 cc engine, which is less powerful than other sports cars) but to reducing the car's weight (e.g., through extensive use of carbon fiber and by stripping the parts and equipment to the essence). The power-to-weight ratio of the 4C is therefore comparable to top (and much more expensive) sports cars such as Ferraris. The concept of the 4C was so appreciated by customers that its first year of production was fully booked a few weeks after market release.

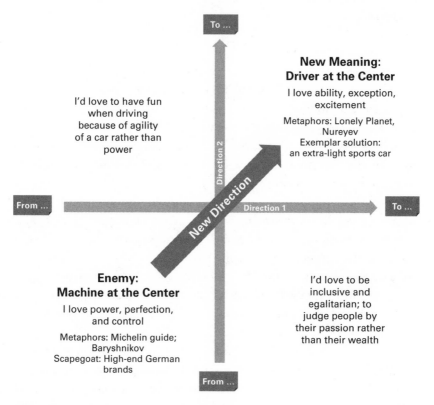

Figure 7.6
Scenario of meaning in the case of Alfa Romeo.

Quartets

Scenarios are based on two contrasting directions. Given that each direction has been explored by a pair, creating scenarios simply implies clashing the work of two different pairs; that is, joining pairs into quartets. A practical way to create quartets is for every pair to indicate which other direction (i.e., which other pair) they would like to work with. In other words: which other direction they would like to clash and fuse with. The important point here is to indicate a direction that is significantly *different* from our own. Not opposite (i.e., focusing on the same subject as us, but taking exactly the contrary direction) but *orthogonal* (i.e., simply unrelated to our direction). A direction that we find inspiring, because we feel there might be a great potential if it were fused with our own. In this process, some direction (and therefore some pair) may receive more than one preference. In such a case the pair that gets more preferences will be the first to choose whom to join.

Enemy first

Once the quartets are formed, they can clash and fuse their two directions and create the scenarios. Given that the directions are orthogonal, here we expect criticism to be more intense. How to transform the critical tensions into creative energy? An effective way is to focus first on where we all do *not* want to go. In other words, start working in the bottom left quadrant of the scenario, which indicates the enemy (figure 7.4). In fact, as we have seen in chapter 5, it is easier to converge first on what we dislike than on what we like.

So start working in the enemy quadrant. Probably the two pairs' definitions of the existing meaning ("from") differ from each other. We need to fuse these two definitions into a coherent picture of why we and customers feel a malaise about the current situation. Two effective ways to support the discussion are to ask the quartet to provide: (1) a name for the enemy; (2) a description of its meaning and myths; (3); a *scapegoat,* i.e., the name of an existing solution (from a competitor or even from ourselves) that epitomizes the existing meaning. This brings the conversation to a very practical and concrete level. The scapegoat should not be unpopular in the market. Rather, it should be a very successful product that people used to find meaningful, but whose values embody a latent malaise. In the case of Alfa Romeo, for example, the scapegoat was represented by high-end German car manufacturers. In the case of Vox, the scapegoat was the traditional bed of elderly people equipped with hospital-like features (e.g., handles that help them to stand up).

FROM POST-ITS TO METAPHORS

If a picture is worth 1,000 words, a metaphor is worth 1,000 pictures!
Thomas J. Shuell[4]

Once you have converged on a common enemy, the next step is to work in the top right quadrant of the scenario, i.e., the new meaning. The point is that if two different directions are there, proposed by different pairs who had time to critically reflect on them, there might be something good behind them: a most promising interpretation that each individual alone could not see.

During this process of clashing different directions, a way to creatively support the critical conversation is to use metaphors. A metaphor is a way of "understanding and experiencing one kind of thing in terms of another" (figure 7.7).[5] For example, we understand (and we do *experience*) "love" as a physical force; indeed we may say "there were sparks in the air when we met" or "I feel attracted by her." Or, using another metaphor, love can be a journey: "look how far we have come in our relationship." If we have never met love in our life but we have met sparks, we can understand better what love is. And, especially, we can better capture how people *experience* it. One *feels* as one does when there are sparks around. George Lakoff and Mark Johnson, in their book *Metaphors we Live By*, illustrate that we use metaphors in our everyday life to express concepts: "Metaphor is pervasive in everyday life, not just in language but in thought and action. Our ordinary conceptual system, in terms of which we both think and act, is fundamentally metaphorical in nature."[6] In other words, we normally think in terms of metaphors. For example when we say "I feel down," we use the metaphor of space ("down") to express a feeling of sadness (probably because people who are sad have drooping shoulders). Metaphors are therefore the most powerful way to express concepts and emotions, especially when these concepts are *new* and *abstract*, such as a new meaning. "Metaphors facilitate thought by providing an experiential framework in which *newly* acquired, abstract concepts may be accommodated."[7]

Metaphor:

Understanding and experiencing one thing in terms of another
Example: Love is a physical force

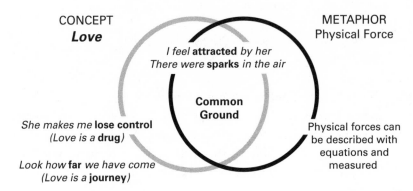

Figure 7.7
Metaphor.

The discussion in the quartet is empowered if every person thinks about two possible metaphors: one for the enemy and one for the new meaning. Take the example of Alfa Romeo. One participant described the existing direction of the premium car industry (the enemy) with the metaphor of the Michelin restaurant guide. A Michelin guide, in fact, suggests top restaurants to inexpert tourists. It ensures a perfectly controllable experience, analogous to the performance of existing high-end cars. The metaphor for the new meaning was instead the Lonely Planet guide; used by expert passionate travelers (often backpackers) to find restaurants outside of traditional paths. The new meaning for Alfa Romeo therefore addresses drivers who are not necessarily well-heeled but are well-wheeled: they have a passion for driving and can appreciate performance in unconventional conditions.

To make meanings tangible and immediate

Using metaphors to clash and fuse different visions has several advantages. First, metaphors enable the quartet to embody meanings in a *tangible* form. Especially, given that a metaphor implies *experiencing* one thing in terms of another, they allow us to powerfully express the emotional and symbolic dimensions of meaning. A metaphor helps keep the conversation at an immediate intuitive level, without losing ourselves in abstract fruitless debates. Aristotle underlines the immediacy of metaphors: "A good metaphor implies an *intuitive* perception of the *similarity* in *dissimilars*."[8] Metaphors are the "basic language" for conversing about meanings. They facilitate criticism, without being a direct critique of someone else's concept. If Post-its are the basic tools in innovation of solutions, then metaphors are the Post-its of innovation of meaning (mmmhhh ... I'm using a metaphor here ...).

Imperfections that let us grow

Second, metaphors are powerful because they are *not perfect*. They do not equal the concept we want to express. Love is not a physical force. The two things ("love" and "physical force") have a common ground (we experience them in a similar way), but they do not totally overlap. There are characteristics of the metaphor (physical force) that do not pertain to the concept (love). For example we cannot describe love with mathematical formulas as we do with forces. And, vice versa, there are characteristics of the concept that do not pertain to the metaphor (we do not kiss a force). The larger the overlap between the two, the more powerful the metaphor is, of course. But the divergence is also very important. Because it helps going deeper, by clarifying what we do *not* have in mind. If I use the metaphor of love as a physical force, you might react, even a little annoyed, saying, "But love cannot be measured, nor does it come from formulas!" "Well, you are right. I did not think about this. And I did not mean it. I liked the metaphor because it captures the inescapable attraction of someone you love." The consequence is that we understand each other better. Then we can decide either that this metaphor captures the most important characteristics of the concept we want to convey, or that it does not work and we had better search for another one. But meanwhile, we have moved deeper in our critical reflection.

Innovating

Third, metaphors facilitate *innovation*. Because of their imperfection, they help us to capture new dimensions and new characteristics of a concept. Let's take a famous example. Nicolas Hayek, the inventor of the Swatch, said "A Swatch is a tie." A powerful metaphor to convey his innovation of meaning: a Swatch watch is like a fashion accessory; like ties, we can have more than one and we can change it according to our mood, style, season. If we checked in the dictionary, we would not find this definition of a watch, but rather "A watch is a device that shows what time it is and that you wear on your wrist or carry in a pocket."[9] However, as Paul Ricoeur, a philosopher of hermeneutics, says, "The dictionary contains no metaphors."[10] Which means that a metaphor exists only in dialogue. It is not static like a definition, but alive. It supports us in the search for *new* understanding. According to Ricoeur, by using metaphors we redescribe the world, and therefore we discover new meaning. And Aristotle: "Ordinary words convey only what we know already; it is from metaphor that we can best get hold of something fresh."[11] This is what Hayek did by creating the metaphor "A watch is a tie." As figure 7.8 illustrates, a metaphor allows us to expand toward novel spaces (Lakoff and Johnson call these extensions entailments). For example, we do not knot a watch to our neck, as we do with a tie. But ... why not? Maybe we could tie a watch to our wrist by using a fabric strap, or we could wear a watch on our neck (for example as a pendant of a necklace).

Indeed, often a change of meaning implies a change of the metaphor we use to experience a thing. We need to stop thinking of watches as jewels (the old metaphor) and consider them as ties or fashion accessories (the new metaphor). Friedrich Nietzsche, in his philosophy of language, warns that "the most accustomed metaphors, the usual ones, now pass for truths and as standards for measuring the rarer ones."[12] Innovating meaning therefore implies challenging established metaphors that have slowly

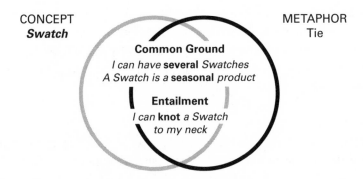

Figure 7.8
Entailments and innovation in the metaphor of the Swatch watch.

become myth, and substituting a new one. "Much of our cultural change arises from the introduction of *new metaphorical concepts* and the loss of old ones," say Lakoff and Johnson.[13] *Without a change of metaphor, we will never be capable of creating a new meaning.*

Communicating

Finally, metaphors are the most powerful way to *communicate* a new meaning, especially to those who did not go through the process of discovering it. Again, this is due to their immediacy. They express not only how we understand a concept, but especially how we *experience* it. They therefore intuitively and immediately convey the symbolic and emotional side of things, which would be hard using any other means.

This implies that there are two kinds of metaphors. We have metaphors for *critical reflection*: they are created during the discussion to help us explore a meaning deeper. We can create several of them, and they are all relevant, even the less powerful ones, because they help us clash and fuse different concepts into new meanings. And then we have metaphors for *communication*. In this case intuitive immediacy is relevant. Take the example of "love is a physical force." This metaphor helped us in the critical reflection: we better understood what we had in mind and what we did not mean. But if your immediate reaction is one of dislike (love cannot be measured!), then this is not a good metaphor for communication. I would suggest searching for another one, even if, after my explanation, you find the metaphor effective. It's not great to communicate through a metaphor whose meaning we always need to explain.

For example, the team of Alfa Romeo found another powerful metaphor: classical ballet dancers. A participant said: "Existing high-end cars are like Baryshnikov, whereas our cars should be like Nureyev." Everyone was surprised. The metaphor was fascinating but hard to grasp. The team asked why. The person explained: "People who are not experts in ballet believe that the greatest ballet dancer in history was Rudolf Nureyev. But the enthusiasts of classical dance maintain that Mikhail Baryshnikov was best. He was perfect in his movements, technically accurate." I noticed a moment of confusion in the team. "So are you claiming we should aim for lower-rank cars?" "Let me finish," he said. "In reality, the real connoisseurs of ballet dancing would tell you that Nureyev was the greatest ever. With his strong personality and identity, he was above perfection. He could be perfect, but he went beyond to be himself." He then showed a photo of Baryshnikov springing into a perfect jump, his body straight, his hands loosened into a graceful effortless pose, his hair neat as if he had just been grooming. Next to it a photo of Nureyev flying in the air, in a bold unconventional figure, his body tensed and wet from the effort, his long unsettled hair covering his face.

Aha! The eyes of people in the team glimmered. It was a great metaphor that helped them clarify what they had in mind for the new Alfa cars: to put the personality of the driver at center stage, rather than the perfection of the machine. Alfa would be for real connoisseurs of driving who want to express their identity, rather than aiming for perfection.[14] The metaphor was perfect in terms of meaning, and also sophisticated. Indeed, too sophisticated. Every time you showed it to someone, you would need to explain its rationale. It was not straightforward. It was effective for supporting critical reflection and moving the discussion deeper. But not for communication. They kept it as a backup, but then created other more effective communication metaphors.

AN INNOVATION FACTORY

Once the quartets have created a new meaning, by clashing and fusing their directions, they can share their scenarios with the entire circle and collect feedback. As always, engaged criticism is crucial during plenary discussions. Everyone should focus on what they like of the new scenario, what they are doubtful about, and what deeper potential may lie underneath. The quartet can take criticism in and refine its vision, or we can reshuffle the quartets to explore new pairs of directions. The process can therefore be iterated, so that different combinations are systematically explored.

Eventually, the output of this phase is typically two or three new, unprecedented meanings. They may imply different strategies and products. At this stage, we do not need to fuse everything further into one single direction. Our internal work has achieved its purpose: to envision a few selected, robust visions about what people could love. The next reflections (which could lead to selecting one of the visions or to further fusing them into another novel comprehensive direction) need to be fueled by new insights. The moment has come to open to outsiders' criticism.

Just a final note about what we have seen in this chapter. One of the myths of innovation processes of the last decade has been the "creative workshop," in which a team of people quickly toss out hundreds of ideas in a very limited time. An ideation workshop tickles the creative spirit that every one of us harbors. We usually find ourselves energized after a fast creative session. Then we leave and go back to our desk and ordinary work. Unfortunately, innovation hardly happens like this. Not even innovation of solutions. Definitely not innovation of meaning. This requires *engaged* deep reflections, in order to see the potential of what we have in front of us. The process described in these pages has different dynamics. It's *deep*. It starts with *intense* work done individually, for about a month. When people come together for a meeting, they have already envisioned their own new directions. The work done by pairs and by the radical circle, during the two-day meeting here described (and summarized in figure 7.7), is not about

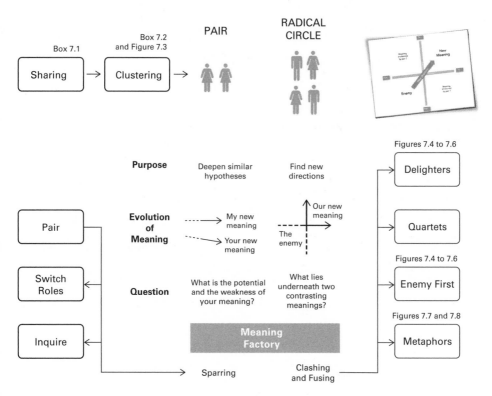

Figure 7.9
Map of chapter 7.

ideation. There is neither brainstorming nor divergent idea generation (the new hypotheses have been envisioned before the meeting begins). It's instead a workshop based on criticism, aimed at clashing different directions, discussing, digging deeper, and converging toward a few visions. It's a process of "fusion": melting through intense hard work. That's maybe why we name it with a different metaphor: the meaning "factory." Yet, as Monet and C. S. Lewis wrote (see chapter 5), an engaged intense debate can be as energizing (and meaningful) as a creative session.

8 The Interpreter's Lab

Outsiders' Criticism

"Where are we going? The examination room is the other way." The team of Philips Design was surprised. They expected Dr. Gorfinkle to show them the MRI area of the hospital. Instead, he turned toward the waiting room where children went before for the exams.

The design team was engaged in a project to create new solutions for the Philips health care business. Philips was one of the main players in the industry, with highly sophisticated imaging products such as CT (computed tomography) or MRI (magnetic resonance imaging). Until that moment, innovation in the imaging industry had focused on scanning performance: fast and accurate. The dominant assumption was that users (both the radiologists and the patients) were primarily interested in having a precise diagnosis and cure. How this diagnosis and cure occurred was secondary. Yet doing an examination could be a stressful experience, even a scary one for children (who needed to be sedated). The design team of Philips was therefore exploring a breakthrough new meaning: to focus on the emotional well-being of the users (the patients and the radiologist). Their assumption was that reducing stress would help patients to heal better, radiologists to be more concentrated and gratified, images more accurate, and examination procedures smoother. In their vision, *how* the examination was conducted had primary importance. This project eventually yielded Ambient Experience for Healthcare, a solution which we have illustrated in chapter 3: Ambient Experience for Healthcare uses "ambient technologies," such as LEDs sources, video animations, and RFID sensors, to create a more relaxing examination context. We have seen that customers loved this solution. But how did the team come to it?

The visit to Dr. Gorfinkle was one of the cornerstone moments in refurbishing the team vision. The team wanted to understand more about the examination experience. Kenneth Gorfinkle, a clinical psychologist, had great expertise on how pain affects children during examination. He had written a book on the subject. Also, he worked at the department of pediatric oncology at Presbyterian Medical Center in New York, where he was the coordinator of psychological services. He definitely looked like an interesting profile. So, halfway through the project, they decided to visit him.

Dr. Gorfinkle guided the Philips designers on a tour of the oncology department. But instead of leading them directly into the examination room and pointing at the devices and instruments, he took another direction: he focused the team's attention on what happens to children before and after they get into the scanning room. He talked of a study where children interviewed four years after the examination considered the sedation injection as the most frightening moment of the whole experience. Sedation typically occurred in a poky claustrophobic space before the exam. Dr. Gorfinkle suggested that this space should instead be as relaxing as possible. In addition, in many hospitals, after the procedure the patient is taken back to the same preparation room. This implies that the last memory fixed in a child's mind is of the same poky room where she had the injection. Given that severely sick children could undergo the same examination several times, ending the procedure in a different room would convey better memories and less stress should they come back.

The visit with Dr. Gorfinkle was eye-opening. On the one hand, it confirmed the team's assumption: the emotional dimension of the examination was important. However, it went beyond. The team realized that the "examination experience" had a much larger span than they had thought. The point was not only making the scanning device less scary (e.g., with smooth rounded lines, or fancy patterns), or the examination room more relaxing and playful. Children came into the scanning room already terrified. What was happening before that room, and after, was as important as what was happening inside.

Eventually, the solution designed by Philips incorporated much of this understanding. For example, the Ambient Experience for Healthcare starts when a child enters the hospital. There, for example, she can choose a puppet, such as an elephant. The puppet includes an RFID sensor. When the child walks the corridors toward the preparation room, the sensor automatically activates video projectors that display animations related to the puppet she has picked (e.g., images and sounds of nature). The child then perceives the hospital as a friendly environment. A hospital that is tuning into her mood, rather than her tuning into the distressing language of the hospital.

Kenneth Gorfinkle proved to be an interpreter for the Philips team. An interpreter is an outsider who looks at our customer from a different perspective. As an expert, an interpreter has been investigating the *same* people who use our product (children and radiologists, in the case of Philips), in the *same* experience (healing), but through a *different* lens (the psychological well-being of patients, especially in relation to pain). When we are engaged in the creation of a new meaningful vision, interpreters such as Kenneth Gorfinkle can be extremely precious.

This chapter illustrates how to tap the power of interpreters in the creation of new meaning. It shows how, after we have generated a tentative new vision, outsiders can help us challenge the vision, make it more robust, reframe it. So that it is not only what *we* love, but also what *people* would love. Innovation of meaning is an inside-out process. This chapter is about the "out."

We will show how to identify interpreters and interact with them through a meeting that we call the "interpreter's lab." We will also briefly discuss the involvement of a second type of outsider: customers. This latter discussion will be shorter, however. Not because customers are less important. Indeed, they are the ultimate givers of meaning, the people we have been working so much for. Simply, customer involvement has been already intensively covered in recent literature. Any attempt here to replicate this richness of tools and methods would provide a poor result. I will refer to material that you can consult in this regard, and that we use ourselves and find effective.

WHY

In her book *On Looking* (which we introduced in chapter 4),[1] Alexandra Horowitz explains why, to see new things, she had decided to walk around her block with eleven experts: "Paying attention is simply making a selection among all the stimuli bombarding you at any moment. ... Psychologists call this the *selective enhancement* of some area of your perceptual field and suppression of other areas. And therein lies my approach to 'paying

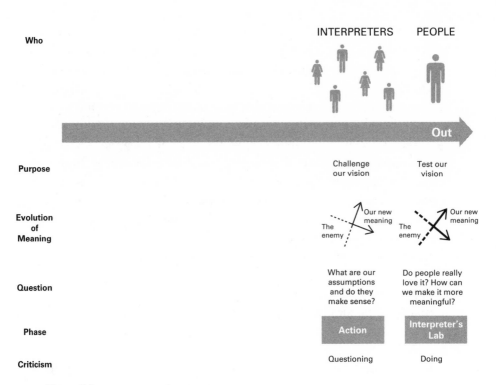

Figure 8.1
Involving outsiders: interpreters and people.

attention' to the block: each of my companions on these walks serves to do the selective-enhancing for us, highlighting the parts of the world that they see, but which we have either learned to ignore or do not even know we can see."[2]

Interpreters are *selective enhancers*. They pay attention to something that we have suppressed (being focused on other things). They shift our attention in other directions. Not because they are better than us, but simply because they have a different mechanism of selective enhancement: their background, their research, their inclination. Dr. Gorfinkle points to the waiting room, rather than the examination room, because of his focus on children's pain and because his research indicates that pain depends significantly on what happens before the exam. This selective enhancement done by the interpreters has two implications.

First, it helps us to *see*: to pay attention to something we would otherwise disregard: to look at the preparation room instead of the imaging devices. For example, one of Horowitz's experts, an illustrator, walks her into a church in her neighborhood she had never entered before. The illustrator liked churches because of the music one can hear inside and because anyone can enter there and sit in the pews.[3]

Thus, interpreters can help us to see things. But seeing is often not enough. We may "see the signs, but not the meaning," says Horowitz. Interpreters can also help us in this second step: they can help us to capture new meaning. Which is what we are eventually looking for. Their greatest contribution is to provide *new interpretation*, even for things we had already noticed. For example, one of Horowitz's walkers is Fred Kent, an expert in urban sociology and founder and president of Project for Public Spaces. When the two walk down the block, they come across one of those large food carts that occupy New York's sidewalks. Alexandra Horowitz notices the protrusions, displays, and containers that widen its girth. She slows down and maneuvers around the cart, almost annoyed by its intrusive presence on the pathway. Fred Kent, instead, stops, takes a photo, and says admiringly: "The vendors add a lot [to the city], because they tend to slow you down ... it's social. That's what a city is." They both saw the same thing, the vendor's cart. But they captured two different meanings. What was annoying for her was positive for him. "I was starkly reminded of the very simple truth that there are *many* ways to look at the *same* event," writes Horowitz. "I tend to see a surfeit of slow walkers and loiterers as hindering my progress on a rushed morning. These same people were viewed by Kent as an essential constituent of the urban landscape." Then something even more interesting happens. She captures a third new meaning: pedestrians as dancing partners: "Might we look at pedestrians not just with tolerance [her original meaning], or with acknowledgment of their role in making the city rich [Kent's meaning], but also as impressive collaborators in an unlikely sidewalk dance [the new meaning]."[4] She describes how people who set forth on a congested sidewalk are astonishingly engaged in a sophisticated, unaware dance to avoid bumping.

This episode also reminds us of the false myth of user observation. Many people naively believe that observation is a powerful and objective method to enable us to see new things. In reality, we see only what we want to (and

can) see: a cart occupying people's way with its protrusions; people annoy-
ingly slowing down; some protesting. That observation would lead us to
design a slimmer cart. This is what *we* see, but it is not necessarily the meaning. Not what is currently meaningful *for people*, nor what *could be more
meaningful*. The same observation, through a different interpreter, could
lead to a totally contrasting meaning (and a totally different design). Which
does not imply that observation is wrong. What is wrong is idealizing its
objectivity and forgetting about the power of our own interpretation over
what we see. And interpreters can unmask and enhance our unconscious
interpretation.

Or, even better, they can *challenge* our interpretation. The best moment
to meet interpreters is *halfway through a project*, when we have already envisioned our new meaning. When we have exposed our own interpretation.
Alexandra Horowitz meets the illustrator and the urban sociologist after she
has taken her first walk alone; after she has noted in her notebook what she
saw, and what she *interpreted*, by herself. The design team of Philips meets
Dr. Gorfinkle after they have had workshops in which they envisioned a
new meaning; when they met him, they already had a hypothesis for a new
meaningful direction.

If we meet interpreters after a meaning factory, we are more likely to
capture their interpretations. Our hidden assumptions then are exposed
and clearer, to us and to others in the team. We can directly target them
by briefing the interpreters and focusing their reflection. Otherwise they
would just talk randomly and anything they said would simply look
flat: seemingly right and wrong. By that time, we also have something to
compare the interpreter's insights with. We learn from differences, from
contrasts.

Therefore, the role of the interpreters is to move us deeper into the art of
criticism. We meet them not to get ideas (as typically suggested by studies
of collective problem solving and crowdsourcing); rather, they *challenge* the
innovative direction that we are exploring, making it stronger and deeper.
They bring good *questions* rather than good ideas.

At the same time, we do not want to meet interpreters at the end of the
project. Especially not after we have met users. We need someone who can
help us rise above existing behavioral patterns. Who can provide novel
interpretations. And we know that users hardly help in this regard. For
example, Philips Ambient Experience for Healthcare does not come from

explicit user needs. Patients were more concerned with how to feel less pain during sedation and could not imagine that the injection could be avoided through the projection of animations. And radiologists were searching for more powerful scanning devices: changing the hospital environment to improve clinical performance was outside the spectrum of what they considered meaningful. They started to consider it only *after* they saw a prototype proposed by Philips at a world radiology congress. User involvement is therefore much more effective *after* we have met interpreters, who can help us give meaning to emerging behaviors.

WHO

How to find good interpreters? Again, what matters is not quantity but quality. Recent theory on open innovation has invited organizations to crowdsource insights from massive numbers of outsiders. This might work for idea generation, but here we are looking for interpretations. Interacting with several interpreters would simply replicate the confusion of the context we want to make sense of. Instead, we need to be *selective*. Pick a few; the right ones, who help us *selectively enhance* our attention in new directions. Our experience is that six to eight interpreters (for any given market context) is a good compromise between variety and depth. Finding fewer then ten interpreters might look like an easy task. Yet finding the right one is a serious task that requires time, attention, and ingenuity. Typically, we contact more than one hundred to eventually have ten. But when we get to the right ones, the feedback they can provide is extremely precious. Box 8.1 illustrates the criteria for identifying them.

The domains
The first step is to identify the domains and fields in which to search for interpreters. Which kind of perspectives do you want to leverage? Which kinds of disciplines and organizations do you want to involve? Do you need experts in chemistry, architecture, TV screens, or web services?

The answer is not trivial. Sometimes organizations believe that it might be helpful to talk to any outsider; "anyone we never talked to," even better if she comes from an outlandish field (e.g., talking to a clown if you are in the business of excavators).[5] Unfortunately, there are thousands of fields and millions of outsiders we have never talked to. Some of them might

Box 8.1

Who: finding the interpreters

Criterion	Question
1. Domain: the field, discipline, industry of the interpreter	What is the customer and "experience of life" we are addressing? Which other domains (industry or field) are looking at our *same customer* in the *same "experience of life"*? Which of these domains are "outside of the network," i.e., are unrelated to our industry? (For the definition of the experience of life, see chapter 6)
2. Categories: the activity of the interpreters	For the selected domains: Which organizations *provide products and services* to the customer (*direct players*, such as manufacturers, retailers, design firms, suppliers of components and technologies)? Which organizations *conduct research on meaning* within that domain (*professionals*, such as professors, researchers, scholars, anthropologists, sociologists, trend analysis agencies)? Which organizations *produce artworks and cultural reflections* on the experience (*cultural interpreters*, such as journalists, directors, writers, priests, critics, curators)?
3. Researcher: the *expertise* of the *person*	For the selected domains and category: Which *person*, within the selected organization, has conducted *research* on the experience and its meaning? Who are the *emerging*, not yet famous, researchers who are exploring *new perspectives*?
4. Critic: the *attitude* of the person	For the selected researchers: Does this person have a *constructive critical attitude*? Does she enjoy reflecting on the why of things? Is she good at inquiring and listening? Is she keen to develop new interpretations herself? Does she *see us as interesting interpreters*?
5. Balance: the right *blend* of interpreters	Concerning the mix of interpreters: Are the domains *heterogeneous*? Are we addressing the *entire experience* of life? In particular, are we involving interpreters *"outside of the network"*? Are we balancing among *categories*: direct players, professionals, and cultural interpreters? Are we involving both considerate and venturesome interpreters (*boundary markers*)?

provide good challenging perspectives; most are simply useless. (Well, a clown can always make us laugh, whichever business we are in, and that is not too bad. But let's go back to meaning). So we cannot simply pick experts from any disparate fields. We need a criterion.

In chapter 6 we explained that meanings pertain to people's experience of life (remember figure 6.7? for example, the meaning of food may pertain to the experience of getting fit, or to the experience of cooking with our partner). The interpreters are therefore *other experts who look at this same life experience*. Simply, they take a different perspective than we do. And this is their value. For example, if we are exploring the meaning of food in the experience of "getting fit," we need interpreters who are investigating how people give meaning to "getting fit." For example: personal trainers, managers in firms that manufacture fitness gear, organizers of sports events, etc. None of them is a food manufacturer. However, they are not just "any" kind of outsiders. All of them have something in common: they deal with people who want to get fit. All of them have to capture how people give meaning to this experience. But they do it from different perspectives than food. And this is what we want.

Hence, the first question in finding interpreters is: Which domains look at our same customer within the *same experience* we want to give meaning to? Typically, there are three types of domains (figure 8.2):

- "Industry" domains: these are experts in our same industry. If we sell cheese, these are other cheese manufacturers, or food manufacturers more generally. They are most similar to us (some of them may even compete with us), and therefore unlikely to provide new perspectives. These are the least interesting interpreters.
- "Adjacent" domains: these are experts in fields that are next to our industry. For example, in the food industry these are the chefs. They do not sell food in supermarkets (at least not as their main mission), but they are very close to the experience of cooking and eating. Adjacent interpreters might be interesting. They provide perspectives that are different from our own. Still, typically, any company in our industry already has connections with adjacent experts. Any food company already talks to chefs. So the perspective these interpreters bring is different but hardly novel compared to what we, and our competitors, already know. This implies that it is worth inviting adjacent interpreters only if they might bring *new* insights that are not yet common knowledge in our industry.

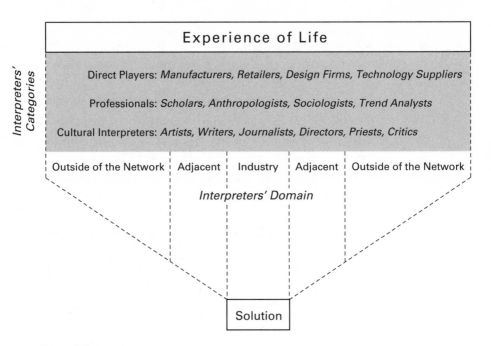

Figure 8.2
Domains and categories of interpreters.

*   "Outside of the network" domains: these are experts in fields that are
    far from our industry, although they are still related to our same experi-
    ence. For example, if we sell cheese, these can be manufacturers of fit-
    ness equipment. Companies in the food industry hardly talk to them.
    Yet free weight manufacturers participate in the experience of "getting
    fit," which is the same experience we, as cheese manufacturers, partici-
    pate in. They can be good interpreters for us (and we can be good inter-
    preters for them). Especially because most likely we will tap into a
    perspective that our competitors miss. *These are the domains we need
    most.*

Take the example of Philips and the AEH project. They interacted
with several interpreters, including doctors, hospital managers, engineers
of health care equipment, marketing experts, who were experts from
adjacent domains whom one could expect to find in any project of a manufacturer of imaging devices. Other interpreters, however, belonged to
domains "outside of the network" who were unusual for projects in this
industry: for example, child psychologists such as Dr. Gorfinkle, architects,

contemporary interior designers, experts in LED technologies and video projection. These most unusual interpreters provided fertile ground for enriching the project's new meaning: that the design of the hospital environment could improve the effectiveness of clinical procedures.

Hence, if a firm is the first to find and attract interpreters from domains "outside of the network" who are disregarded by the firm's competitors, it will be more likely to access novel interpretations. Figures 8.3 and 8.4 illustrate examples of interpreters in two different projects. The first refers to Alfa Romeo (we introduced this project in chapter 7). Here the referenced experience was "travel" for premium-segment customers. We can recognize some interpreters in the same industry (a manufacturer of tires); in adjacent industries (a provider of mobile telecommunication services); and especially, interpreters from "outside of the network": a manufacturer of leather goods (such as bags and computer backpacks), a CEO of high-end resorts, or a manufacturer of fitness equipment (how do you keep fit when you travel and fight back pain?).

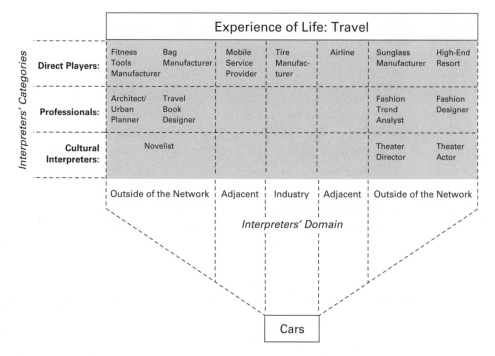

Figure 8.3
Interpreters in the case of Alfa Romeo.

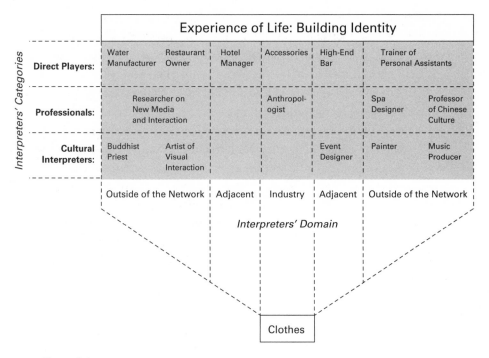

Figure 8.4
Interpreters in the case of a high-end fashion retailer.

The second example refers to a high-end fashion brand that wanted to reconceive its stores. Here the referenced experience is building identity (shoes and clothes are just sliders in the experience of building one's own personality and image). Here again we can find several interpreters from "outside of the network." For example, a brand manager for high-end mineral waters (yes … people pick a brand of water according to their own identity), a company that trains personal assistants to CEOs (personal assistants know a lot about how wealthy people give meaning to their identity), or a spa designer.

The categories

Once we have identified the domains, we need to pick the players and organizations that could serve as interpreters. As figure 8.2 shows, within a given domain there are three categories of interpreters:

• *Direct players*: these are experts who actively operate by *producing products and services*. For example a manufacturer of fitness gear, or a fitness club, is an active player in the domain of getting fit. They have to interpret how people give meaning to that experience, because they *provide people with things to use* during the experience. Typically, active players may be manufacturing firms, retailers, design firms, suppliers of components and technologies. These interpreters are extremely effective, since their interpretations come from direct experience. They are not just reflective: they need to create real value for people. They reflect, *act*, then reinterpret their actions, and so on. In particular, suppliers of novel technologies can be extremely valuable, since they tend to look ahead and have a glimpse of novel experiences enabled by disruptive technologies.

- *Professionals*: these are experts who *conduct research* on meaning within the domain. These can be professors, researchers, scholars, anthropologists, sociologists, trend analysis agencies. They do not provide products and services directly to people. Rather, their profession is to do research and develop new interpretations (which they would usually sell as a service to the direct players). In the example of the fashion brand (figure 8.4), we can see among the interpreters a researcher in new media and interaction, an anthropologist, a professor of modern Chinese culture. These interpreters may be interesting for providing a broad perspective on a given experience (direct players instead are usually more focused on a specific product).

- *Cultural interpreters*: these are players from *artistic and cultural domains*, such as journalists, directors, writers, priests, critics. They do not conduct "formal" research, but their profession is, by definition, to give meaning to things. They are precious interpreters especially of *emotions* and *symbols*. In the Alfa Romeo project we can notice a theater director, who had just written an irreverent piece on how "premium" people perceive themselves; or a young writer whose novels talk about contemporary professionals in modern cities. Among cultural interpreters, the fashion firm chose to involve an artist in visual interaction, a music producer, and a Buddhist priest who is often approached by wealthy people who search for meaning and identity. These interpreters usually bring a *provocative* perspective, outside the dynamics of business. They are capable of capturing hidden malaise in people and making it visible. They often tell us, and even more *make us feel*, what we would prefer not to hear.

Researchers on meaning

Once you have identified the domains and categories, you need to find the best interpreters within each domain. I mean: *the best people*. Interpreting meanings is not an exercise that is accessible to any player. There are thousands of chefs and thousands of personal trainers, but not all of them are interpreters. Only a few can provide good insights. Others only add noise. And the worst thing that can happen, when we are engaged in making sense of things, is to have more noise. *A useless interpreter is not just useless, she is bad.*

In choosing the right person within a domain, an important factor to consider is that she needs to have investigated meanings in the field and have developed her own interpretation. Possibly, a *novel* interpretation that captures the latest changes in people's lives. In other words, within a given domain and category, we need to find the *researchers on meaning*.

Philips did not randomly pick a child psychologist for the AEH project. It searched carefully. Dr. Kenneth Gorfinkle is not a generic child psychologist. Through years of studies as a clinical professor of psychology he had developed robust knowledge on how pain affects children, and had proposed novel interpretations. In his book *Soothing Your Child's Pain*[6] he explains how different techniques such as visualization, distraction, and narrative could improve children's relaxation, and how parents may play an important role, for example by telling a story. These insights from his studies supported the creation of animated projections used in the AEH solutions, whose theme can be selected by children as they are getting ready for their examination. Also, his studies led to conceiving a scaled-down version of a CT scan to be located in the waiting room. Children use this "Kitten Scanner" to build their own stories of the exam by doing a clinical scan of a variety of soft toys. They can also see that if a toy is shaken during the scan, the image distorts, so they learn the importance of lying still to get a good image.

Note that looking for researchers does not mean you have to go to the most popular experts in a field. Sometimes well-known experts get stuck in their past explorations and struggle to challenge dominant assumptions in a field (which they have probably contributed to creating themselves). They are also easily accessible to all your competitors: their interpretation will hardly make a significant difference. Instead, untapped novel researchers may prove to be more effective.

Note also that by "researcher" we do not necessarily mean someone with a PhD. Rather, we refer to experts who act as *researchers on meaning*: they have, *explicitly* or *implicitly* (through their daily work), empirically analyzed how people give meaning to an experience, and they have *reflected* upon it. They have *evidence* (quantitative data, or simply case studies from their personal projects). They have *produced* novel interpretations (new products, research reports, or artworks based on their insights).

Critics

Once we have identified the domains and categories and, within them, those interpreters who have expertise through research, we have a final criterion: the *personality* of the interpreter.

During a project with a large corporation, we conducted a test to assess the effectiveness of interpreters.[7] To this purpose, we asked the corporation's innovation team to value how much each interpreter contributed to a better understanding of meaning. The result of the test was interesting. Expertise of the interpreters (the research they conducted on meaning in the field) emerged as an important factor. But it was not enough. The assessment of the team was strongly correlated also with another parameter: the personality of the interpreter. Especially the team appreciated those interpreters who were good at taking a critical stance, i.e., who were good at reflecting, debating, challenging the team. On the other hand, interpreters who simply presented their research but did not engage in critical reflection were rated low. Similarly, interpreters who appeared extremely creative and proposed extemporary solutions were hardly appreciated. Solutions were not what the team was looking for.

Interpreters therefore are not just experts or idea generators. They are critics. They are precious insofar they challenge us and our interpretations. A great interpreter is someone who displays characteristics that we have already searched for when assembling our internal team (box 6.1): they enjoy reflecting on the why of things. They are not only good at answering our questions but also, and especially, at asking us unconventional questions. They appreciate going deeper, giving feedback. They also appreciate being criticized. They are keen to meet us and listen, in order to sharpen their own interpretation. A good interpreter leaves the meeting with novel learning.

Balancing

In identifying the interpreters, the blend is also important. Here again we can think as we did when forming our internal radical circle (box 6.2). Enhance heterogeneity: by combining different disciplines (especially from experts outside of the network); by balancing between direct players, professionals, and cultural interpreters; by ensuring the presence of boundary markers (namely considerate interpreters who are more aligned with existing interpretations, and venturesome interpreters who are exploring outlandish directions).

Of course, if we are investigating different market segments, geographies, or experiences, we may need to find specific interpreters for each context. For example, the fashion retailer in the case of figure 8.4 selected 14 different interpreters because it was addressing two different cultural contexts. It indeed organized two separate meetings with seven interpreters each, focusing on the two market segments

How to find them

Finding the right interpreter is a serious task. To meet 14 interpreters, the high-end fashion retailer identified 102 candidates, contacted 23, and, after a preliminary phone interview aimed at explaining the purpose of the meeting and assessing their critical attitude, picked the best 14.

To find interpreters we can use a combination of methods. Initially we may search broadly: by leveraging our own network of contacts, and the network of others in our organization; by searching through social media, such as LinkedIn; by accessing diverse databases (e.g., publications and patents). Then, when we have a starting base of interesting people, the search may become more focused. For example we may use a simple snowball method: asking people in our starting base about others who fit our specific search, and so on.

Often, a good interpreter can be a good mediator. Mediators are players who are well connected in a domain and who can therefore point us toward the most appropriate experts. Interpreters' novel perspectives, in fact, likely come from their immersion in novel networks. Interpreters can especially help us to search for experts in a new domain where we do not have established relationships. For example Dr. Gorfinkle suggested that Philips approach the Child Life Council, a nonprofit organization that promotes reduction of stress and trauma in hospitals. Experts from the Child Life

Council underlined how the environment should facilitate positive interactions among the patients, the staff, and the relatives. They described for example how in situations in which parents could not stay in the examination room with their child, some staff tied a long thread to the finger of the child and gave the other end to the parents outside the room, to maintain connection. This inspired the creation in AEH of two-way visual and audio communication via a camera between patients in the treatment room and staff and/or loved ones waiting nearby.

MEETING THE INTERPRETERS

There are two ways to interact with the interpreters. We can meet them independently of each other, or we can group them in a single meeting, which we call an interpreter's lab. The first option enables us to focus more on the contribution of the individual. The second leverages their mutual interactions and insights; also, it tends to be appreciated by the interpreters themselves, who value the possibility of learning from several perspectives.

Preparing the interpreter's lab

The role of the interpreters is to challenge our assumptions about what is meaningful to people. We search for *depth* of reflection, rather than extemporaneous ideas. This depth of reflection can be achieved only by careful preparation of the meeting.

For this reason, it is important to brief the interpreters well in advance (usually 2–3 weeks before the meeting). A central part of the brief is to clarify the specific focus of the meeting: the assumptions that we want to challenge. To this purpose, we can elaborate the results of the meaning factory. The radical circle had envisioned a few new directions. We do not want to disclose these directions to the interpreters (they have strategic value for us). And it is not even necessary to do so. What we can instead share with them are the *assumptions* that underpin those directions.

For example, in the case of Vox, the direction was the "living bedroom," i.e., transforming the bedroom of elderly people into a central social place in the home. Examples of assumptions underpinning this direction are: we assume that elderly people spend a significant amount of time in their beds at home, and that they still will; we assume that they would like to be more active rather than resting; that they would accept less intimacy (sleeping and even being medically treated in a bed placed in a central room), for the benefit of having a home that fosters socialization; that they are willing to spend more on a large nice bed (and maybe save on sofas); that their apartments will have one large central room, or an open space, in which to host a larger bed, rather than several small rooms.

All these assumptions can be transformed into *assumption questions* (e.g., the last assumption might turn into the following questions, which might be addressed for example to an architect: "How would elderly people love to organize their house in terms of spaces? What do you understand of their aspirations? And how much are they willing to reorganize their apartment when they get older?"). Assumption questions do not disclose our strategic intention, so they can be shared with the interpreters. Also, they are less specific than our direction, so the interpreters are more free to elaborate their insights without being biased by our interpretation. (If we were to simply ask, "Would elderly people like to have a large bed in the middle of their living room, where they can host relatives and children during a visit?," we would limit the space of freedom of the interpreters. They could only answer yes or no, which is not what we want. We do not involve them in order to poll their preferences, but to have them reflect openly.)

Typically, after a meaning factory, a team has envisioned three to five possible strategic directions, each of which is underpinned by ten to twenty assumption questions. These questions usually have some overlap. So we can cluster questions around major themes and share them with the interpreters, asking them to pick the theme they would like to focus on during the meeting according to their insights and expertise. Box 8.2 provides guidelines to help the interpreters reflect on the assumption questions they have picked, and prepare their talk for the meeting.

The meeting

The interpreter's lab is aimed at challenging our assumptions and developing deeper insights. As said, a typical lab gathers six to eight interpreters. Box 8.3 illustrates the dynamics of the meeting. The discussion is organized around the themes that we have used to brief the interpreters. An

Box 8.2

Briefing for the interpreters

In order to brief the interpreters for the interpreter's lab, we should clarify:

1. People: Who are the targets of our reflection, the people whose meaning we are investigating? E.g., elderly people in Europe, in the case of Vox.
2. Experience: What is (are) the life experience(s) we will discuss during the meeting? E.g., how elderly people give meaning to life in their home; how they socialize with others; how they take care of their health.

Then, to help the interpreters prepare their contributions, we can provide the following guidelines.

Guideline	Explanation to the Interpreter
1. Interpretation, not creativity	The point is not to be creative. We are not looking for solutions or ideas, but for *robust interpretations*. Your talk will have the highest value for the meeting if you leverage your deep understanding of people's experience. You may base your discussion on your research, but also on your guts. Just be yourself and bring your own vision. The simple fact that you look at things from your perspective may enable others in the meeting to see new things.
2. Pragmatic, not only theoretical	Do not worry if you have not conducted extensive formal research on the topic. You have been invited because of your perspective and your understanding of people's experience, which can be definitely based on *practical applications* (your products and services). Simply address the questions exposing your insights.
3. Criticism, not negativity	Unfortunately we often associate a negative meaning with the word "criticism." In reality the word critic means "able to discern": it is not about being negative, but about going *deeper*. By "critical" we mean going beyond the first-glance appearance of phenomena to question existing assumptions, without being necessarily "against" or "beyond" but rather "underneath": to dig deeper.
4. Why, not what	The meeting focuses on the *meaning* that people give, not on specific solutions. In giving a critical discussion of the assumptions, try to dig deeper: move from what you see people doing (the what) into why they do it (the needs), i.e., their purpose.

Box 8.2 (continued)	
5. Discern	There is probably a significant heterogeneity among different people and their search for meaning. If so, please specify how your insights differ according to the type of people and *segments* they are applied to.
6. Metaphors	Please pick an object (or a song, a poem, a picture) that best represents your interpretation of the theme. This metaphor will help to capture your insights from an emotional and symbolic perspective. It's the *crisp and immediate* way you address the questions.
7. Further references	Please indicate any additional material, studies, readings, people, and other sources that could be interesting for further investigation of your insights.

interpreter picks a theme that is close to her interest and introduces it. Then the other interpreters and our internal team further contribute with their perspectives, feedback, inquiries. The purpose is not to converge on a common vision. Rather, to compare different insights on similar phenomena, to understand why these differences are there, to develop novel interpretations.

What happens after the lab is as important as what happens during it. Typically, the day after the meeting, the internal team meets again for an intense debriefing session in which all insights are reorganized according to the direction they pertain to. In this regard, the Post-its where all participants have indicated their major insights are extremely useful. They were arranged according to themes. Now they can easily be rearranged according to the meaning directions envisioned in the meaning factory.

Then the team is ready to reflect on each direction and reframe its interpretations: Is this direction still meaningful? Should we redefine it? Or should we even abandon it? Is there any new direction that emerged during the discussion with the interpreters that we had overlooked? (This typically happens if a Post-it with insights from the interpreter's lab cannot be traced back to any of our preliminary directions. It implies that there is probably a meaning we are currently missing.) The result of these reflections is a new scenario of meaning, and possible solutions that we can feed into the next step: texting with users.

Box 8.3

The dynamics of the interpreter's lab

After the typical introduction and warm-up exercises, an interpreter's lab can be organized according to this structure.

Discussing the themes:

Our assumption questions can be clustered into a few themes (typically, as many themes as the number of the interpreters). In preparation for the meeting each interpreter has picked a theme in which she will act as lead interpreter, i.e., the person who will start the reflection on the theme. After the lead interpreter has been introduced by the facilitator, the discussion, for each theme, can be structured as follows.

1. Metaphor	The lead interpreter starts from her emotional/symbolic interpretation of the theme: the metaphor she picked (object, song, picture, etc.; see box 8.2). She first shows it, without commenting, and then explains the meaning of this metaphor.
2. Inspirations by the lead interpreter	The lead interpreter introduces the discussion. First, she provides background about her own research or experience on the question. Has she or her organization conducted research in the field? Why and how? Then she inspires the discussion by bringing her own interpretation of the theme.
3. Reflections by participants	The reflection is then opened up to the participants (both other interpreters and our internal team). Some may provide their view on the theme, and especially address different insights than the lead interpreter (clashing). Others may provide possible explanations for these different perspectives (fusing).
4. Summary of the theme	Every participant (interpreters and internal team) write on a Post-it the two major insights captured from the reflection, and place them on a board where all comments on a theme are collected.

Wrap-up:

The concluding session can reflect across the different themes. Every participant writes two major insights that summarize her learning from the meeting.

INVOLVING PEOPLE

We are now ready to work directly with people, i.e., the customers we are addressing. Do people really love our vision? How can we make it more meaningful?

We involve people at this later stage not because they are not important. On the contrary, they are the core of our reflections. The recipients of our gift. Simply, as discussed in detail in chapter 4, we want to be sure that this gift is meaningful for them. And to be meaningful, we have to love it first, otherwise they will smell our lack of love. People can only love a gift that is proposed with love by us. Now we have the proposal that we love. And we have made it robust through our process. We are ready to take customers' criticism. For this purpose there are several approaches. Indeed, there is an extensive literature and tools we can tap here.

Understanding users

One approach is to apply classic methods for analyzing user needs, from quantitative (e.g., surveys) to qualitative tools (focus groups, ethnography, etc.); an overview of these methods has been provided in box 6.5. These methods could be even more effective if we reflect on their results together with the interpreters. They can point to things that we would otherwise disregard. This was for example the case of the team of Philips Design that visited Presbyterian Medical Center in New York and did an ethnographic user observation together with Dr. Gorfinkle.

Probing and beta testing

A more active approach is to test our hypothesis with customers. This implies embedding the meaning into tentative solutions, creating a proto-type, and letting them try. We call this activity "probing." A probe is a prototype quickly developed that people can use to provide feedback. For example the team of Philips developed a probe of the Ambient Experience for Healthcare system. The probe included various solutions, some based on real technologies and others simply simulated (where the technology was still not ready). Philips Design finds probes more useful than textual description or slideshows to illustrate the potential of a new radical mean-ing. Especially in this case, since Philips had never designed hospital envi-ronments before. It was therefore difficult for executives and customers to capture in abstract terms the value of the new proposal. Probes instead are "experience demonstrators" that allow us to see the radical shifts in product meanings because they embed insights into a *tangible* and *visible* output. Therefore on the one hand they focus the work of the team on real outcomes, and on the other hand they facilitate the communication of this new vision to top executives, potential clients, and other partners. Indeed, it is only after a probe of AEH was presented at the Radiology World Congress in Chicago in 2003 that customers started to see its potential, which made the project gain further support from executives of the Philips health care division.

Minimal viable product

Even more advanced, and effective, is to move directly into action and provide (selected) users a simplified version of our product, or minimal viable product (MVP). This can enable us to start interacting with users, learn, and then iterate. There are two different kinds of MVP:[8]

- Validating MVP: its performance is lower than the final expected solution, typically because it is missing some features. If people find an MVP meaningful notwithstanding its limits, then we can move on with more confidence. If instead customers are puzzled by the concept, then we need to reflect on whether the negative feedback is due to a wrong direction, or because the solution is wrong, or because the MVP is too simplified.

- Invalidating MVP: it has better performance then the final expected solution. This happens for example when the final solution will be based on automation (software, machines, etc.) but the MVP is delivered by employees (to minimize upfront investment). Employees are more responsive and offer a better, customized solution compared to machines. If customers do not like this experience, even though it is better than the expected final product, then we may seriously consider stopping; if instead people like it, we can reflect on whether their appreciation is because the direction if right, or because the MVP is too overperforming.

Another framework that we find extremely helpful at this stage is the "Sprint" process, masterfully illustrated by Jake Knapp, John Zeratsky, and Braden Kowitz.[9]

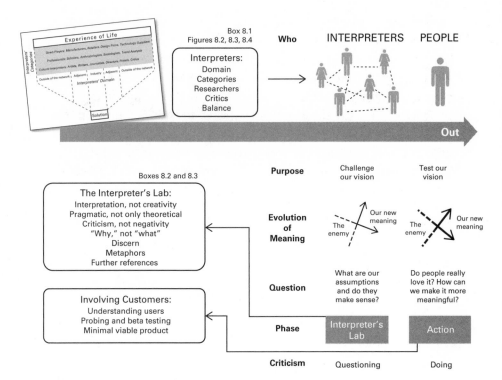

Figure 8.5
A map of chapter 8.

One great advantage of the process we have described in this book is that it fits perfectly with the principles of lean product development. The more we come to this stage with a robust vision, the greater our ability to make sense of the results of quick tests, probes, and MVPs.[10] Once we have a new clear frame, we have a direction for our experimentation, and we are more capable of interpreting feedback from customers because we have a hypothesis to compare it with. Indeed, the more we want to be lean and fast in development, the more we need to start with a robust vision.

ACTION

Definitely the approach I prefer most for this later stage of the process is to move directly into action.

And it is time to move into action also for us. I mean, you and me. We have reflected together through these pages. We have hopefully captured the value of meaning, and how we could create it.

There is no time to write a conclusion for this book. There is no time for further reading. The world is changing. Rapidly. We do not want to navigate a world whose meaning we can only endure passively, whatever it is. We want to create meaning, accomplishing what we believe could be better, could make the life of people more meaningful.

We want to make gifts. For people. And for ourselves. It's only through the *making* that we deliver the gift. It's only through the *making* that we enjoy the extreme pleasure of creating meaning. The gift is for people. The act of making the gift is for us.

Sorry for rushing away so fast from these pages. It's time to act. I have some sense of malaise. A will to change a part of the world that pertains to me. The world of education. The world of personal growth: how people and organizations today can learn and express their potential in a more meaningful way, which, I'm afraid, current institutional education is dramatically missing. I have an inescapable striving for meaning. And you?

Appendix: New Meanings Are Everywhere

Cases of Innovation of Meaning

Innovation of meaning is a major driver of value in all industries. This appendix provides examples from a broad variety of contexts: consumer markets or industrial markets, product- or service-based, profit or not-for-profit organizations, large or small businesses (see figure 9.1 for an overview). Its purpose is not to address any possible contexts (which would be impossible), but to provide empathy between your specific situation and others that are close to you in terms of typology of organization and industry. They illustrate how meanings move the creation of wealth from former leaders to new players. And they show that, in the face of the continuous change of meaning in your industry, you only have two choices: either you drive this change and capture its value, or you observe other players becoming relevant. Missing a transition of meaning implies becoming marginal, doomed to compete on the small profitability of performance-driven competition.

Da Vinci Surgical Robot
BtB product
2013

The Da Vinci system is a surgical robotic system that does not substitute for doctors but enables them to do complex prostatectomy surgery, even remotely or when an old doctor has shaky hands. It has become the leading prostatectomy procedure.

Old meaning	**New meaning**
I use robots because I want to *substitute for doctors and hospital personnel*	I use robots because I want to *enable doctors to do complex surgical procedures*

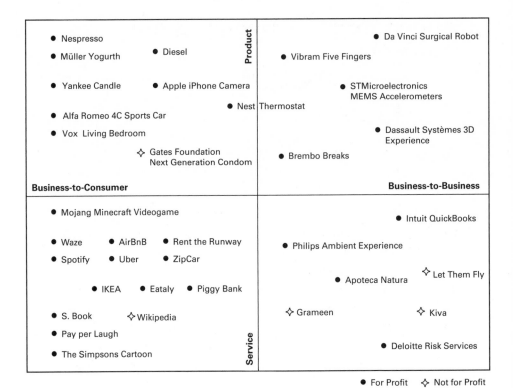

Figure 9.1
Cases of innovation of meaning that have disrupted competition in different industries.

| **Vibram Five Fingers** | BtB product |
| | 2005 |

Vibram is a supplier of rubber outsoles for footwear producers. FiveFingers is a shoe with an extremely thin and flexible sole. It is inspired by barefoot running and it works like a glove for feet: the shoe is contoured to each individual toe. The shoe comes in bright colorful shades, bringing a touch of fashion and style into the rugged outdoor footwear industry.

Old meaning
I use outdoor shoes because I want to *cushion my feet from the ground*

New meaning
I use outdoor shoes because I want to *bring my feet as close as possible to the ground*

STMicroelectronics MEMS accelerometers   BtB product

2006

MEMS accelerometers are small electronics components that are sensitive to movement and position. In 2006 they were supplied by STMicroelectronics to Nintendo for realizing the Wii, the first game console that teenagers used by moving (e.g., playing tennis by swinging their arm). This change of meaning enabled Nintendo to lead competition in game consoles for five years, beating giants such as Sony and Microsoft.

Old meaning
I use a game console because I want to
enter into a virtual world

New meaning
I use a game console because I want to
stay real, move and socialize with others

Dassault Systèmes 3D Experience   BtB product

2012

Dassault Systèmes is the leading provider of software products for design and development. Its recent new platform of applications (the 3D Experience) enables its users (mainly designers and engineers usually involved downstream) to move upstream into the creation of new concepts (e.g., using 3D software to enable end consumers to design their own products), therefore transforming 3D applications from tools for development to enablers of business model innovation.

Old meaning
I use 3D applications because I want to
develop a new product effectively

New meaning
I use 3D applications because I want to
create new business models

Brembo Brakes   BtB product
                                                                        1980

Brembo is the leading supplier of brakes for high-end sport cars. Its aluminum brakes are made visible (typically in red) through the wheels of the car.

Old meaning   **New meaning**
I use brakes because I want to   I use brakes because I want to
be safe when I drive   *show my skill in driving faster*

Intuit Quickbooks   BtB service
                                                                        2005

Quickbooks is an accounting application targeted to small businesses. Thanks to its simplicity, it can be used by people who have no expertise in accounting and do not even like to do accounting. Quickbooks has more than 80% of the US market share for accounting applications.

Old meaning   **New meaning**
I use an accounting application   I use an accounting application
because I want to   because I want
be precise in my bookkeeping   *accounting to be as smooth and painless
                                             as possible*

Philips Ambient Experience for Healthcare   BtB service
                                                                        2004

Philips AEH is a system for the imaging departments of hospitals (CAT scanning, MRI, etc.). It uses ambient technologies, such as LED sources, projection of video animations, and RFID sensors, to help patients (especially children) to be more relaxed during examinations. When patients are more relaxed, they move less and the image is less blurred. 50% of children who undergo examinations through this system do not even need to be sedated.

Old meaning   **New meaning**
I use an imaging system because I   I use an imaging system because I
want to   want to
*achieve precise images through the   achieve precise images through a
power of the device*   relaxing environment for patients and
                                             staff*

Apoteca Natura   Service
                                                                     2016

Apoteca Natura is a concept of pharmacies focused on natural health. Instead of traditional pharmacies that look like supermarkets (and pharmacy staff who look like inventory managers), Apoteca Natura gives products a minor level of importance in the experience, and instead enhances the personal contact between a professional pharmacist and the customers.

Old meaning	**New meaning**
I visit a pharmacy because I want to *buy a medicine*	I visit a pharmacy because I want to *meet an expert who can advise me about a more aware path to health*

Deloitte Risk Services   BtB service
                                                                     2006

Deloitte Australia launched a new line of risk services in 2011, under the slogan "Know the worth of risk," that, alongside traditional services relating to compliance with regulations, also provided advisory services targeted to the upper levels of their client organizations, such as the CEO and the board. Deloitte's vision is that in a world inherently characterized by uncertainty, those who can manage risk better might also afford to capture valuable chances that are inaccessible to others. In three years its revenues from risk services rose by 30% and, thanks to the higher value provided, profitability rose by 80%, in a market where most competitors were downsizing.

Old meaning	**New meaning**
I use a risk service because I want to *minimize concern (risk is negative)*	I use a risk service because I want to *create value (risk is positive)*

The Grameen Bank   BtB service
                                                                    1983

The Grameen Bank is a microfinance organization founded in Bangladesh. It makes small loans without requiring collateral. In 2006 the bank and its founder, Muhammad Yunus, were jointly awarded the Noble Peace Prize.

Old meaning   **New meaning**
I get a loan from a bank because I   I get a loan from a bank because I
want to   want to
make more money than what I already   *rise out of poverty with the support of*
have (collateral)   *my community*

Kiva Microfunds   BtB service
                                                                    2005

Kiva is a microfinance organization located in San Francisco based on the concept of peer-to-peer microlending, i.e., a direct connection between a specific borrower and a specific lender, blurring the lines between donations and loans.

Old meaning   **New meaning**
I lend money because I want   I lend money because I want to
the world to be a better place   *help a specific person whose project I*
                                          believe in

Nestlé Nespresso   BtC product
                                                                    1986

Nespresso is a popular coffee system based on coffee machines and single-use capsules with different flavors.

Old meaning   **New meaning**
I drink coffee because it is a way   I drink coffee because it is a way
to take a break, enjoy preparation, and *to show my identity, through the flavor*
share with others   *I pick, in an easy way*

Diesel Jeans   BtC product
                                                                        1978

Diesel introduced variety in jeans, through different ways of processing the fabric and different styles and fittings. In an industry dominated by long-established US brands, where jeans were the symbol of conforming with others, Diesel brought a focus on individual identity that anticipated big changes in culture and society.

Old meaning   **New meaning**

I use jeans because I want to   I use jeans because I want to
have convenience and be uniform with   *stand apart and make a fashion*
others   *statement*

Snapchat   BtC application
                                                                        2011

Snapchat is a video messaging application based on impermanent photos: posted images disappear once one watches them. A company's blog describes its mission: "Snapchat isn't about capturing the traditional Kodak moment. It's about communicating with the full range of human emotion—not just what appears to be pretty or perfect."

Old meaning   **New meaning**

I take photos because I want to   I take photos because I want to
capture the moment   *converse better*

Müller Yogurt   BtC product
                                                                        1971

In a crowded industry like that of dairy products (in particular yogurt), Müller has brought a total new vision: rather than simply searching for new flavors, it has transformed yogurt into a dessert, creamy, sweet.

Old meaning   **New meaning**

I eat yogurt because I want to   I eat yogurt because I want to
be healthy   *indulge in taste*

Yankee Candle   BtC product
                                                                    1975

Yankee Candle produces scented candles, often poured within a thick jar. Though it is a newcomer to the conservative and long-stable candle industry, Yankee Candle is the fastest-growing firm, with a 40% share in premium candles.

Old meaning	New meaning
I use candles because I want to *illuminate (in case there's no electric power)*	I use candles because I want to *create a welcoming atmosphere*

Alfa Romeo 4C   BtC product
                                                                    2013

The 4C is an affordable sports car whose driving experience is more exciting than that of luxury supercars, such as a Ferrari with a more powerful engine. The secret: a body in carbon fiber and a streamed-to-the-essence configuration so that the car weights less than 900 kilos. Launched in September 2013, it sold out the first two years of production.

Old meaning	New meaning
I use a sports car because I want to *show wealth and the muscles. Performance comes from power (engine and money)*	I use a sports car because I have *a passion for exciting driving. I'm less powerful (not wealthy and I do not care for big engines), but I'm so agile that I have more excitement than with supercars*

Vox Living Bedroom BtC product
2012

Vox is a Polish furniture manufacturer that has reconceived the role of bedrooms in homes, especially to address the European market where the population is aging. Its vision is that the bedroom becomes a central space of a house where elderly people could meet relatives and friends, socialize with them, and pleasurably spend time, just as normally happens in a living room (and as teenagers do with their own bedrooms). One of the products that came out of this process, for example, is a bed incorporating a large bookshelf (something that typically belongs in the living room), space for holding visitors' shoes, and even an unfolding screen to watch movies in company.

Old meaning
I have to stay in my bedroom
because I have to
sleep and heal from sickness. My
bedroom is a secluded private space

New meaning
I want to stay in my bedroom
because I can
meet friends and socialize. My bedroom
is a living space

Nest Thermostat BtC product
2011

The Nest thermostat is informed by smart simplicity: it does not require programming because it learns by itself what temperature the user likes. One just needs to start up the thermostat by simple manual regulation (using a straightforward rotary interface that acts as an on/off switch), and after three days its software learns the family's temperature habits. The thermostat is also equipped with sensors that understand when there's no one home, so that the heating is automatically turned down. Nest Labs was acquired by Google in 2014 for US $3.2 billion.

Old meaning
I use a thermostat because I want to
control the temperature

New meaning
I use a thermostat because I want to
feel comfortable without having to
control the temperature

Mojang *Minecraft* Videogame   BtC software
                                                                          2009

Minecraft is a sandbox videogame where players build their own virtual world. By combining simple blocks, they build everything from shelters to tools to human characters and animals. This videogame, created by a small Swedish start-up, has reached a greater diffusion in one year than classic videogames such as *Call of Duty*.

Old meaning   **New meaning**
I use videogames because I want to   I use videogames because I want to
show my abilities (e.g., in driving a car,   *express my imagination*
or in killing enemies)

Gates Foundation Next Generation Condom   Not-for-profit product
                                                                          2013

In order to prevent the spread of sexually transmitted diseases, in 2013 the Bill & Melinda Gates Foundation launched a challenge for ideas to reinvent the condom. With a totally new meaning: a condom that makes intercourse even more pleasurable, so that couples are more willing to use it.

Old meaning   **New meaning**
I use condoms because I want to   I use condoms because I want to
feel safe and protected   *feel more pleasure*

Waze Navigator   BtC application
                                                                          2006

Waze is a GPS-based geographical navigator that provides turn-by-turn information based on user-submitted travel times and current route conditions. Waze was acquired by Google in 2013 for US $1.1 billion.

Old meaning   **New meaning**
I use a navigator because I want to   I use a navigator because I want to
get to an unknown destination   *get to a known destination in the fastest*
                                           way now

AirBnB   BtC application
                                                              2008

AirBnB is a peer-to-peer application that enables people to list, find, and rent lodging. It has raised US $795 million from investors and has around 1.5 million listings.

Old meaning   **New meaning**
I use a travel service because I   I use a travel service because I
want to   want to
find a safe and good-quality hotel room *be immersed in the authentic*
                                          sociocultural life of a place

---

Rent the Runway   BtC application
                                                              2009

Rent the Runway lends high-end women's clothing. Its concept is based on the context of an experience economy, where wearing a dress matters more than owning it. It has a community with more than 4 million members.

Old meaning   **New meaning**
I shop for clothes because I want to   I rent clothes because I want to
own them   *be always different and dare to afford*
                                          dresses I would never buy

---

Spotify Mood Music   BtC application
                                                              2012

As music-streaming services enable access to the whole library of music, people find themselves lost in the choice of millions of songs. Which one to pick? How to find new music that I like? Spotify has addressed this wish with a breakthrough approach: organizing music according to moods instead of music genres. A mood refers to the context the music is listened to (e.g., a party, a dinner, a morning commute) rather than a style of music production (e.g., rock, pop, reggae, …)

Old meaning   **New meaning**
I listen to a music-streaming service   I listen to a music-streaming service
because I want to   I want to
have easy access to music   *discover new music according to the*
                                          situation I am in at this moment

Uber   BtC application
                                                                                     2009

Uber offers peer-to-peer transportation services. Customers deliver a trip request to an Uber driver who uses her own car to provide the service. One can rate the driver (and the rider). It is often mentioned as the quintessential example of a disruptive newcomer in an industry.

Old meaning   **New meaning**
I choose a taxi because I   I choose a taxi because I
trust the taxi company   *trust the driver*

Zipcar   BtC application
                                                                                     2000

Zipcar is a car-sharing company. Members pay for the use of a car only for the time they reserve it. Zipcar has been sold to Avis for about US $500 million.

Old meaning   **New meaning**
I buy a car because   I use car sharing because I want to
it's one of the most important things a   *move without the annoyance of owning*
person owns   *a car*

IKEA Seasonal Furniture   BtC service
                                                                                     2010

IKEA is bringing the world of furniture into fashion. Whereas in the past a piece of furniture was considered a durable good that one bought every several years, IKEA with its low prices and seasonal product design (especially in fabric, but also in furniture, as epitomized by its popular catalog) is transforming furniture into a nondurable product, whose purchase is driven by the need in the moment.

Old meaning   **New meaning**
I buy furniture because   I buy furniture because I like it
it's an investment in my home   *for my life as it is now*

Eataly Grocery Store   BtC service
                                                                        2004

Eataly is a grocery store that sells high-quality food items from Italy, typically not found in normal supermarkets and unknown to consumers. People can try some of the products in the restaurants hosted in the store. Which makes Eataly a full immersion into an Italian food experience.

Old meaning

I go to a grocery store because I want to
buy the food I know

New meaning

I go to a grocery store because I want to
discover and taste good food

GetDreams   BtC application
                                                                        2014

GetDreams is a Swedish start-up that is changing the way we look at financial services. Usually people save money in a bank for later use. The idea of GetDreams is to define a specific dream, e.g., something we want to buy or an experience we want to have. Then the application acts as a coach to help us slowly save the funds to get there (e.g., every time one turns down a specific purchase to save money for one's dream, the app automatically saves that money in the dream savings account).

Old meaning

I avoid purchasing something today because I want to
save money for any future use

New meaning

I avoid purchasing something today because I have a
specific experience I want to have in the future

S. (Novel)   BtC media
                                                                      2013

S. is a novel written by Doug Dorst and conceived by J. J. Abrams. It is indeed a story within a story, since it is composed of the novel *Ship of Theseus* by a fictional author and of hand-written notes filling the book's margins as a dialogue between two college students hoping to uncover the author's mysterious identity and the novel's secret. The book includes loose supplementary materials tucked in between pages.

Old meaning	**New meaning**
I read a book because	I read a book because
it contains a story	*the book is the story itself*

The Simpsons Cartoon   BtC media
                                                                      1989

The Simpsons is a popular animated sitcom. Its authors merged for the first time ever the language of cartoons (typically targeted to a younger audience) with a satirical sitcom of a working-class lifestyle in the United States.

Old meaning	**New meaning**
I do not watch cartoons because	I watch a cartoon because
they are for children	*it spurs a funnier and more acid satire of adults' lifestyles*

Wikipedia   Not-for-profit
                                                                      2001

Wikipedia is a collaborative online encyclopedia. It's among the ten most visited websites on the web.

Old meaning	**New meaning**
I use an encyclopedia because I want	I use an encyclopedia because I want
static information certified by am inaccessible cultural élite (to which I would like to belong)	*dynamic accessible information certified by people like me*

Notes

CHAPTER 1

1. The conversation between Tony Fadell and Matt Rogers comes from a combination of different interviews: mainly the narration of Matt Rogers at Startup Grind Silicon Valley (https://www.startupgrind.com/events/details/startup-grind-silicon-valley-hosted-matt-rogers-nest, accessed 11 November 2014), and other interviews cited below.

2. Roberto Verganti, *Design-Driven Innovation: Changing the Rules of Competition by Radically Innovating What Things Mean* (Boston: Harvard Business Press, 2009).

3. Jessica Salter, "Tony Fadell, Father of the iPod, iPhone and Nest, on Why He Is Worth $3.2bn to Google," *Telegraph*, 14 November 2014, http://www.telegraph.co.uk/technology/people-in-technology/10892436/Tony-Fadell-father-of-the-iPod-iPhone-and-Nest-on-why-he-is-worth-3.2bn-to-Google.html, accessed 25 August 2015.

4. Austin Carr, "The $3.2 Billion Man: Can Google's Newest Star Outsmart Apple?," *Fast Company*, 9 September 2014, http://www.fastcodesign.com/3035239/innovation-by-design-2014/nest-hatches-a-connected-home-boom, accessed 25 August 2015.

5. Simon Sinek, *Start with Why: How Great Leaders Inspire Everyone to Take Action* (New York: Portfolio, 2009).

6. Adam Lashinsky, "Is Tony Fadell the next Steve Jobs or … the next Larry Page?," *Fortune*, 12 June 2014, http://fortune.com/2014/06/12/tony-fadell-nest/, accessed 25 August 2015.

7. Carr, "The $3.2 Billion Man."

8. Eco-Structure, "The Sustainable Suite Design Competition Announces Winners," *EcoBuilding Pulse*, 2 November 2009, http://www.ecobuildingpulse.com/news/the-sustainable-suite-design-competition-announces-winners_o accessed 14 November 2014.

9. Katie Fehrenbacher, "Honeywell Killed Off Its Learning Thermostat 20 Years Ago," *GigaOm*, 2 February 2012, https://gigaom.com/2012/02/02/honeywell-20 -years-ago-we-killed-off-our-learning-thermostats/, accessed 18 November 2014.

10. Steve Wozniak, interview with the author, Milan, 28 October 2014.

11. Lashinsky, "Is Tony Fadell the next Steve Jobs or ... the next Larry Page?"

12. Carr, "The $3.2 Billion Man."

13. "Tony Fadell: On Setting Constraints, Ignoring Experts & Embracing Self-Doubt," https://vimeo.com/43497548, accessed 26 August 2015.

14. Carr, "The $3.2 Billion Man."

15. Tony Fadell recently announced his departure from Nest Lab (Tony Fadell, "Leaving the Nest," *Inside Nest*, 3 June 2016, https://nest.com/blog/2016/06/03/ leaving-the-nest/, accessed 20 June 2016). As always in these cases, the real reasons for such a step are multifaceted and out of the public eye. However, the situation at Nest before his departure was tense and, reportedly, marked by a too "harsh corporate culture." Richard Nieva and Anne Dujmovic, "CEO Tony Fadell Announces He's Leaving Nest," *c|net*, 3 June 2016, http://www.cnet.com/news/ceo-tony-fadell -announces-hes-leaving-nest/, accessed 20 June 2016; Kia Kokalitcheva, "Nest CEO Tony Fadell Is Resigning," *Fortune*, 3 June 2016, http://fortune.com/2016/06/03/ tony-fadell-leaves-nest/, accessed 20 June 2016.

16. On the concept of an innovation portfolio and strategy, see Gary Pisano, "You Need an Innovation Strategy," *Harvard Business Review* (June 2015). Innovation of meaning, in particular, refers to what Pisano indicates as an innovation that "Requires a *New* Business Model" (either leveraging existing competences or creating new ones).

17. Sinek, *Start with Why*.

18. W. Chan Kim and Renée Mauborgne, *Blue Ocean Strategy* (Boston: Harvard Business School Press, 2005).

19. Clayton M. Christensen, *The Innovator's Dilemma: When New Technologies Cause Great Firms to Fail* (Boston: Harvard Business School Press, 1997).

20. Clayton M. Christensen and Michael E. Raynor, *The Innovator's Solution: Using Good Theory to Solve the Dilemmas of Growth* (Watertown, MA: Harvard Business School Press, 2003); Anthony Ulwick, *What Customers Want: Using Outcome-Driven Innovation to Create Breakthrough Products and Services* (New York: McGraw-Hill, 2005); Clayton M. Christensen, Scott D. Anthony, Gerald Berstell, and Denise Nitterhouse, "Finding the Right Job for Your Product," *MIT Sloan Management Review* (April 2007): 2–11; Anthony Ulwick and Lance A. Bettencourt, "Giving Customers a Fair Hearing," *Sloan Management Review* 49, no. 3 (2008): 62–68.

21. Alexander Osterwalder, Yves Pigneur, Greg Bernarda, Alan Smith, and Trish Papadakos, *Value Proposition Design: How to Create Products and Services Customers Want* (Hoboken, NJ: John Wiley, 2015).

22. In reality, the framework of the jobs to be done is halfway between innovation of solutions (the how of things) and innovation of meaning (the why of things). It focuses on the intermediate level of "experiences" (the what of things), which, as Sinek explains, is not the same as the why that makes people fall in love.

23. Ash Maurya, *Running Lean: Iterate from Plan A to a Plan That Works* (Sebastopol, CA: O'Reilly Media, 2012); Jake Knapp, John Zeratsky, and Braden Kowitz, *Sprint: How to Solve Big Problems and Test New Ideas in Just Five Days* (New York: Simon and Schuster, 2016).

CHAPTER 2

1. Micheline Maynard, "Millennials in 2014: Take My Car, Not My Phone" *Forbes*, 24 January 2014, http://www.forbes.com/sites/michelinemaynard/2014/01/24/ millenials-in-2014-take-my-car-not-my-phone/, accessed 3 October 2014.

2. In this book, I will often use the phrase "*search* for meaning." But perhaps Andrew Solomon's expression would be more appropriate: "*forge* meaning." Says Solomon: "I've heard the popular wisdom that that has to do with finding meaning. And for a long time, *I thought the meaning was out there, some great truth waiting to be found.* But over time, I've come to feel that the truth is irrelevant. *We call it finding meaning, but we might better call it forging meaning.* ... Forge meaning, build identity, forge meaning and build identity. That became my mantra. Forging meaning is about changing yourself. Building identity is about changing the world. All of us with stigmatized identities face this question daily: how much to accommodate society by constraining ourselves, and how much to break the limits of what constitutes a valid life? Forging meaning and building identity does not make what was wrong right. It only makes what was wrong precious." Andrew Solomon, "How the Worst Moments in Our Lives Make Us Who We Are," TED talk, March 2014, http://www.ted.com/talks/andrew_solomon_how_the_worst_moments_in_our_lives_make_us_who_we_are/transcript?language=en#t-41912, accessed 21 July 2015 (my italics).

3. The number of confirmations in Italy has decreased by 10% in just 10 years between 2000 and 2010. Riccardo Benotti, "Cresime in Italia. Numeri e orientamenti," *Rogate Ergo*, April 2013.

4. http://smallbusiness.chron.com/big-candle-industry-69541.html, accessed 8 October 2014.

5. Elaboration of the European Candle Association, on data from Eurostat, for consumption of candles in the European Union (EU28), July 2014, http://www

.eca-candles.com/index.php?rubrik=19&topnav=8&sprach_id=en, accessed 8 October 2014.

6. Serena Ng, "Yankee Candle Agrees to $1.75 Billion Deal," *Wall Street Journal*, 3 September 2013, accessed 9 October 2014.

7. See for example http://www.oxfordlearnersdictionaries.com/definition/english/meaning_1 or http://www.macmillandictionary.com/dictionary/british/meaning (accessed 12 October 2014). For a deeper analysis of meaning and its connection with innovation and products, see Åsa Öberg, "Striving for Meaning: A Study of Innovation Processes," PhD dissertation, School of Innovation, Design and Engineering, Mälardalen University, October 2015.

8. The concept of "meaning as the idea that a sign represents" is the subject of investigation of entire disciplines, and in particular of semiotics (the theory of what signs and symbols mean) and linguistics (what language means), whose reflections date back to the fundamental studies of Ferdinand de Saussure and of Charles Sanders Peirce in the late nineteenth and early twentieth centuries. These theories have strong application in the domain of artifacts such as products, services, software, graphics, and brands and create an entire field of study on product language. See for example Steffen Dagmar, "On a Theory of Product Language: Perspectives on the Hermeneutic Interpretation of Design Objects," *FormDiskurs* 3, no. 2 (1997): 17–27; Giampaolo Proni, "Outlines for a Semiotic Analysis of Objects," *Versus* 91/92 (January-August 2002): 37–59; Toni-Marti Karjalainen, *Semantic Transformation in Design: Communicating Strategic Brand Identity through Product Design*, published doctoral thesis (Helsinki: University of Arts and Design Helsinki, 2004); or Josiena Gotzsch, "Product Talk," *Design Journal* 9, no. 2 (2006): 16–24.

9. Klaus Krippendorff, *The Semantic Turn: A New Foundation for Design* (Boca Raton, FL: CRC Press, 2006).

10. From a philosophical perspective, this interpretation of the evolution of society is aligned with *existentialism*, in particular what Søren Kierkegaard anticipated in his reflections: that meaning cannot be prescribed, and that everyone has to find her or his own meaning in life.

11. The understanding that the search for meaning deeply affects our everyday experiences, not merely our theoretical reflections, is a major standpoint of pragmatism, in particular of the studies of Charles Sanders Peirce.

12. Abraham Maslow, *Motivation and Personality* (New York: Harper, 1954).

13. Abhijit V. Banerjee and Esther Duflo, *Poor Economics: A Radical Rethinking of the Way to Fight Global Poverty* (New York: Public Affairs, 2012).

14. Barry Schwartz, *The Paradox of Choice: Why More Is Less* (New York: Harper Perennial, 2005).

15. Ibid., 5.

16. Claudio Dell'Era and Roberto Verganti, "Strategies of Innovation and Imitation of Product Languages," *Journal of Product Innovation Management* 24 (2007): 580–599.

17. Joel Stein, "Millennials: The Me Me Me Generation," *Time*, 20 May 2013.

18. Anthony Giddens, *Modernity and Self-Identity: Self and Society in the Late Modern Age* (Palo Alto, CA: Stanford University Press, 1991).

19. Zygmunt Bauman, *Liquid Modernity* (Cambridge: Polity, 1999).

20. Anthony Elliot, *The Contemporary Bauman* (Abingdon, UK: Routledge, 2013), 37.

21. The concept of vision is connected to the concept of a "value proposition" (the promise of value that a business makes to its customers) and to the concept of customer benefits. They all refer to value creation, i.e., to what worth is. My emphasis on vision highlights its nature as an interpretation, a way of seeing, a direction in a complex environment.

22. For an extended discussion of design as a meaning-making process, see Roberto Verganti, *Design-Driven Innovation: Changing the Rules of Competition by Radically Innovating What Things Mean* (Boston: Harvard Business Press, 2009). See also Klaus Krippendorff, "On the Essential Contexts of Artifacts or on the Proposition that 'Design Is Making Sense (of Things),'" *Design Issues* 5, no. 2 (Spring 1989): 9–38.

23. In this case innovation creates a "dominant design" of vision, on the analogy of the dominant design of technological architectures investigated by Jim Utterback in his model of the dynamics of innovation in industries: James M. Utterback, *Mastering the Dynamics of Innovation* (Boston: Harvard Business School Press, 1994).

24. Evidence shows indeed that people are looking for more than mere solutions to problems. Ravindra Chitturi and coauthors state that "more than 60% of customers who switch to another brand would classify themselves as 'satisfied' [with their old brand]. These findings point to a theoretically and substantively interesting research question: why does customer satisfaction with products translate into such low levels of customer loyalty? Moreover, how can we improve it? One possibility is that customers are looking for more than mere satisfaction—perhaps they are looking to be *delighted* in exchange for greater loyalty." Ravindra Chitturi, Rajagopal Raghunathan, and Vijay Mahajan, "Delight by Design: The Role of Hedonic versus Utilitarian Benefits," *Journal of Marketing* 72, no. 3 (May 2008): 48–63.

25. I refer here to love as a metaphor. As we will see later in this book, metaphors help us better understand a concept, without being an exact definition of it. They enhance some attributes while downsizing others. Same here for this metaphor of love, which is a magnificently multifaceted feeling that escapes any definition. And, most of all, it's a subjective feeling. Even more, its meaning evolves as our life does.

Inspiring snapshots and reflections on the meaning of love today are offered in the *New York Times* column "Modern Love": http://www.nytimes.com/video/modern -love/ (accessed 13 November 2014).

CHAPTER 3

1. http://www.innovationmanagement.se/imtool-articles/open-innovation-and -the-bp-oil-spill-what-went-wrong/, accessed 24 November 2014.

2. http://opensource.com/education/13/11/linux-kernel-community-growth, accessed 24 November 2014.

3. Sometimes a massive number of ideas is not even necessary to solve a problem. The Deepwater Horizon spill was indeed eventually solved not thanks to the 20,000 ideas sourced from the crowd (to assess and test which would have required enormous investment and time) but thanks to a small consortium of experts from ExxonMobil, BP, and few other oil and gas companies: http://www .innovationmanagement.se/imtool-articles/open-innovation-and-the-bp-oil-spill -what-went-wrong/, accessed 24 November 2014.

4. Joel Stein, "Some French Guy Has My Car," *Time*, 29 January 2015, 28–33.

5. http://data.worldbank.org/, accessed 21 March 2015.

6. http://www.statista.com/statistics/200005/international-car-sales-by-region -since-1990/, accessed 21 March 2015. Sales of cars in western countries and South America are flat. Only Asia is growing, although there are already signs of saturation in the Chinese market.

7. Stein, "Some French Guy Has My Car."

8. Ibid.

9. W. Chan Kim and Reneé Mauborgne, *Blue Ocean Strategy* (Boston: Harvard Business School Press, 2005); W. Chan Kim and Reneé Mauborgne, "Blue Ocean Strategy," *Harvard Business Review* (October 2004): 1–9; Gary Hamel, *The Future of Management* (Boston: Harvard Business School Press, 2007).

10. Noriaki Kano, Nobuhiku Seraku, Fumio Takahashi, and Shinichi Tsuji, "Attractive Quality and Must-Be Quality," *Journal of the Japanese Society for Quality Control* (in Japanese) 14, no. 2 (April 1984): 39–48.

11. Stefano Marzano, interview with the author, Eindhoven, November 2010.

12. The case of Philips's Ambient Experience for Healthcare will be further discussed later in this book. See also Roberto Verganti, "Designing Breakthrough Products," *Harvard Business Review* 89, no. 10 (October 2011): 114–120.

13. See chapter 4 in Roberto Verganti, *Design-Driven Innovation: Changing the Rules of Competition by Radically Innovating What Things Mean* (Boston: Harvard Business Press, 2009). A theoretical discussion of the link between meaning and technologies is developed in Donald A. Norman and Roberto Verganti, "Incremental and Radical Innovation: Design Research versus Technology and Meaning Change," *Design Issues* 30, no. 1 (Winter 2014): 78–96.

14. For further insights on technology epiphanies driven by digital technologies, see Tommaso Buganza, Claudio Dell'Era, Elena Pellizzoni, and Roberto Verganti, "Unveiling the Potentialities Provided by New Technologies: Technology Epiphanies in the Smartphone App Industry," paper presented at the EIASM International Product Development Management Conference, Limerick, Ireland, 22 June 2014.

15. http://news.yahoo.com/waze-sale-signals-growth-israeli-high-tech-174533585.html, accessed 23 March 2015.

16. http://www.forbes.com/sites/petercohan/2013/06/09/google-to-spite-facebook-buy-waze-for-1-3-billion/, accessed 23 March 2015.

PART II

1. Gary Pisano, "You Need an Innovation Strategy," *Harvard Business Review* (June 2015).

CHAPTER 4

1. The sentence of Tim Brown comes from the interview Drake Baer, "IDEO's 3 Steps to a More Open, Innovative Mind," *Fast Company*, 12 June 2013, http://www.fastcompany.com/3012824/dialed/ideos-3-steps-to-a-more-open-innovative-mind. The sentence of David Kelley comes from the ABC *Nightline* video "The Deep Dive." The sentence of Steve Jobs comes from the interview Gary Wolf, "Steve Jobs: The Next Insanely Great Thing," *Wired*, February 1996, http://archive.wired.com/wired/archive/4.02/jobs_pr.html. The sentence of Steve Wozniak comes from an interview he gave me during a speech at the World Business Forum in Milan, 28 October 2014.

2. In the field of open innovation, the most influential scholar has definitely been Henry W. Chesbrough with his book *Open Innovation: The New Imperative for Creating and Profiting from Technology* (Boston: Harvard Business School Press, 2003). On crowdsourcing see Jerff Howe, *Crowdsourcing: Why the Power of the Crowd Is Driving the Future of Business* (New York: Crown Business, 2009). Indeed the myth of outside-in change can be traced back even earlier to sociotechnical principles of organization design. See for example David P. Hanna, *Designing Organizations for High Performance* (Reading, MA: Addison-Wesley, 1988).

3. Karim R. Lakhani and Jill A. Panetta, "The Principles of Distributed Innovation," *Innovations* 2, no. 3 (2007): 97–112.

4. Larry Huston and Navil Sakkab, "Connect and Develop: Inside Procter & Gamble's New Model for Innovation," *Harvard Business Review* 84, no. 3 (2006): 31–41.

5. On user-centered design see for example Karel Vredenburg, Scott Isensee, and Carol Righi, *User-Centered Design: An Integrated Approach* (Upper Saddle River, NJ: Prentice Hall, PTR, 2002); Robert W. Veryzer and Brigitte Borja de Mozota, "The Impact of User-Oriented Design on New Product Development: An Examination of Fundamental Relationships," *Journal of Product Innovation Management* 22 (2005): 128–143.

6. Eric Von Hippel, *Democratized Innovation* (Cambridge, MA: MIT Press, 2005).

7. For the article and the following debate, see Roberto Verganti, "User-Centered Innovation Is Not Sustainable," *Harvard Business Review* on-line magazine, 19 March 2010, https://hbr.org/2010/03/user-centered-innovation-is-no.

8. Alexandra Horowitz, *On Looking: Eleven Walks with Expert Eyes* (New York: Scribner, 2013), 8.

9. https://www.youtube.com/watch?v=eywi0h_Y5_U, accessed 14 July 2015.

10. Paul McNamara, "Five Years Ago They Said the iPhone Would Be a Flop ... Now?," *NetworkWorld*, 27 June 2012, http://www.networkworld.com/article/2289240/smartphones/five-years-ago-they-said-the-iphone-would-be-a-flop-----now-.html, accessed 14 July 2015.

11. Horowitz, *On Looking*.

12. Brown is not alone in this perspective. For example, see also Mark Stefik and Barbara Stefik, "The Prepared Mind Versus the Beginner's Mind," *Design Management Review* 16, no. 1 (Winter 2005): 10–16; Michael R. Bokeno, "Marcuse on Senge: Personal Mastery, the Child's Mind, and Individual Transformation," *Journal of Organizational Change Management* 22, no. 3 (2009): 307–320; John Kao, *Clearing the Mind for Creativity* (Upper Saddle River, NJ: New World City, 2011).

13. Clayton M. Christensen, *The Innovator's Dilemma: When New Technologies Cause Great Firms to Fail* (Boston: Harvard Business School Press, 1997).

14. Roberto Verganti, *Design-Driven Innovation: Changing the Rules of Competition by Radically Innovating What Things Mean* (Boston: Harvard Business School Press, 2009).

15. Donald A. Norman and Stephen W. Draper, *User Centered System Design: New Perspectives on Human-Computer Interaction* (Mahwah, NJ: Lawrence Erlbaum Associates, 1986).

16. Donald A. Norman, "Technology First, Needs Last: The Research-Product Gulf," *Interactions* 17, no. 2 (2010): 38–42; Donald A. Norman and Roberto Verganti, "Incremental and Radical Innovation: Design Research versus Technology and Meaning Change," *Design Issues* 30, no. 1 (Winter 2014): 78–96; Donald Norman and Roberto Verganti, "Hill Climbing and Darwinian Evolution: A Response to John Langrish," *Design Issues* 30, no. 3 (Summer 2014): 106–107.

17. Hans-Georg Gadamer, *Truth and Method*, 2nd ed. (1960; New York: Continuum, 1998).

18. Susann M. Laverty, "Hermeneutic Phenomenology and Phenomenology: A Comparison of Historical and Methodological Considerations," *International Journal of Qualitative Methods* 2, no. 3 (2003), article 3, https://www.ualberta.ca/~iiqm/backissues/2_3final/html/laverty.html, accessed 8 July 2015.

19. Annie Dillard, *Pilgrim at Thinker Creek* (New York: Harper Collins, 1974), 23.

20. Horowitz, *On Looking*, 4.

21. E. E. Cummings, "Since Feeling Is First," in *Selected Poems*, ed. Richard S. Kennedy (New York: W. W. Norton, 2007), 99.

22. There are at least two ways of looking at preconception and preunderstanding. First through the lens of psychology, and in particular through the frameworks of the theory of perception and theory of cognition. In this perspective, our past experience creates frameworks that affect our way of perceiving and understanding things. We tend to see what we can and want to see, and what we can and want to understand. There is a copious literature in this field. My early reflections in this chapter, with the support of Alexandra Horowitz's journey, surface this psychological perspective. However, the deepest part of my argument, and deepest motivation for inside-out innovation, come from a second perspective, which is philosophical. In this perspective, connected to hermeneutics, our preunderstanding, our horizon, is a powerful source of learning if properly dealt with. Inside-out innovation is therefore a way to make sense of our presence in the world, to give meaning and offer meaning. I align more with this second philosophical stance. Hence my references to Hans-Georg Gadamer and, later, to Paul Ricoeur.

23. John Green, "The Gift of Gary Busey," clip, https://www.youtube.com/watch?v=j22qA39eHvw, uploaded on YouTube on 25 August 2009, accessed 7 July 2015.

24. Coldplay (Guy Rupert Berryman, William Champion, Christopher Anthony John Martin, and Jonathan Mark Buckland), "Fix You," 2005 by Universal Music Publishing Group, CD.

25. When innovating solutions, one should anyway question whether the existing parameters of value are indeed good. We should always wonder about the morality of what we do, even if it is already accepted in the market and searched for.

26. Stefano Marzano, interview with the author, Eindhoven, November 2010.

27. The figure of the good father or *bonus pater familias* is used in law as the archetype of the ultimate standard of care for someone.

28. Gary Hamel, "Innovation Starts with the Heart, Not the Head," *Harvard Business Review* online magazine, 12 June 2015, https://hbr.org/2015/06/you-innovate-with-your-heart-not-your-head, accessed 8 July 2015.

29. Simon Sinek, *Start with Why: How Great Leaders Inspire Everyone to Take Action* (New York: Portfolio, 2009).

30. Maria Popova, "How to Get Rich: Paul Graham on Money vs. Wealth," *BrainPickings*, http://www.brainpickings.org/index.php/2014/07/02/how-to-make-wealth-paul-graham-hackers-painters/, accessed 7 July 2015.

31. Birger Wernerfelt, "A Resource-Based View of the Firm," *Strategic Management Journal* 5 (1984): 171–180.

32. Laverty, "Hermeneutic Phenomenology and Phenomenology."

33. Horowitz, *On Looking*, 264.

CHAPTER 5

1. The story of the Xbox is based on personal interviews with Microsoft's management and on the precious book by Dean Takahashi, *Opening the Xbox: Inside Microsoft's Plan to Unleash an Entertainment Revolution* (Roseville, CA: Prima Publishing, 2002).

2. Takahashi, *Opening the Xbox*, ix.

3. Ibid., 123.

4. Umberto Galimberti, *I miti del nostro tempo* [The myths of our time] (Milan: Feltrinelli, 2011).

5. In the following sections we will often refer to "judgment." There are two kinds of judgments: of *facts* and of *values*. "A Judgment of fact affirms that something is true or false, correct or not. A judgment of value affirms that something is good/bad, valuable/valueless" (Abraham [Rami] B. Shani, Dawn Chandler, Jean-François Coget, and James B. Lau, *Behavior in Organization: An Experiential Approach*, 9th ed. [New York: McGraw-Hill/Irwin, 2009], 51). Criticism is related to judgment of value. It therefore refers to the second perspective: judging whether something is good or bad, which is beyond the question of whether it is true or false. Here the purpose is not to define what is true (as might a judge in court, who is not a critic), but to understand and set a direction.

6. Bertrand Russell, *The Autobiography of Bertrand Russell, 1944–1969* (New York: Simon and Schuster, 1969).

7. Takahashi, *Opening the Xbox*, 167.

8. The body of studies here is extensive. See, for example, Kurt Lewin, "Frontiers in Group Dynamics: Concept, Method and Reality in Social Science, Social Equilibria and Social Change," *Human Relations* 1 (June 1947): 5–41; Amir Levy, *Organizational Transformation: Approaches, Strategies and Theories* (New York: Praeger, 1986); Rosabeth Moss Kanter, *The Challenge of Organizational Change* (New York: Free Press, 1992); Chris Argyris and Donald A. Schön, *Organizational Learning II: Theory, Method and Practice* (Reading, MA: Addison-Wesley, 1996); Edgar H. Schein, *Organizational Culture and Leadership*, 4th ed. (San Francisco: Jossey-Bass, 2010).

9. François Thiébault-Sisson, "Claude Monet, an Interview," *Le Temps*, 27 November 1900; as quoted by Michael P. Farrell, *Collaborative Circles: Friendship Dynamics and Collaborative Work* (Chicago: University of Chicago Press, 2001), 44. The case of the impressionists in this book is significantly based on Farrell's narrative, given his focus on the group dynamics and their creative production.

10. Ambroise Vollard, *Renoir, an Intimate Record* (New York: Alfred A. Knopf, 1925), 33–34; cited in Farrell, *Collaborative Circles*, 35.

11. Vollard, *Renoir, an Intimate Record*, cited in ibid.

12. I warmly thank Karim Lakhani for suggesting that I read Farrell's book, which has been such a rich source of inspiration.

13. On the role of pairs in innovation, see for example Lawrence McGrath, "When Pairing Reduces Scaring: The Effect of Dyadic Ideation on Evaluation Apprehension," *International Journal of Innovation Management* 19, no. 4 (August 2015): 1–36.

14. On the power of frank (or honest) feedback, see also Ed Catmull, "How Pixar Fosters Collective Creativity," *Harvard Business Review* 86, no. 9 (September 2008): 64–72.

15. Farrell, *Collaborative Circles*, 34–35.

16. Ibid., 51.

17. Ibid., 46.

18. Gary Tinterow and Henri Loyrette, eds., *Origins of Impressionism* (New York: Metropolitan Museum of Art, 1994); cited in Farrell, *Collaborative Circles*, 39.

19. John Gage, *Color and Culture: Practice and Meaning from Antiquity to Abstraction* (Berkeley: University of California Press, 1993), 209.

20. Takahashi, *Opening the Xbox*, vii.

21. Farrell, *Collaborative Circles*, 6.

22. We will explore some criteria in chapter 6. For inspiring theories on how individuals can think deeper, see the studies Donald Schön and his theories on *reflection-on-action*: Donald A. Schön, *The Reflective Practitioner: How Professionals Think in Action* (London: Temple Smith, 1983), and the framework of double-loop learning, proposed by Argyris: Chris Argyris and Donald A. Schön, *Organizational Learning: A Theory of Action Perspective* (Reading, MA: Addison-Wesley, 1978).

23. Takahashi, *Opening the Xbox*, vii.

24. Many theories of innovation underline the importance of giving people resources to experiment with ideas they believe in, without asking for preliminary top management support. These resources can be in the form of free time that employees can dedicate to innovation (an extreme example was Google's famous policy of offering its employees 20% of their working hours for free explorations); or in the form of a budget to pay for prototypes; or in terms of space for meetings; or, again, in the form of facilitating contacts with experts and players who could support idea development. Microsoft did not have similar policies. Yet it was tolerant of deviants who wanted to dedicate their overtime to exploring new paths. And the case of the Xbox shows that when it comes to developing a new vision, committed employees can often find time and resources to work on it, even if there are no formal organizational supports.

25. C. S. Lewis, *The Four Loves* (New York: Harcourt Brace, 1960); cited in Farrell, *Collaborative Circles*, 16.

26. Ibid.

27. Humphrey Carpenter, *Tolkien* (Boston: Houghton Mifflin, 1977); cited in Farrell, *Collaborative Circles*, 11.

28. Takahashi, *Opening the Xbox*, vii.

29. An appreciation of the importance of mutual "respect" and "esteem" has been pointed to me by Rami Shani, a professor at Calpoly, after a two-hour-long critique on this chapter. He is right. If I think about my own connections, those who provide me most with affinitive encouragement are people I most respect and esteem. Like Rami indeed.

30. Jeffery M. Masson, ed., *The Complete Letters of Sigmund Freud to Wilhelm Fliess* (Cambridge: Belknap Press of Harvard University Press, 1985); cited in Farrell, *Collaborative Circles*, 14.

31. Farrell, *Collaborative Circles*, 8.

32. Humphrey Carpenter, *The Inklings: C. S. Lewis, J. R. R. Tolkien, Charles Williams, and Their Friends* (Boston: Houghton Mifflin, 1979); cited in Farrell, *Collaborative Circles*, 8.

33. Trust to talk is one of the most relevant forms of trust. According to Patrick Lencioni, expert on organizational behavior, "Trust is not the ability of team members to predict one another's behaviors ... trust is all about vulnerability. Team members who trust one another learn to be comfortable being open, even exposed, to one another around their failures, weaknesses, even fears." Patrick Lencioni, *Overcoming the Five Dysfunctions of a Team: A Field Guide* (San Francisco: Jossey-Bass, 2005).

34. Trust is one of the most widely investigated subjects in psychology and organizational behavior. My perspectives here tap three aspects of theories of trust. First, I align with the basic acceptation of trust, as relying that another person will behave *as expected* and that she will eventually *not harm* us (Erik H. Erikson, *Childhood and Society* [New York: Norton, 1950]). In the case of a radical circle, this expectation is corroborated by a shared intention: a malaise with the status quo and a will to change. Second, however, trust in a radical circle does not necessarily come from a belief in the other person's honesty (which typically depends on the length of their relationship), but from a belief in her *intentions* and *confidence* in her *competence* (here I connect trust to the previous comment on respect and esteem). Third, prediction of behavior is not the only component of trust. *Vulnerability*, i.e., the willingness of members of a radical circle to share a half-baked work and therefore to expose its likely defects, is a major element in the process of trust building (Lencioni, *Overcoming the Five Dysfunctions of a Team*). In this, a radical circle resembles the dynamics of group therapy, where openness toward the group is a major ingredient for personal development (William C. Schutz, *Elements of Encounter: A BodyMind Approach* [Big Sur, CA: Joy Press, 1973]).

35. Vollard, *Renoir, an Intimate Record*, 64; cited in Farrell, *Collaborative Circles*, 33.

36. Anne Kane, "Lonergan's Philosophy as Grounding for Cross-Disciplinary Research," *Nursing Philosophy* 15 (2014): 125–137, 130. For the studies of Lonergan, see Bernard J. F. Lonergan, *Insight: A Study in Human Understanding*, 5th ed., rev. and aug., in *Collected Works of Bernard Lonergan*, vol. 3 (1957; Toronto: University of Toronto Press, 1992). About the importance of *wonder* see also the most recent works by Finn Thorbjørn Hansen at Aalborg University: Hansen, "The Call and Practices of Wonder: How to Evoke a Socratic Community of Wonder in Professional Settings," in Michael Noah Weiss, ed., *The Socratic Handbook* (Zurich: Lit Verlag, 2015).

37. Jean Renoir, *Renoir, My Father* (San Francisco: Mercury House, 1988); cited in Farrell, *Collaborative Circles*, 30.

38. Takahashi, *Opening the Xbox*, 63.

39. I'm currently exploring, together with Naiara Altuna, the dynamics of innovative communities in various domains. Early results show that breakthrough movements and communities have at their core a radical circle, i.e., an initial small group of trusted and knowledgeable people who share a sense of malaise about the

established meaning. Examples are Slow Food in food, Homebrew in computing, Memphis in furniture. For early insights see: Naiara Altuna, Claudio Dell'Era, Paolo Landoni, and Roberto Verganti, "Moving beyond Creative Geniuses and Crowdsourcing: The Contribution of Radical Circles in the Development of New Visions," EIASM Innovation Product Development Management Conference, Copenhagen, 22–23 June 2015.

40. See the well-known theory of Bruce Tuckman on the stages of group development: Bruce W. Tuckman, "Developmental Sequence in Small Groups," *Psychological Bulletin* 63 (1965): 384–399.

41. It is interesting to notice that a radical circle moves outside of formal organizational arrangements, and therefore it enjoys a partial separation from the establishment. This separation favors the nourishment of a vision that is not in line with the existing one and prevents its watering down during the delicate phase when the vision is still weak and not public. Research has shown that breakthrough change benefits from separation from existing organizational and social arrangements. What is interesting about a radical circle, however, is that it is only partially separated. Unlike skunk works (Everett M. Rogers, *Diffusion of Innovations* [New York: Free Press, 1962]) or internal ventures (Robert A. Burgelman, "Managing the Internal Corporate Venturing Process," *Sloan Management Review* [Winter 1984]: 33–48; Robert A. Burgelman and Modesto A. Maidique, *Strategic Management of Technology and Innovation* [Homewood, IL: Irwin, 1988]), people who create a radical circle are still physically and organizationally immersed in the daily organization. However, they act separately (almost like a secret society) when they work together. Being still immersed in the organization enables them to have a close sense of what is happening "inside the box" instead of jumping into adventurous journeys outside the organizational box, which happens in skunk works that are isolated organizations (and whose ideas typically get killed by the establishment when finally exposed).

42. For further insights on the role of visionary leaders, see Jean-François Coget, Abraham B. (Rami) Shani, and Luca Solari, "The Lone Genius, or Leaders Who Tyrannize Their Creative Teams: An Alternative to the 'Mothering' Model of Leadership and Creativity," *Organizational Dynamics* 43, no. 3 (2014): 105–113.

43. Takahashi, *Opening the Xbox*.

44. Nicholas Sparks, *Safe Haven* (New York: Grand Central Publishing, 2010), 106.

45. Farrell, *Collaborative Circles*, 35.

PART III

1. Examples of others books that propose processes based on similar principles (inside-out innovation and criticism) are Paul Hekkert and Matthijs B. van Dijk, *Vision in Design: A Guidebook for Innovators* (Amsterdam: BIS publishers, 2011); and

Kees Dorst, *Creating Frames: A New Design Practice for Driving Innovation* (Cambridge, MA: MIT Press, 2015).

CHAPTER 6

1. The initiator of the concept of focusing on the output (the purpose) rather than the product was Theodore Levitt, in his seminal article "Marketing Myopia," *Harvard Business Review* 38, no. 4 (1960): 22–47. More recently, the concept of jobs to be done has been developed by Christensen and Ulwick: Clayton M. Christensen and Michael E. Raynor, *The Innovator's Solution: Using Good Theory to Solve the Dilemmas of Growth* (Watertown, MA: Harvard Business School Press, 2003); Anthony Ulwick, *What Customers Want: Using Outcome-Driven Innovation to Create Breakthrough Products and Services* (New York: McGraw-Hill, 2005); Clayton M. Christensen, Scott D. Anthony, Gerald Berstell, and Denise Nitterhouse, "Finding the Right Job for Your Product," *MIT Sloan Management Review* (April 2007): 2–11; Anthony Ulwick and Lance A. Bettencourt, "Giving Customers a Fair Hearing," *Sloan Management Review* 49, no. 3 (2008): 62–68.

2. Some supermarkets went in a similar direction, but instead of a rolling basket simply opted for a half-sized cart.

3. As of today, no one has ever scientifically demonstrated the superiority of one of the tools listed in box 6.4 to the others.

4. Tom Kelley, *The Art of Innovation: Lessons in Creativity from IDEO, America's Leading Design Firm* (New York: Doubleday, 2001); Tim Brown, *Change by Design: How Design Thinking Transforms Organizations and Inspires Innovation* (New York: Harper-Business, 2009).

5. For the strategy canvas and four-action framework, see W. Chan Kim and Renée Mauborgne, *Blue Ocean Strategy* (Boston: Harvard Business School Press, 2005). For jobs to be done and the customer-centered innovation map see Christensen and Raynor, *The Innovator's Solution*, and Ulwick, *What Customers Want*. For the value proposition canvas see Alexander Osterwalder and Yves Pigneur, *Value Proposition Design* (San Francisco: Wiley, 2014). For the Kano model see Noriaki Kano, Nobuhiku Seraku, Fumio Takahashi, and Shinichi Tsuji, "Attractive Quality and Must-Be Quality," *Journal of the Japanese Society for Quality Control* (in Japanese) 14, no. 2 (April 1984): 39–48. For empathy maps, see Kelley, *The Art of Innovation*. For discovery-driven innovation see Rita Gunther McGrath and Ian C. MacMillan, *Discovery-Driven Growth: A Breakthrough Process to Reduce Risk and Seize Opportunity* (Boston: Harvard Business School Press, 2009). For the customer experience and customer journey mapping see Joseph B. Pine and James H. Gilmore, *The Experience Economy* (Boston: Harvard Business School Press, 1999). For inside-the-box innovation, see Kevin Coyne, Patricia Gorman Clifford, and Renée Dye, "Breakthrough Thinking from Inside the Box," *Harvard Business Review* (December 2007): 70–78.

6. Dennis Haseley (and Ed Young, illustrator), *Twenty Heartbeats* (New York: Roaring Brook Press, 2008).

7. http://www.wikigallery.org/wiki/painting_300429/Italian-Unknown-Master/Madonna-of-Large-Eyes

8. https://en.wikipedia.org/wiki/Madonna_del_cardellino

9. https://en.wikipedia.org/wiki/Solly_Madonna

10. https://en.wikipedia.org/wiki/Madonna_del_Granduca

11. https://en.wikipedia.org/wiki/Small_Cowper_Madonna

12. https://en.wikipedia.org/wiki/Madonna_del_Prato_(Raphael)

13. Many studies address the practice of self-reflection, or reflective practice. Probably the most notable is the study of Schön about reflection *on* action: Donald A. Schön, *The Reflective Practitioner: How Professionals Think in Action* (London: Temple Smith, 1983).

CHAPTER 7

1. http://www.bbc.com/news/uk-politics-10377842, accessed 12 August 2015.

2. This spiral form of interaction is based on Hegel's dialectic, and in particular on the concept of *Aufheben* or "sublation," which means to abolish and at the same time to preserve: criticism preserves the useful portion of a direction and, by moving beyond its limitation, makes it richer and more robust.

3. For the concept of "delighters" see Noriaki Kano, Nobuhiku Seraku, Fumio Takahashi, and Shinichi Tsuji, "Attractive Quality and Must-Be Quality," *Journal of the Japanese Society for Quality Control* (in Japanese) 14, no. 2 (April 1984): 39–48.

4. Thomas J. Shuell, "Teaching and Learning as Problem Solving," *Theory into Practice* 29, no. 2 (Spring 1990): 102–108.

5. George Lakoff and Mark Johnson, *Metaphors We Live By* (Chicago: University of Chicago Press, 1980), 27.

6. Ibid., 3.

7. Ibid.

8. Aristotle, *The Poetics*, trans. Gerald F. Else (Ann Arbor: University of Michigan Press, 1967, 1970), 1459a, 5–8.

9. http://www.merriam-webster.com/dictionary/watch, accessed 13 August 2015.

10. Paul Ricoeur, *The Rule of Metaphor* (Toronto: University of Toronto Press, 1977), 97. According to Ricoeur the dictionary contains no metaphor, or better, it contains

faded metaphors: things that used to be metaphors and now have become established metaphorical uses of words.

11. Aristotle, *Rhetoric*, trans. William Rhys Roberts, book III, chapter 10, 12 (New York: Dover, 2004), 135.

12. Friedrich Nietzsche, *The Birth of Tragedy and Other Writings*, ed. Raymond Geuss and Ronald Speirs, trans. Ronald Speirs (Cambridge: Cambridge University Press, 1999), 50.

13. Lakoff and Johnson, *Metaphors We Live By*, 145.

14. http://www.fcagroup.com/investorday/PresentationList/Alfa_Brand.pdf, accessed 13 August 2015.

CHAPTER 8

1. Alexandra Horowitz, *On Looking: Eleven Walks with Expert Eyes* (New York: Scribner, 2013).

2. Ibid., 14.

3. Ibid., 87.

4. Ibid., 143.

5. Nathan Myhrvold, "Funding Eureka," *Harvard Business Review* (March 2010): 40–50.

6. Kenneth Gorfinkle, *Soothing Your Child's Pain* (Lincolnwood, IL: Contemporary Books, 2013).

7. Naiara Altuna, Åsa Öberg, and Roberto Verganti, "Interpreters: A Source of Innovations Driven by Meaning," IPDMC 21st International Product Development Management Conference, EIASM, Limerick, Ireland, 15–17 June 2014.

8. N. Taylor Thompson, "Building a Minimum Viable Product? You're Probably Doing It Wrong," *HarvardBusinessReview.org*, 11 September 2013, https://hbr.org/2013/09/building-a-minimum-viable-prod, accessed 24 August 2015.

9. Jake Knapp, John Zeratsky, and Braden Kowitz, *Sprint: How to Solve Big Problems and Test New Ideas in Just Five Days* (New York: Simon and Schuster, 2016).

10. Alan MacCormack, Roberto Verganti, and Marco Iansiti, "Developing Products on 'Internet Time': The Anatomy of a Flexible Development Process," *Management Science* 47, no. 1 (January 2001): 133–150.

Design Thinking, Design Theory:
About the Series

As professions go, design is relatively young. The practice of design predates professions. In fact, the practice of design—making things to serve a useful goal, making tools—predates the human race. Making tools is one of the attributes that made us human in the first place.

Design, in the most generic sense of the word, began over 2.5 million years ago when *Homo habilis* manufactured the first tools. Human beings were designing well before we began to walk upright. Four hundred thousand years ago, we began to manufacture spears. By forty thousand years ago, we had moved up to specialized tools.

Urban design and architecture came along ten thousand years ago in Mesopotamia. Interior architecture and furniture design probably emerged with them. It was another five thousand years before graphic design and typography got their start in Sumeria with the development of cuneiform. After that, things picked up speed.

All goods and services are designed. The urge to design—to consider a situation, imagine a better situation, and act to create that improved situation—goes back to our prehuman ancestors. Making tools helped us to become what we are—design helped to make us human.

Today, the word "design" means many things. The common factor linking them is service, and designers are engaged in a service profession in which the results of their work meet human needs.

Design is first of all a process. The word "design" entered the English language in the 1500s as a verb, with the first written citation of the verb dated to the year 1548. *Merriam-Webster's Collegiate Dictionary* defines the verb "design" as "to conceive and plan out in the mind; to have as a specific purpose; to devise for a specific function or end." Related to these is the act of drawing, with an emphasis on the nature of the drawing as a plan or map, as well as "to draw plans for; to create, fashion, execute or construct according to plan."

Half a century later, the word began to be used as a noun, with the first cited use of the noun "design" occurring in 1588. *Merriam-Webster's* defines the noun as "a particular purpose held in view by an individual or group; deliberate, purposive planning; a mental project or scheme in which means to an end are laid down." Here, too, purpose and planning toward desired outcomes are central. Among these are "a preliminary sketch or outline showing the main features of something to be executed; an underlying scheme that governs functioning, developing or unfolding; a plan or protocol for carrying out or accomplishing something; the arrangement of elements or details in a product or work of art." Today, we design large, complex process, systems, and services, and we design organizations and structures to produce them. Design has changed considerably since our remote ancestors made the first stone tools.

At a highly abstract level, Herbert Simon's definition covers nearly all imaginable instances of design. To design, Simon writes, is to "[devise] courses of action aimed at changing existing situations into preferred ones" (Simon, *The Sciences of the Artificial*, 2nd ed., MIT Press, 1982, p. 129). Design, properly defined, is the entire process across the full range of domains required for any given outcome.

But the design process is always more than a general, abstract way of working. Design takes concrete form in the work of the service professions that meet human needs, a broad range of making and planning disciplines. These include industrial design, graphic design, textile design, furniture design, information design, process design, product design, interaction design, transportation design, educational design, systems design, urban design, design leadership, and design management, as well as architecture, engineering, information technology, and computer science.

These fields focus on different subjects and objects. They have distinct traditions, methods, and vocabularies, used and put into practice by distinct and often dissimilar professional groups. Although the traditions dividing these groups are distinct, common boundaries sometimes form a border. Where this happens, they serve as meeting points where common concerns build bridges. Today, ten challenges uniting the design professions form such a set of common concerns.

Three performance challenges, four substantive challenges, and three contextual challenges bind the design disciplines and professions together as a common field. The performance challenges arise because all design professions:

1. act on the physical world;
2. address human needs; and
3. generate the built environment.

In the past, these common attributes were not sufficient to transcend the boundaries of tradition. Today, objective changes in the larger world give rise to four substantive challenges that are driving convergence in design practice and research. These substantive challenges are:

1. increasingly ambiguous boundaries between artifacts, structure, and process;
2. increasingly large-scale social, economic, and industrial frames;
3. an increasingly complex environment of needs, requirements, and constraints; and
4. information content that often exceeds the value of physical substance.These challenges require new frameworks of theory and research to address contemporary problem areas while solving specific cases and problems. In professional design practice, we often find that solving design problems requires interdisciplinary teams with a trans-disciplinary focus. Fifty years ago, a sole practitioner and an assistant or two might have solved most design problems; today, we need groups of people with skills across several disciplines, and the additional skills that enable professionals to work with, listen to, and learn from each other as they solve problems.

Three contextual challenges define the nature of many design problems today. While many design problems function at a simpler level, these issues affect many of the major design problems that challenge us, and these challenges also affect simple design problems linked to complex social, mechanical, or technical systems. These issues are:

1. a complex environment in which many projects or products cross the boundaries of several organizations, stakeholder, producer, and user groups;

2.   projects or products that must meet the expectations of many organi-
     zations, stakeholders, producers, and users; and

3.   demands at every level of production, distribution, reception, and
     control.These ten challenges require a qualitatively different approach
     to professional design practice than was the case in earlier times. Past
     environments were simpler. They made simpler demands. Individual
     experience and personal development were sufficient for depth and
     substance in professional practice. While experience and development
     are still necessary, they are no longer sufficient. Most of today's design
     challenges require analytic and synthetic planning skills that cannot
     be developed through practice alone.

Professional design practice today involves advanced knowledge. This
knowledge is not solely a higher level of professional practice. It is also a
qualitatively different form of professional practice that emerges in response
to the demands of the information society and the knowledge economy to
which it gives rise.

In a recent essay ("Why Design Education Must Change," *Core77*,
November 26, 2010), Donald Norman challenges the premises and practices of the design profession. In the past, designers operated in the belief
that talent and a willingness to jump into problems with both feet gives
them an edge in solving problems. Norman writes:

In the early days of industrial design, the work was primarily focused upon physical
products. Today, however, designers work on organizational structure and social
problems, on interaction, service, and experience design. Many problems involve
complex social and political issues. As a result, designers have become applied behavioral scientists, but they are woefully undereducated for the task. Designers often
fail to understand the complexity of the issues and the depth of knowledge already
known. They claim that fresh eyes can produce novel solutions, but then they wonder why these solutions are seldom implemented, or if implemented, why they fail.
Fresh eyes can indeed produce insightful results, but the eyes must also be educated
and knowledgeable. Designers often lack the requisite understanding. Design schools
do not train students about these complex issues, about the interlocking complexi-
ties of human and social behavior, about the behavioral sciences, technology, and
business. There is little or no training in science, the scientific method, and experi-
mental design.

This is not industrial design in the sense of designing products, but
industry-related design, design as thought and action for solving problems

and imagining new futures. This new MIT Press series of books emphasizes strategic design to create value through innovative products and services, and it emphasizes design as service through rigorous creativity, critical inquiry, and an ethics of respectful design. This rests on a sense of understanding, empathy, and appreciation for people, for nature, and for the world we shape through design. Our goal as editors is to develop a series of vital conversations that help designers and researchers to serve business, industry, and the public sector for positive social and economic outcomes.

We will present books that bring a new sense of inquiry to the design, helping to shape a more reflective and stable design discipline able to support a stronger profession grounded in empirical research, generative concepts, and the solid theory that gives rise to what W. Edwards Deming described as profound knowledge (Deming, *The New Economics for Industry, Government, Education*, MIT, Center for Advanced Engineering Study, 1993). For Deming, a physicist, engineer, and designer, profound knowledge comprised systems thinking and the understanding of processes embedded in systems; an understanding of variation and the tools we need to understand variation; a theory of knowledge; and a foundation in human psychology. This is the beginning of "deep design"—the union of deep practice with robust intellectual inquiry.

A series on design thinking and theory faces the same challenges that we face as a profession. On one level, design is a general human process that we use to understand and to shape our world. Nevertheless, we cannot address this process or the world in its general, abstract form. Rather, we meet the challenges of design in specific challenges, addressing problems or ideas in a situated context. The challenges we face as designers today are as diverse as the problems clients bring us. We are involved in design for economic anchors, economic continuity, and economic growth. We design for urban needs and rural needs, for social development and creative communities. We are involved with environmental sustainability and economic policy, agriculture, competitive crafts for export, competitive products and brands for micro-enterprises, developing new products for bottom-of-pyramid markets, and redeveloping old products for mature or wealthy markets. Within the framework of design, we are also challenged to design for extreme situations, for biotech, nanotech, and new materials, and design for social business, as well as conceptual challenges for worlds that do not yet exist such as the world beyond the Kurzweil singularity—and for new visions of the world that does exist.

The Design Thinking, Design Theory series from the MIT Press will explore these issues and more—meeting them, examining them, and helping designers to address them.

Join us is this journey.

Ken Friedman   Erik Stolterman
Editors, Design Thinking, Design Theory Series

Index